IDENTITY
and INDIVIDUATION

Edited by

Milton K. Munitz

New York: NEW YORK UNIVERSITY PRESS
1971

Introduction

MILTON K. MUNITZ

The distinction between what it is to be an individual or a particular instance on the one hand, and what it is to be general, repeatable, or common on the other, is as fundamental as any distinction in philosophy. It is central to the conceptual scheme with which the human mind operates. It is reflected, for example, in the distinction we draw in ordinary language between the use of proper names (such as, 'the Eiffel Tower', 'Socrates') and common nouns and adjectives (for example, 'building', 'wise'). Yet, having noted the distinction, the problem of how to make it precise and of how to bring out all its subtle ramifications and repercussions is a matter of the utmost difficulty and complexity. It is a theme that has engaged the attention of philosophers from the Greeks to the present day.

Involved in the attempt to work out this distinction is another central pair of concepts, namely, sameness and difference. To be able to identify an individual requires that we be able to say it is that very same individual and no other. How are we able to accomplish this, not merely practically, but by way of satisfying some adequate *theory* of individual identity? How *do* we differentiate individuals from one another, even when they very closely resemble one another? Moreover, the problem of establishing the identity of an individual involves not only differentiating that individual from other *coexisting* individuals. We should also wish to know in what the identity of the individual consists that warrants the belief that it is the *same* individual that has persisted over a stretch of time. Why do we sometimes say an individual has retained his (or its) identity, amidst all sorts of marked changes and transformations, whereas in other cases, the changes and transformations have been so great we are ready to acknowledge the individ-

iii

ual's identity *qua* that individual is no longer preserved? (The challenge to make explicit and cogent on what basis we affirm that, despite marked changes, something remains *the same,* is already present in the famous thesis of Heraclitus that we cannot step into *the same river* twice.)

Meanwhile, in the other direction, as we seek to bring out what constitutes the common or the repeatable, again we inevitably fall back on the notions of 'the same and the different'. To say what distinguishes one kind or type from another and makes it the very kind or type that it is calls for a criterion of identity that would apply to that which is general or repeated. How is this to be formulated? The latter problem broadens out into a series of related questions. For example, what are we to make of philosophical talk of "universals"? What view shall we adopt with respect to the question of the possibility of definitional synonymy in the specification of the meaning of general terms? How are we to construe the role of predicative expressions in propositional discourse?

Because the above distinction is as fundamental as it is, it cannot serve the purposes of clarity to cover them both by speaking of a single "law" or "principle" of identity, or to assert that the notion of "the same" is used in the same way, now in connection with individuals, now in connection with what is general. The temptation to assimilate these under a general formula is what leads many philosophers — Plato the first of a long line — to treat concepts as themselves a type of *object.* The formula "$a = a$" read as "Everything is identical with itself" is then taken by these philosophers to encompass not only ordinary things such as tables, rocks, or persons, but such rarified "objects" as numbers or triangles (and universals or Forms generally). The identity belonging to a concept, universal, predicative term, or common noun and adjective, however, is a different sort of thing from what is involved in specifying wherein the identity of an individual consists.[1] To cover both of these ideas by the formula "$a = a$" without specifying whether the "a" stands for some general concept or whether it is being used to designate an individual is misleading. The symbol "$=$" need not be taken as having *the same* meaning of "identity" or "the same" in both cases.

Of the two broad sets of questions thus far distinguished — that having to do with the sameness or identity of individuals, and that having to do with the sameness of concepts — it is, in any case, the

---

[1] "The Aristotelian law of identity Aaa, where A means 'every — is' and a is a variable universal term, is different from the principle of identity Ixx where I means 'is identical with' and x is a variable individual term." Jan Lukasiewicz, *Aristotle's Syllogistic,* Oxford University Press, p. 149.

former kind of question that is normally meant when philosophers allude to the "problem of identity." Without in any way minimizing the importance of the kinds of questions raised by the second line of inquiry sketched above, we shall follow current philosophic usage in dealing with the problem of identity by concentrating on the sets of questions raised in the first of the topics mentioned. The title of this volume is intended to call attention to the selection thus being made; the essays that follow examine a variety of issues related in one way or another to this broad underlying theme.

We must now try to state somewhat more precisely what, in fact, are some of the issues that do arise in connection with the problem of identity when thought of as principally connected with the identity of individuals. The point to be made at once, of course, is that there is no single question here, but rather a cluster of them.

(1) The grown man I see before me today is *the same person,* I say, I knew as a child twenty years ago; the table at which you are eating your lunch now is *the very same table* you bought a number of years ago and have used ever since. What is it that justifies us in describing this sameness or identity to an individual object, or to a person? Why is it that despite the many changes and transformations which that object or person has undergone, we are nevertheless able to say that it is the same individual that has persisted from t_0 to t_n? In what does the identity of an individual through time consist? How shall we characterize the persistence of an object or a person through time? Is there something that remains permanent or unchanging in virtue of which we say it is the same individual? And, if so, how shall this be described? What role is to be assigned to the notion of *spatiotemporal continuity* or to the possession of *essential* properties as defining such identity? Is it the case, moreover, that in answering these questions, we shall provide the same set of answers both for material objects as well as for persons? Is the identity of a material object, for example a table, basically of the same type as the identity of a person? On all these interrelated questions philosophers, as might be expected, have offered widely different answers: and ever since the days of Locke and Hume, to go no further back, the issues revolving around the notions of material-object identity and personal identity have been in the forefront of philosophic concern. (The essays by Coburn, Hirsch, Shoemaker, and Chisholm deal with various aspects of this question.)

(2) Another central question that calls for attention was given prominence in the philosophy of Leibniz. In ordinary talk about individuals, we normally say of a given individual that it has this or that

property. The question that Leibniz raised may be put as follows: Is it the case that there can be two or more individuals that differ only numerically, but that possess exactly the same properties? Is it possible for individuals *A* and *B* to have exactly the same properties and yet be numerically distinct? Leibniz himself answered this question in the negative. "It is not true," he says in his *Discourse on Metaphysics* (IX), "that two substances may be exactly alike and differ only numerically, *solo numero.*" Another way of formulating this general idea, sometimes referred to as the Principle of the Identity of Indiscernibles, asserts that a necessary condition for an object *x* to be identical with an object *y* is that every property of *x* is a property of *y*. For Leibniz the truth of these principles rested on a broad factual claim of a metaphysical sort, according to which the world is so constituted that no two individuals, in fact, are identical with respect to the properties that characterize them. It may be seriously questioned, however, whether indeed Leibniz' principle does state a factual truth about the world, since when we examine the way in which the principle functions, it turns out that in order for us to be able to numerically distinguish individuals, they must, in Leibniz' formulation, possess different characteristics in some respect. It would appear that the Principle of the Identity of Indiscernibles is a 'grammatical rule' (in Wittgenstein's sense) as to how we are to use the term 'individual'. That is, anything to which we are going to apply the term 'individual' *must* be different in some respect from anything else so distinguished. As such, this statement no longer can be considered a factual statement, one that is either true or false.

Another principle, also bearing Leibniz' name, sometimes identified with the aforementioned Principle of the Identity of Indiscernibles, is the *Principle of Substitutivity.* "Two terms are the *same* if one can be substituted for the other without altering the truth of any statement. If we have *A* and *B* and *A* enters into some true proposition, and the substitution of *B* for *A* wherever it appears, results in a new proposition which is likewise true, and if this can be done for every such proposition, then *A* and *B* are said to be the *same;* and conversely, if *A* and *B* are the same, they can be substituted for one another as I have said." Here, it will be noted, a shift in our concern with the properties of substances, to the terms we use to describe substances, has been effected. It may be questioned, however, whether indeed the Principle of the Identity of Indiscernibles does, in fact, reduce to the Principle of Substitutivity, that is, whether they are so related that the Principle of Identity implies the Principle of Substitutivity. (See Cartwright's essay.)

(3) The dominance in much of contemporary analytic philosophy of linguistic and semantical considerations is a commonplace. On the general subject of identity, the shift from predominantly metaphysical to linguistic considerations is nowhere more evident than in the pioneering paper by Frege, "Über Sinn und Bedeutung," a paper that serves as the springboard for most contemporary discussions of the subject. Frege there raises the question whether equality (the term he uses for what we shall hereafter designate as 'identity'), as expressed by the equation "$a = b$" (read as "a is the same as b" or "a and b coincide"), is a relation between objects or between the names or signs of objects. He argues for the view that identity is best approached as a relation holding between the names or signs of objects. Frege's problem is best viewed as one having to do with the kind of analysis we are to give to *statements of identity*. Thus if the symbol "=" is used to represent identity, the normal or typical identity statement will consist of two expressions on either side of this identity sign. In some cases, the expressions involved may be proper names; in other cases, they may be definite descriptions. For example, an identity statement may consist of an identity asserted to hold between that which is meant or referred to by two proper names flanking the identity sign, as in the statement "Tully = Cicero," or it can be exemplified by a statement in which we have two definite descriptive phrases flanking the identity sign, as in the statement "the Morning Star = the Evening Star," or finally one in which we may have a combination of a proper name and a definite descriptive phrase, as in the statement "Pablo Casals is the most renowned elderly living cellist."

To say $a = a$ (where a is used to symbolize either a proper name or definite descriptive phrase) is commonly thought not to pose any special problems for the identity being asserted and is said to be a "trivial identity." Of course, the question is not a trivial one if, indeed, we ask wherein the identity of any object consists, as we have seen in a brief review of earlier stated questions. However, the typical problems of analysis concerning identity statements revolve, not about statements of the general form "$a = a$," but rather of the general form "$a = b$" where 'a' and 'b' are different expressions. One of the puzzles arising in the analysis to be given to this kind of statement was first noted by Frege and led to his famous distinction between sense and reference. It has to do with the cognitive value of an identity statement. For, as Frege pointed out, to say "The morning star is the morning star" is a trivial identity and is cognitively uninformative, whereas to say "The morning star is identical with the Evening Star" is not at all trivial and represents an astronomical discovery. Yet, if the expressions "the Morning Star" and "the Evening Star" do somehow signify the same object, how can such a statement be cognitively informative since it should then presumably reduce to the trivial identity "$a = a$"? Or, to put the question in modal terms: Whereas the statement "The Morning Star is the Evening Star" is contingent, and *might* have been false, the statement "The Morning Star is the Morning Star" is necessary (*must* be true). In what sense, if at all, can there be, however, *contingent* identity statements? Frege's solution to this puzzle consisted in drawing a distinction between the sense and reference of a term, and in the claim that in the case of the nontrivial identity, $a = b$ ("The Morning Star = the Evening Star" case, for example) while, indeed, the two terms refer to the same object, they do not have the same sense, and to bring these different senses into juxtaposition can be cognitively informative. The examination of the worth of this answer has been a mainstay of philosophic concern ever since Frege's epoch-making paper. (Various aspects of this whole question are discussed in the papers by Lockwood, Kripke, and Woods.)

(4) Most of the papers in this volume (and following these our own brief summary thus far) focus on the questions of identity as these emerge from and relate to individual identity and to statements having to do with this. Out of the considerations of these complex questions, a number of ancillary issues emerge, and philosophers have in various directions sought to extend, apply, and extrapolate these considerations by applying them to fresh topics. Typical of such an enterprise are the matters taken up in the group of three essays (those by Margolis, Ruddick, and Hiz) with which the volume concludes. Thus, the much-debated topic of mind-body identity, the possibility of getting insight into the character of equations in physical science, and the problem of bringing to bear certain semantic considerations in defining what it is to be an individual are the matters touched on respectively in these essays.

The following papers include those presented during a seminar on "Identity and Individuation," *held during the academic year 1969–1970, under the auspices of the New York University Institute of Philosophy. None of the papers have previously been published.*

Contents

IDENTITY
and INDIVIDUATION

Problems of Identity

RODERICK M. CHISHOLM

I

IDENTITY AND PERSISTENCE

1. I shall discuss what is, for me at least, an extraordinarily difficult and puzzling topic: that of persistence, or identity through time. I
have discussed this topic on other occasions when, I regret to say, I
have been even more confused than I am now. But I find that other
philosophers are confused, too. I think I have made some progress.
And so I feel justified, therefore, in taking up the topic once again.

I will begin by formulating three different puzzles, Puzzle A,
Puzzle B, and Puzzle C, and by describing a uniform way of treating
all three puzzles. The treatment in question is reasonably plausible in
connection with Puzzle A, which has to do with identity through space.
It is fairly plausible in connection with Puzzle B, which has to do with
the identity of a familiar type of physical thing through time. But, I will
try to suggest, the treatment is entirely implausible in connection with
Puzzle C, which has to do with the identity of persons through time.
I will also try to suggest that by contemplating the nature of a person,
or, better, by contemplating upon the nature of *oneself,* we will be led
to a more adequate view of the nature of persistence, or identity
through time. My approach to these questions is very much like that
of Leibniz, Bishop Butler, and Thomas Reid.[1]

---

[1] See Leibniz' *New Essays concerning Human Understanding,* Book II, Chapter
XXVII ("What Identity or Diversity Is"); Bishop Butler's dissertation "Of Personal
Identity"; and Thomas Reid, *Essays on the Intellectual Powers of Man,* Essay III,
Chapters IV and VI. I have discussed these questions in "The Loose and Popular and

2. We begin, then, with Puzzle A. We will depict, somewhat schematically, a dispute about the identity of roads. In the northern part of the city, there is a road composed of two parts: A, which is the

$$AB$$
$$CD$$
$$EF \quad GH$$
$$IJ \quad KL$$

south-bound lane, and B, which is the north-bound lane. Proceeding down the south-bound lane, we come to another area where the road is composed, in a similar way, of C and D. Then we arrive at a fork in the road: one can go in a southeasterly direction through GH to KL, or one can go in a southwesterly direction through EF to IJ. The road from AB to IJ is called "Elm Street" and the road from AB to KL is called "Route 42." Elm Street has been in approximately the same place for more than 100 years, while Route 42 is less than 10 years old. But Route 42 is a three-lane highway with the same kind of topping from one end to the other, while Elm Street switches at the fork from tar to concrete and from three lanes to two. We can imagine now that a dispute could develop over the question: "If you start out at AB and stay on the same road, will you end up at IJ or at KL?" The Elm Street faction insists that you will end up at IJ and the Route 42 group insists that it will be at KL. They consult a metaphysician and he gives them this advice:

"Your dispute has to do with the following six objects among others: (1) the northern stretch of road AB; (2) the southwestern stretch IJ; (3) the southeastern stretch KL; (4) a road which begins at AB and ends at IJ, that is, Elm Street; (5) a road which begins at AB and ends up at KL, that is, Route 42; and (6) a Y-shaped object with AB as its handle and IJ and KL as the ends of its forks. These objects overlap in various ways but they are six different things. IJ is not identical with KL; neither of these is identical with AB or with Elm Street or with Route 42 or with the Y-shaped object; and Elm Street, Route 42, and the Y-shaped object are different things despite their overlap. These six different things are equally respectable ontologically. No one of them is any less genuine an entity than any of the others.

the Strict and Philosophical Senses of Identity," in Norman S. Care and Robert H. Grimm, eds., *Perception and Personal Identity* (Cleveland: The Press of Western Reserve University, 1969), and in "Identity Through Time," in Howard Keifer and Milton K. Munitz, eds., *Language, Belief, and Metaphysics* (Albany: State University of New York Press, 1970).

"Now there is no dispute about any observational data. You have agreed about what it is that is called 'Elm Street', about what it is that is called 'Route 42', about the number of lanes in the various places, and about what parts are composed of what. Your dispute, then, has to do with criteria for *constituting the same road* or, as we may also put it, with criteria for applying the expression '*x* constitutes the same road as does *y*'. Both groups should be able to see that the members of the other side have correctly *applied* the criterion they happen to be using. That is to say, given the criterion of the Elm Street faction, it would be true to say that if you start at *AB* and continue on the same road you will end up at *IJ*. And given the criterion of the Route 42 group, it would be true to say that you would end up instead at *KL*. It's just a matter, therefore, of your employing conflicting criteria. You have different standards for applying such expressions as 'the same road' and '*x* constitutes the same road as does *y*'.

"I realize you may be inclined to say that you have the 'right' criterion and that the other people have the 'wrong' one. But think more carefully and try to see just what it is you would be trying to express if you talk that way. For once you see what it is, we can call in other experts—in all probability nonphilosophers this time—and they will settle the dispute for you.

"Thus if you think you are using the expression 'the same road' the way the majority of people do or the way the traffic experts of our culture circle or some other more select group uses it and if you think the other group is not using the expression that way, then we can call in the linguists. They can work up questionnaires and conduct surveys and, it may be hoped, you will soon find out who is right. Or perhaps your concern is not with the ways in which other people may happen to use 'the same road'. You may think only that your way of using it is the most convenient one. If you think, say, that we can handle traffic problems more efficiently by using the expression your way than by using it the other way, then the traffic experts and psychologists should be able to help. Or if you think that your use is the better one for promoting some other kind of good, there will be some expert who will know better than any of us.

"Finally, keep in mind that if people had quite different interests from those that any of us now happen to have and if we had been brought up to play some language game very different from this one, there might be no temptation at all to use *either* of the present criteria. If you were grasshoppers, for example, you might be arguing whether the road from *C* to *K* goes through *E* or goes through *I*."

I think now we can leave the dispute about the road. As philosophers, surely, we have little or no interest in the outcome. I hope we can agree that, in this instance, the metaphysician's advice is fairly reasonable and that there is little more to be said.

But let us now consider what happens when he applies a similar treatment to two analogous problems having to do with identity or persistence through time. I will formulate Puzzle B and Puzzle C. It may be tempting to follow the metaphysician in his treatment of Puzzle B, but something is clearly wrong, I think, with his treatment of Puzzle C. I suggest that, it is not until we have seen what is wrong with his treatment of Puzzle C, that we can really appreciate the problem of identity through time.

3. Puzzle B is a version of the ancient problem of the Ship of Theseus. We now consider a dispute that might arise about the identity of ships through time. The ship when it first set sail was composed of two parts A and B. Parts of parts were replaced and at a later point in its history it was composed of C and D where previously it had been composed of A and B. At a certain point it underwent fission and went off, so to speak, in two different directions — one ship being composed of E and F going off toward the southwest and another ship being composed of G and H going off toward the southeast. The ship that went southwest ended up being composed of I and J and the one that went southeast

$$AB$$
$$CD$$
$$EF \quad GH$$
$$IJ \quad KL$$

being composed of K and L. This time the question arises: "Had you boarded AB when it first set sail and remained on the same ship, would you now be on the southwesterly IJ or on the southeasterly KL?" The IJ faction may point out that, if you end up on IJ, you will have remained throughout on a wooden ship called "*Theseus*" and that, if you end up on KL, you will now be on an aluminum ship called "*The East Coast Ferry*." The KL group may point out, to the contrary, that if you end up on KL, you will have remained throughout on a ship having the same daily schedule, the same crew, and the same traditions and that, if you end up on IJ, you will be on a weekend cruise ship having an amateur crew and nothing worth calling a tradition. Being impressed by the way in which our metaphysician handled the problem of the roads, the two parties turn to him for advice. And this is what he tells them:

"There is no difference in principle between the present problem and the problem of the roads. For just as an object that is extended through space at a given time has, for each portion of space that it occupies, a *spatial part* that is unique to that portion of space at that time, so, too, any object that persists through a period of time has, for each subperiod of time during which it exists, a *temporal part* that is unique to that subperiod of time.

"Taking our cue from the problem of the roads, we see that in this case, too, there are six objects which are of special concern. Just as a road that extends through space has different spatial parts at the different places at which it exists, a ship that persists through time has different temporal parts at the different times at which it exists. So we may distinguish: (1) the earlier temporal part AB; (2) the present southwestern part IJ; (3) the present southeastern part KL; (4) that temporally extended object now called the "*Theseus*" with the early part AB, the later part IJ, and CD and EF falling in between; (5) that temporally extended object now called "*The East Coast Ferry*" with the early part AB, the later part KL, and CD and GH falling in between; and (6), what you may not have noticed, a Y-shaped temporal object with AB as its root and IJ and KL as the ends of its forks. As in the previous case, these are different things despite their overlap and they are all on a par ontologically.

"There is no dispute about any of the observational data. You are in agreement about crews, schedules, stuff, and traditions, and about what things are called what. Your dispute has to do with *criteria* for constituting the same ship, or, as we may now also put it, with criteria for applying the expression 'x constitutes the same ship as does y'. The members of each faction have correctly applied their own criteria. If you are inclined to say that your criterion is the right one and that the other one is the wrong one, reflect a little further and I'm sure we can find some nonphilosophical expert who can help you settle the question. Do you think, for example, that you are using 'the same ship' the way the majority of people do or the way the nautical people do? The linguists can check on that for you. Or do you think you are using it the way it's used in the courts? Then we can call in the lawyers. Or do you think that your way of using it is the most convenient one given your purposes or given the purposes of most people? State as clearly as you can what the purposes in question are and then we can find an expert who will help you out.

"Keep in mind that, if people had quite different interests and played a different language game, then there might be no temptation to use either of the present criteria. After all there are still other temporal objects involved here: for example, the temporally scattered object made up of A, F, and L, the one made up of C, H, and J, and so on. Some one of those might be what you would call a ship—if *you* were a different type of temporal object."

Let us not pause to evaluate this advice. For our interest in Puzzle B and its treatment is only transitional. I have spelled out the account only to prepare us for Puzzle C.

4. Puzzle C: Mr. Jones has learned somehow that he is about to undergo fission. Or, more accurately, he has learned that his body will undergo fission. It is now made up of parts A and B. Presently it will be made up of C and D. Then there will be fission; one body will go off as EF and end up as IJ, and the other will go off as GH and end up as KL. Then there will be the two men, IJ and KL. Or, to be more cautious, there will be a man who has IJ as his body and there will be a man who has KL as his body.

$$AB$$
$$CD$$
$$EF \quad GH$$
$$IJ \quad KL$$

Mr. Jones knows that the man who ends up with IJ will have the distinctive physical characteristics — brain waves, fingerprints, and all the rest — that he, Mr. Jones, now has, and that the man who ends up as KL will not. He also knows that the inner parts of IJ will have evolved in the usual manner from the inner parts he has now, that is, from the inner parts of AB, whereas a number of the crucial organs within KL will have been transplanted from outside. But he knows further that the man who has KL as his body will have the memories, or a significant part of the memories, that he, Mr. Jones, now has, and what is more that the man will remember doing things that only Mr. Jones has ever done. Or perhaps we should say, more cautiously, that the man will *seem* to himself to remember — will *think he remembers* — having done those things. And the memory, or ostensible memory, will be extraordinarily accurate in points of detail. Mr. Jones now puts this question: "Will I be the one who ends up as IJ or will I be the one who ends up as KL?"

It has been said that there are "two main competing answers" to the question "What are the criteria for the identity of a person through time?" One of these is that "the criterion of the identity of a person is the identity of the body that he has." And the other is that "the criterion of the identity of a person is the set of memories which he has." [2] We will suppose that, according to the first of these criteria ("the bodily criterion") the man who has IJ as his body is the same person as Mr. Jones; and according to the second of these criteria ("the memory cri-

[2] See Terence Penelhum's article, "Personal Identity," in *The Encyclopedia of Philosophy*, ed. Paul Edwards (New York: Macmillan, 1967), Vol. VI.

terion") the man who has KL as his body is the same person as Mr. Jones.

To make sure that Mr. Jones's interest in the question is not purely theoretical, let us suppose further that he has the following information: Though both men will languish during their final phases, the IJ and the KL phases, the man who ends up as KL will lead the most wretched of lives during his GH phase, and the man who ends up as IJ will lead a life of great happiness and value during his EF phase. And so Mr. Jones asks with some concern: "Which one am I going to be?"

The approach of the metaphysician should now be familiar. He will note that, for each portion of space that Mr. Jones's body now occupies there is a spatial part of Mr. Jones's body that is now unique to that portion of space. He will then point out that, for any period of time during which Mr. Jones will have existed, there is a *temporal part* of Mr. Jones that is unique to that period of time. Turning to the problem at hand, he will distinguish the following things among others: AB; IJ; KL; the thing that begins as AB and ends as LJ; the thing that begins as AB and ends as KL; and the Y-shaped object that begins as AB and ends as IJ in one place and KL in another. He will note that Mr. Jones is raising a question about criteria: "Is 'the memory criterion' or 'the bodily criterion' the correct criterion of what it is for someone at one time to constitute the same person as does someone at some other time?" He will point out to Mr. Jones that, in asking which is the correct criterion, he is in fact concerned with some more specific question. If he is asking how the majority of people, or how certain people, use the expression "same person," he should consult the linguists. If he is asking how the courts would deal with the question, he should look up the law books. And if he is asking, with respect to certain definite ends, what linguistic uses would best promote those ends, there will be authorities who can give him at least a probable answer. (*We* might remind Mr. Jones, however, that if he asks these empirical authorities how *he*, Mr. Jones, could best promote certain ends after the fission has taken place, then he should look very carefully at the answer.)

As before, the metaphysician will conclude with some general advice: "Keep in mind that, if people had quite different interests and played a different language game, there might be no temptation to use either the bodily criterion or the memory criterion. After all, there are still other temporal objects involved in your problem. With different interests and a different makeup, you might be more concerned with two of *them* instead of with the two that you happen to have singled out. You claim to know that the EF phase is going to be good and that the GH phase is going to be bad. You haven't noticed, apparently, that there is more than one person who will go through the EF phase and more than one person who will go through the *GH* phase. What other persons? For example, there is the one that goes from *AB* to *EF* to *KL*, and then there is the one that goes from *CD* through *GH* to *IJ*. If you had a different makeup, you might wish you were one of *those* and hope you're not the other."

If Mr. Jones is at all reasonable, he will feel at this point that something has gone wrong. However many persons the problem involves, if there is a person who starts out as *AB*, goes through *CD* and *EF* to *IJ*, there is not also *another* person who starts out as *AB*, goes through *EF*, and ends up as *KL*. And if there is a person who starts out as *AB*, goes through *CD* and *GH* to *KL*, there is not *another* person who goes through *GH* and ends up as *IJ*. (It would hardly be just to punish *two* persons for the sins that someone committed during the *GH* phase.) And, what is more important, after Mr. Jones has consulted the various empirical authorities, he will still wonder whether he has an answer to his question: "Which one am I going to be?"

Where did the metaphysician go wrong?

5. Going back for a moment to Route 42 in Puzzle A, consider what is involved when we say there is a Buick and an Oldsmobile on the road, the former a mile behind the latter. We are saying, of course, that there exists an x, namely, Route 42, which is such that a Buick is on x and an Oldsmobile is on x, a mile in front of the Buick. But this is to say that there is a y and a z which are distinct from x and from each other and which are such that the Buick is on y and not on z and the Oldsmobile is on z and not on y. And so we are referring to *three* different things in addition to the Oldsmobile and the Buick. We are referring, first, to Route 42 which both the Oldsmobile and the Buick are on; we are referring, secondly, to that portion of Route 42 which the Oldsmobile but not the Buick is on; and we are referring, thirdly, to that portion of Route 42 which the Buick but not the Oldsmobile is on. Our metaphysician assumes that temporal differences are analogous.

What is involved when we say that a ship had been red and then subsequently became blue? According to our metaphysician we are, once again, referring to three different things. We are saying, of course, that there was an x, namely, the ship, which was such that x was red and then x became blue. And this, according to our metaphysician, is to say that there was a y and a z, each distinct from x and from each other, which were such that y was red and not blue and z was blue and not red. In addition to the ship, there was that "temporal part" of it which was red and that other "temporal part" of it which was blue.

It is very important to note that, according to the metaphysician, his thesis will be true whether or not any of the parts of the ship are ever replaced — or, more exactly, it will be true whether or not anything occurs that would *ordinarily* be described as replacement of the parts of the ship. Let the ship be such that we could describe it in our ordinary language by saying it has kept all its parts intactly, down to the smallest particles. Our metaphysician will nevertheless say that that temporal part of the ship which is red is other than that temporal part of the ship which is blue and that each of these is other than the ship itself.

And he maintains a similar thesis with respect to Puzzle C. Consider now the man who began with the body made up of *A* and *B* and ended up with *I* and *J*. What is involved in saying that he is sad one day and happy the next? Again, there will be an *x*, the man, such that *x* is sad and subsequently *x* is happy. And to say this, according to our metaphysician, is to say that there is also a *y* and a *z* each distinct from *x* and from each other and such that *y* is sad and *z* is happy. But is this true?

It may be instructive to compare the doctrine of our metaphysician with what Jonathan Edwards says in defense of the doctrine of original sin. Edwards is concerned with the question whether it is just to impute to you and me the sins that were committed by Adam. And he wishes to show that it is *as* just to attribute Adam's sins to us now as it is to attribute any *other* past sins to us now.

He appeals to the doctrine, which he accepts, that God not only created the world *ex nihilo* but constantly preserves or upholds the things which he creates. Without God's continued preservation of the world, all created things would fall into nothingness. Now Edwards says that "God's upholding created substance, or causing its existence in each successive moment, is altogether equivalent to an immediate *production out of nothing*, at each moment." In preserving the table in its being a moment from now, God will get no help from the table. It isn't as though the table will be there waiting to be upheld. If it were there waiting to be upheld, if it were available to God and ready for preservation, he would not *need* to uphold or preserve it. God does not uphold the table by making use of matter that is left over from an earlier moment. Edwards compares the persistence of such things as the table with that of the reflection or image on the surface of a mirror. "The image that exists this moment, is not at all *derived* from the image which existed the last preceding moment . . . . If the succession of new *rays* be intercepted, by something interposed between the object and the glass, the image immediately ceases; the *past existence* of the image has no influence to uphold it, so much as for one moment. Which shows that the image is altogether completely remade every moment; and strictly speaking, is in no part numerically the same with that which existed in the moment preceding. And truly so the matter must be with the *bodies* themselves, as well as their images. They also cannot be the

same, with an absolute identity, but must be wholly renewed every moment. . . ." Edwards summarizes his doctrine of preservation this
way: "If the existence of created *substance*, in each successive moment, be wholly the effect of God's immediate power, in *that* moment,
without any dependence on prior existence, as much as the first creation out of *nothing,* then what exists at this moment, by this power, is a
new effect, and simply and absolutely considered, not the same with
any past existence. . . ." [3]

This conception of persisting physical things, though not its the-
ological basis, is also defended by a number of contemporary philosophers. It may be found, for example, in the axiom system concerning things and their parts that is developed in Carnap's *Introduction to
Symbolic Logic.*[4] Carnap's system is derived from the systems developed by J. H. Woodger and Alfred Tarski, in Woodger's *The Axiomatic
Method in Biology.*[5] These authors say that, for every moment at which
a thing exists there is a set of momentary parts of the thing; none of
these parts exists at any other moment; and the thing itself is the sum
of its momentary parts.[6]

The thing that constitutes you now, according to this view, is diverse from the things that have constituted you at any other moment,
just as you are diverse from every other person who exists now. But
God, according to Jonathan Edwards, can contemplate a collection of
objects existing at different times and "treat them as one." He can
take a collection of various individuals existing at different times and
think of them as all constituting a single individual. Edwards appeals to
a doctrine of truth by divine convention; he says that God "*makes
truth* in affairs of this nature." Like our metaphysician, God could regard temporally scattered individuals — you this year, me last year, and
General De Gaulle the year before that — as comprising a single individual. And then he could justly punish you this year and me last year
for the sins that General De Gaulle committed the year before that.

---

[3] The quotations are from Edwards' *Doctrine of Original Sin Defended* (1758), Part IV,
Chapter II.
[4] Rudolf Carnap, *Introduction to Symbolic Logic* (New York: Dover Publications,
1958), p. 213 ff.
[5] J. H. Woodger, *The Axiomatic Method in Biology* (Cambridge: Cambridge University
Press, 1937); see especially pp. 55–63, and Appendix E by Alfred Tarski (pp. 161–172).
[6] A thing *a* is said to be the *sum* of a class *F*, provided only every member of the class *F*
is a part of *a*, and every part of *a* has a part in common with some member of the class.
If, as these authors postulate, every nonempty class has a sum, there would be, for example, an *individual thing* which is the sum of the class of men: Every man would be a
part of this collective man and every part of this collective man would share a part with
some individual man. The same would hold for that class the only members of which are
this man and that horse. An opposing view is that of Boethius: a man and a horse are not
one thing. See D. P. Henry, *The Logic of Saint Anselm* (Oxford: The Clarendon Press,
1967), p. 56.

And so, Edwards concludes, "no solid reason can be given, why God . . . may not establish a constitution whereby the natural posterity of Adam . . . should be treated as *one* with him, for the derivation, either of righteousness, and communion in rewards, or of the loss of righteousness, and consequent corruption and guilt."

Like our metaphysician, Edwards is impressed by what he takes to be the analogy between space and time. To persuade his reader that God could reasonably regard Adam's posterity as being one with Adam, he asserts that there would be no problem at all if Adam's posterity *coexisted* with Adam. If Adam's posterity had "somehow *grown out of him*, and yet remained *contiguous* and literally *united to him*, as the branches to a tree, or the members of the body to the head; and had all, before the fall, existed together at the *same time*, though in *different places*, as the head and members are in different places," surely then, Edwards says, God could treat the whole collection as "one moral whole" with each of us as its parts. And if a collection of persons existing in different places can be thought of as a single moral whole, why not also a collection of persons existing at different times?

6. What are we to say of all this? What Jonathan Edwards and our metaphysician have left out, if I am not mistaken, is what has traditionally been called the *unity* of every real thing. Leibniz said that we acquire this notion of unity by reflecting upon our own nature.[7] I suggest that this is so and that if we reflect "upon our own nature," we will see what is wrong with the Edwardian doctrine and with the solution to Puzzle C.

Edwards was even mistaken in his spatial figure. If we think of Adam's posterity as growing out of Adam's body, with me here and you there and Adam some place in between, we cannot properly regard the resulting whole as "a moral unity." Though there may be just one body involved there will be irreducibly many persons if one of them is me, another you, and a third Adam.

Let me quote to you from the chapter "On the Unity of Consciousness" from Franz Brentano's *Psychologie vom empirischen Standpunkt*. Brentano asks whether when we consider our own consciousness at any moment we find a real unified whole or a bare multiplicity — what he called a mere *collectivum* and not a unity or unitary whole. Suppose you find yourself hearing a certain sound and seeing a certain color, as you do now, and you realize that these are two different experiences. Could one conceivably say that the thing that is doing the seeing is *other* than the thing that is doing the hearing? "If the presentation of the color is to be ascribed to one thing and the presentation

---

[7] *New Essays Concerning Human Understanding,* Book II, Ch. I, sec. 8.

of the sound to another, is the presentation of the difference to be as-cribed to the one, or to the other, or to both together, or to a third thing?" If one thing is doing the hearing and another thing is doing the seeing, how would either of *those* things become aware of the fact that there are two different experiences going on, one the hearing and the other the seeing? It wouldn't do, Brentano says, to attribute the per-ception of the difference to some *third* thing — some thing other than the thing that's doing the seeing and other than the thing that's doing the hearing. Should we ascribe the perception of the difference then to the *two* different things — to the seer and to the hearer? "This, too, would be ridiculous. It would be as though one were to say that, although nei-ther a blind man nor a deaf man can perceive the difference between a color and a tone, the two of them can perceive it together when the one sees and the other hears. . . . When we combine the activities of the blind man and the deaf man, we have only a *collectivum*, not a real uni-tary thing [*immer nur ein Kollektiv, niemals ein einheitliches wirkliches Ding*]. Whether the blind man and the deaf man are close together or far apart makes no difference. It wouldn't make any difference whether they lived in the same house, or whether they were Siamese twins, or whether they had developed even more inseparably together. It is only when the color and the sound are presented to one and the same indi-vidual thing, that it is thinkable that they may be compared with each other." [8]

In short, when you see and hear something at the same time, the experience cannot be adequately described by saying "There exists an x and a y such that x sees something, y hears something, and x is other than y." We can use just one personal variable ("There exists an x such that x sees something and x also hears it") or if we use two ("There exists an x such that x hears something and there exists a y such that y hears it"), then we must add that their values are one and the same ("x is identical with y").

Brentano discussed the kind of unity that is involved when we are aware of ourselves as having two different experiences, seeing and hearing, at the same time. Let us now consider, analogously, the kind of unity that is involved when we are aware of ourselves as having dif-ferent experiences throughout an interval of time. This is what happens when, as now, you are listening to someone talking, or what happens when you are listening to a melody. But consider an experience of even shorter duration: one hears the birdcall "Bob White." The experience might be described by saying "There exists an x such that x hears 'Bob'

[8] Franz Brentano, *Psychologie vom empirischen Standpunkt*, Vol. I (Leipzig: Felix Meiner, 1924), pp. 226–227.

and x hears 'White'." But we want to make sure we are not talking about the experience wherein one hears two sounds at once—'Bob' from one bird and 'White' from another. And so we might say "There exists an x and two times, t^1 and t^2, such that t^2 is later than t^1, and such that x hears 'Bob' at t^1 and x hears 'White' at t^2." If we are not to reify times, we will put the matter another way, perhaps as "There exists an x such that x hears 'Bob' *before* x hears 'White' " or as "There exists an x such that x hears 'Bob' *and then* x hears 'White'." But we are not now concerned with what is philosophically the best way to describe the passage of time. Our present concern is with the variable 'x' and the thing that it refers to.

We will say, then, "There exists an x such that x hears 'Bob' and then x hears 'White'." Jonathan Edwards and our metaphysician would say that the experience could be adequately described by using two variables: "There exists a y and a z such that y hears 'Bob' and z hears 'White'." But the latter sentence is *not* adequate to the experience in question. The man who has the experience knows not only (1) that there is someone who hears 'Bob' and someone who hears 'White'. He also knows (2) that the one who hears 'Bob' is *identical with* the one who hears 'White'. And, what is crucial to the present problem, he knows (3) that his experience of hearing 'Bob' and his experience of hearing 'White' were not *also* had by two other things, each distinct from himself and from each other.

7. What are we to say, then, of the doctrine of "temporal parts," of the doctrine according to which, for every period of time during which an individual thing exists, there is a temporal part of that thing which is unique to that period of time? We can point out, as I have tried to do, that it is not adequate to the experience we have of ourselves. We can also point out that the doctrine multiplies entities beyond necessity. And, finally, we can criticize the case *for* the doctrine of temporal parts.

What is this case? It is based, presumably, upon the assumption that whatever may be said about spatial continuity and identity may also be said, *mutatis mutandis,* about temporal continuity and identity. If this assumption is correct, then the doctrine of temporal parts would seem to be true. We may say, as our metaphysician did: "Just as an object that is extended through space at a given time has, for each portion of space that it occupies, a *spatial part* that is unique to that portion of space at that time, so, too, any object that persists through a period of time has, for each subperiod of time during which it exists, a *temporal part* that is unique to that subperiod of time." But is it correct to assume that whatever may be said about spatial continuity and identity may also be said, *mutatis mutandis,* about temporal continuity and identity? I would say that there is a fundamental *disanalogy* between space and time.

The disanalogy may be suggested by saying simply: "One and the same thing cannot be in two different places at one and the same time. But one and the same thing can be at two different times in one and the same place." Let us put the point of disanalogy, however, somewhat more precisely.

When we say "a thing cannot be in two different places at one and the same time," we mean that it is not possible for *all* the parts of the thing to be in one of the places at that one time and *also* to be in the other of the places at that same time. It *is* possible, of course, for *some* part of the thing to be in place at a certain time and *another* part of the thing to be in another place at that time. And to remove a possible ambiguity in the expression "all the parts of a thing," let us spell it out to "all the parts that the thing ever will have had."

Instead of saying simply "a thing cannot be in two different places at one and the same time," let us say this: "It is *not* possible for there to be a thing which is such that all the parts it ever will have had are in one place at one time and also in another place at that same time." And instead of saying "a thing can be at two different times in one and the same place," let us say this: "It *is* possible for there to be a thing which is such that all the parts it ever will have had are in one place at one time and also in that same place at another time."

It seems to me to be clear that each of these two theses is true and therefore that there is a fundamental disanalogy between space and time. And so if the case *for* the doctrine of temporal parts presupposes that there is no such disanalogy, then the case is inadequate. (We may, of course, appeal to the doctrine of temporal parts in order to *defend* the view that there is no such disanalogy. We may use it, in particular, to criticize the second of the two theses I set forth above, the thesis according to which it is possible for there to be a thing which is such that all the parts it ever will have had are in one place at one time and also in that same place at another time. But what, then, is the case *for* the doctrine of temporal parts?)

The doctrine of temporal parts is sometimes invoked as a solution to this type of puzzle. "(i) Johnson was President five years ago but is not President now. Therefore (ii) something can be truly said of the Johnson of five years ago that cannot be truly said of the Johnson of now. Hence (iii) the Johnson of five years ago is other than the Johnson of now. How, then, are they related?" The proposed solution is: "They are different temporal parts of the same person." But it is simpler just to note that (ii) is false. *Nothing* can truly be said of the Johnson of five years ago that cannot be truly said of the Johnson of now.

The Johnson of now, like the Johnson of five years ago, *was* President five years ago, and the Johnson of five years ago, like the Johnson of now, is *not* President now. But if (ii) is false, then the derivation of (iii) is invalid. And so the puzzle disappears.

8. Mr. Jones's problem, the problem of Puzzle C, is much more difficult than our metaphysician thought it was. I fear that we cannot help him either, but we may point out, in conclusion, certain considerations which would be relevant to the solution of his problem.

Let us say that an "Edwardian object" is an individual thing such that, for any two different moments at which it exists, there is a set of things making it up at the one moment and another set of things making it up at the other moment and the two sets of things have no members in common. According to Jonathan Edwards and to the doctrine of temporal parts, *every* individual thing is Edwardian. I have suggested that some things that persist through time, namely, we ourselves, are *not* Edwardian. Some persisting things have a kind of *unity* through time that Edwardian objects, if there *are* any Edwardian objects, do not have.[9] How are we to characterize this unity?

We might characterize it by reference to "intact persistence." Let us say that a thing "persists intactly" if it has continued, uninterrupted existence through a period of time and if, at any moment of its existence, it has precisely the same parts it has at any other moment of its existence. Thus a thing that persists intactly would exist at at least two different times; for any two times during which it exists, it also exists at any time between those times; and at no time during which it exists does it have any part it does not have at any other time during which it exists. We might now define a "primary thing" as a thing that persists intactly during every moment of its existence. The simplest type of unity through time, then, would be that possessed by primary things. Other types of unity could then be described by reference to it.

It is tempting to say, in Leibnizian fashion: "There are things. Therefore there are primary things." But a somewhat more modest thesis would be this: Every extended period of time, however short,

---

[9] I have attributed to Carnap the view that every individual thing is Edwardian; see Carnap, *op. cit.,* p. 213 ff. I should note, however, that he is quite aware of what I have called the problem of the unity of a persisting thing through time. He is aware, for example, that such an object as the one that is composed of my temporal parts of this year, yours of last year, and General De Gaulle's of the year before that does not have the type of unity through time that other objects do. To secure the latter type of unity he introduces the concept of *genidentity.* "Following Kurt Lewin, we say that world-points [temporal slices] of *the same particle* are *genidentical*"; *op. cit.,* p. 198. (I have italicized "the same particle.") But if we do not multiply entities by assuming that every concrete individual is Edwardian, we need not multiply relations by supposing that there is a concept of *genidentity* in addition to that of identity, or persistence through time.

is such that some primary thing exists during some part of that time. I would suggest that it is only by presupposing this thesis that we can make sense of the identity or persistence of any individual thing through time.

So far as Mr. Jones's problem is concerned, we may note that it is at least possible that persons are primary things and hence that Mr. Jones is a primary thing. This would mean, of course, that we could not identify Mr. Jones with that object that persists without remaining intact which is his body. But for all anyone knows he might be identical with some physical thing which is a *part* of that body. We should also note that it is logically possible for a primary thing to persist from one time to another without there being any *criterion* by means of which anyone who had identified it at the earlier time could also identify it at the later time. Hence if Mr. Jones is a primary thing, it is possible that *he* will be the one who has bodily parts *IJ* even though neither he nor anyone else will ever know, or even have good reason to believe, that the man who now has bodily parts *AB* is also the man who will have bodily parts *IJ*.[10]

II

The Identity of Events and States of Affairs

1. In addition to concrete individual things and their properties, there are also such things as events, such things as propositions, and such things as states of affairs. I shall present and attempt to defend one way of looking at these things, one theory about the nature and interrelations of events, propositions, and states of affairs.[11]

Any theory about the nature and interrelations of events, propositions, and states of affairs should be adequate to the fact of *recurrence,* the fact that there are some things that recur or happen more than once. We begin, then, with this concept.

To make clear what is here intended by "recurrence," let us note that, for every finite number n, there are exactly four ways in which an event p may occur exactly n times. This point is illustrated by the accompanying diagrams. We let "$=$" represent an occurrence of p that has no beginning or ending, "$\sqsubset$" an occurrence of p that has a beginning and no ending, "$\sqsupset$" an occurrence of p that has an ending but no beginning and "$\square$" an occurrence of p that has both a beginning and an ending. (I use the expressions "beginning" and "ending" rather

---

[10] Compare Sydney S. Shoemaker, "Comments," and Roderick M. Chisholm, "Reply," in *Perception and Personal Identity,* Norman S. Care and Robert H. Grimm, eds. (Cleveland: The Press of Case Western Reserve University, 1969).

[11] Parts of this section are adapted from "Events and Propositions," *Nous,* Vol. IV (1970), 15–24. I am indebted to Ernest Sosa, Michael Corrado, and Robert Keim.

than "coming into being" and "passing away," for, given the ontology that is here defended, it is not correct to say that events come into being when they occur or that they pass away, or cease to be, when they cease to occur.) If we let the direction from left to right represent that from past to future, our three diagrams will indicate, respectively, the four ways in which p could occur just once, the four ways in which p could occur just twice, and the four ways in which p could occur just three times.

Once	Twice	3 times
⚌	⊐⊏	⊐▢⊏
⊏	▢⊏	▢▢⊏
⊐	⊐▢	⊐▢▢
▢	▢▢	▢▢▢

Thus the first diagram depicts these four ways in which an event may occur exactly once. (1) The event may occur without beginning and without ending; an ancient example would be the being in motion of the heavenly spheres. (2) The event may occur without ending but with beginning; if St. Thomas is right, there being light would be an example. (3) The event may occur without beginning but with ending; there being total darkness may be an example. And, finally, (4) the event may occur with ending and with beginning; presumably this group of people being in this room is an example. If for every event there is also that event which is its negation, then, in the first of these four cases, the negation of p does not occur at all; in the second and third it occurs just once; and in the fourth it occurs just twice. To depict the ways in which an event may occur n times, where n is greater than or equal to 2, we construct two columns as in the second diagram and insert between them n minus 2 columns of squares.

How are we to describe the recurrence of an event? There seem to be four coherent theories of recurrence. (1) We might consider saying that there are three different *times* such that the event occurs at the earliest and at the latest and not at the one in the middle. But this will not do if we are reluctant to suppose or if we are reluctant to *begin* by supposing, that, in addition to events, there are such things as "times." (2) We might consider saying that there are three different *occasions* such that the event occurs on the earliest and on the latest and not on the one in the middle. But what are the things we would then be calling "occasions"? (3) We might say that, if an event p recurs, then there are events q, r, and s of this kind: r occurs after q, and s occurs after r, and p is *exemplified* or *instantiated* in q and in s and not in r. In this case, we would appeal to two quite different sets of entities: "*abstract events*," or "*event types*," such as *p*, which may be exemplified or instantiated in "*concrete events*" such as *q*, *r*, and *s*. This, surely, would be to multiply entities at a very early point. (4) Using tenses, we might define "*p* recurs" by saying "It is, was, or will be the case that: *p* did occur, *p* is not occurring, and *p* will occur." I shall not investigate this possibility, for the fifth method seems to me to have advantages that it does not have. (5) I suggest that, instead of positing such entities as "times," "occasions," or "concrete events," and instead of making essential use of tenses, we describe recurrence by making use of the concept of *conjunctive events* and the concept of the *negation of an event*.

If an event *p* occurs *while* an event *q* is occurring, then the *conjunctive event p & q* occurs. If John sometimes sings while he walks, then the conjunctive event with John walking and John singing occurs, but if he never sings while he walks, then, even though John's walking occurs and John's singing occurs, John's walking and John's singing does not occur.

We shall distinguish between saying that a certain event does *not* occur and saying that the *negation* of that event *does* occur, between saying "*p* does not occur" and saying "not-*p* does occur." If *p* is "it's raining in Chicago," and not-*p* is "it's not raining in Chicago," it is true to say that *p* sometimes occurs and also true to say that not-*p* sometimes occurs. Hence, though "*p* does not occur" implies "not-*p* does occur," it is not the case that "not-*p* does occur" implies "*p* does not occur." (The *negation* of an event might be defined in the following way by reference to conjunctive events: "not-*p* occurs" for "There is a *q* such that *q* occurs and *q & p* does not occur.") [12]

Now we may say, tenselessly, that an event *recurs* if and only if the event occurs and then after that the negation of the event occurs and then after that the event occurs.

Before setting forth this theory in detail, let us compare the *occurrence* of events with the *truth* of propositions. We will use "to occur" as short for "to occur, hold, obtain, happen, or take place."

2. Consider these truths that hold of any proposition *p*:

(a) *p* is true or the negation of *p* is true;
(b) *p* is true if and only if the negation of the negation of *p* is true;
(c) If the negation of *p* is true, then *p* is not true.

If we replace "is true" by "occurs," the first two will also hold of any event. But the third will not. For if an event recurs, then the event

---

[12] This suggestion is due to Michael Corrado.

occurs and its negation also occurs. And consider these truths about conjunctive propositions:

(d) If p & q is true, then p is true and q is true;

(e) p & q is true if and only if q & p is true;

(f) p & (q & r) is true if and only if q & (p & r) is true;

(g) If p is true and p & $\sim q$ is not true, then p & q is true;

(h) If p is true and q is true, then p & q is true;

(i) If p & q is true, and q & r is true, then q & r is true;

(j) If p & q is true, then p & $\sim q$ is not true.

The first four of these, (d) through (g), remain true if we take them to pertain to events and replace "is true" by "occurs"; but the last three, (h) through (j), become false. For, as we have noted, the conjunctive event p & q does not occur unless p and q overlap in time — unless p occurs *while* q occurs.[13]

Thus "Lincoln being President" has occurred and "Agnew being Vice President" has occurred, but "Lincoln being President and Agnew being Vice President" has not occurred. (I use quotation marks, of course, only to make reading more convenient.) "Franklin Roosevelt being President and Harry Truman being Senator" has occurred, as has "Franklin Roosevelt being President and Harry Truman being Vice President," but "Harry Truman being Senator and Harry Truman being Vice President" has not occurred. And just as "Franklin Roosevelt being President and Harry Truman being Vice President" has occurred, "Franklin Roosevelt being President and Harry Truman not being Vice President" has also occurred. (We may note, incidentally, that "Franklin Roosevelt being President" occurred exactly once even though he served more than three terms, and "Grover Cleveland being President" occurred exactly twice even though he served less than three terms.)

3. If an event p recurs, we may be able to single out its various *occurrences* and say things of some of them we cannot say of others. For example, we might be able to say of the third occurrence of p, but not of any of its other occurrences, that it came after a certain event r, or that it contributed causally to a certain event q. Must we say, therefore, that in addition to events there are such things as the *particular occurrences* of events? Or can we reduce talk that is ostensibly about the particular occurrences of events to talk that refers just to events,

---

[13] Should we add "unless p occurs *where* q occurs"? If we do not, we must countenance a further disanalogy between events and propositions: p may occur while not-p occurs (somewhere else); hence p & p may occur. But for simplicity we ignore this possibility.

attributes, and individual things? I shall describe one way in which such reduction might be carried out.

If an event p recurs, that is, if p occurs at least twice, then p occurs, p is followed by its negation, and p follows its negation. I shall make two metaphysical assumptions about such recurrence. The first is that no event is followed by its negation unless some individual thing alters or comes into being or ceases to be. And the second is that nothing, in Locke's terms, is capable of "two beginnings of existence." If a thing ceases to be, then _it,_ itself, does not come into being again. We may also note a third general principle, namely, that everything is such that, for any two moments during which it exists, it has some properties at the one moment it does not have at the other. I believe that, given an adequate conception of time, this third principle can be seen to be analytic.[14] The principles guarantee that, as long as there are individual things, there will be no "eternal recurrence," and that, for any interval of time, _something_ is occurring throughout that interval that does not occur at any other interval.

Let us introduce the location "p occurs before q begins." We may abbreviate this as "pBq," reading "$\sim pBq$" as "not-p occurs before q begins," and reading "$pB \sim q$" as "p occurs before not-q begins." Since events may recur, the relation indicated by "pBq" is not asymmetrical. (If p occurs twice, then "$pB \sim p$" and "$\sim pBp$," as well as "pBp" will be true.) Nor is the relation transitive. (Suppose q occurs, then r occurs, then p occurs, then q occurs again, and r does not occur again and p occurs just once. In this case "pBq" and "qBr" will be true and "pBr" will be false.)

Among the essential properties of the relation expressed by "p occurs before q begins" are those expressed in the following axioms:

(A1) $pBq \supset \sim qBq$.
(A2) p occurs and q occurs $\equiv (pBq$ or qBp or p & q occurs).
(A3) $[pBq$ and qBr and $\sim (qBp)] \supset pBr$.
(A4) $pBp \supset pB \sim p$.
(A5) $\sim (p)(pB \sim p)$.

The second axiom enables us to deduce "p occurs and q occurs" from "pBq." Perhaps we do some slight violence to ordinary language, since it is not clear that "p occurs before q begins" would ordinarily

---

[14] Can we put this assumption without quantifying over times? We might say: Every individual thing x is such that, if there occur two different events p and q, such that p & q does not occur (that is, p does not occur while q occurs), and such that x exists while p occurs and also while q occurs, then x has a certain property while p occurs that x does not have while q occurs.

be taken to imply that q occurs. I propose now the following definitions:

D1. p recurs (or p occurs at least twice) $= Df\ pBp$.

D2. p always occurs $= Df$ Not-p does not occur.

D3. p occurs exactly once $= Df\ p$ occurs and $\sim(pBp)$.

If an event occurs exactly once, we might call it, not a "unique event" (for everything is unique), but a "one-shot event," or a "nonrecurring event."

The strategy of the definitions that follow is this. We first say what it is for something to occur *during* p's *first occurrence*, but without using any term purporting to designate p's first occurrence. In terms of that, we next say what it is for something to occur during what is at least p's second occurrence; and so on, for any finite number n. And then we can say what it is for p to occur exactly n times.

D4. s occurs during p's first occurrence $= Df$. There is a q such that q occurs exactly once, q & s occurs, q & $\sim p$ does not occur, and $\sim(pBq)$.

D5. There is something that occurs during what is at least p's nth occurrence $= Df$. There is an s such that s occurs exactly once, and there is a q and an r such that q occurs exactly once, r occurs exactly once, q occurs during p's occurrence $n - 1$, qBr, rBs, p & s occur, and p & r does not occur.

Thus if p occurs at least two times, there will be three "one-shot events" such that no two of them occur together and p occurs together with the earliest and the latest but not with the one in the middle.

D6. p occurs exactly n times $= Df$. There is something that occurs during what is at least p's nth occurrence and nothing that occurs during what is at least p's occurrence $n + 1$.

Other possible definitions are these: "s is unique to an occurrence of p" for "s occurs exactly once, p & s occurs, and $\sim p$ & s does not occur"; "s is unique to p's nth occurrence for "s occurs during what is at least p's nth occurrence, s does not occur during what is at least p's occurrence $n + 1$, and s is unique to an occurrence of p"; "s occurs before p's nth occurrence" as "For every q, if q is unique to p's nth occurrence, then sBq"; "p's nth occurrence is prior to an occurrence of s" as "For every q, if q is unique to p's nth occurrence, then qBs"; "p's seventh occurrence is prior to s's ninth occurrence" for "For every q, if q is unique to p's seventh occurrence, there is an r such that r is unique to s's ninth occurrence and qBr"; and, given the concept of causal contribution, "the nth occurrence of p contributes causally to an occurrence of e" for "There is an s such that s occurs during p's nth occurrence, there is a q such that q is unique to an occurrence of e, p & s contributes causally to q & e, p & s does not contribute causally to q, and s does not contribute causally to e."

In some such way as the above, if I am not mistaken, we can reduce talk about particular occurrences of events to talk just about events.

4. What are the things we have been calling "propositions"? The term may be taken in a broad or in a narrow sense. Taking it in its broad sense, we might identify the class of things to which it refers by saying that it comprises those things which are capable of being the objects of propositional attitudes. Thus a proposition, in this sense, would be anything capable of serving as the object of belief, or of hope, of wonderment, or of any of those other intentional attitudes that take things other than attributes or individuals as their objects.

Consider such true statements as these: "There is something he knows that we do not know"; "There are things he believes that no other rational person would believe"; "What Jones desires is the very thing that Smith fears"; "I've been thinking about what it is that obsesses him"; and "There is something we have all wished for at one time or another that only he has had the courage to try to bring about." So far as I know, there is no adequate analysis of such statements which does not presuppose that there *are* certain things — other than attributes and individuals — which the attitudes in question may take as their objects.[15] The following seems to me to be a sound procedure methodologically: if (1) there are certain true sentences which can be taken to imply that there *are* certain things other than attributes and concrete individual substances, and if (2) we are unable to paraphrase these sentences into other sentences which can be seen *not* to imply that there are those things, then (3) it is not unreasonable to suppose that there are in fact those things. I shall assume, then, that there are the things in question.

This intentional approach to propositions, incidentally, throws some light upon the problem of "individuating" them. What would be a

---

[15] Compare W. V. Quine: ". . . it is the propositional attitudes above all, it seems to me, and not modal logic, that clamor for positing propositions and the like." *Word and Object* (Cambridge: Cambridge University Press, 1960), p. 202.

nontrivial condition for saying that a proposition p is identical with a proposition q? One such would be this: "It is necessary that, if anyone accepts p, he accepts q, and conversely; if anyone is pleased about p, then he is pleased about q, and conversely; if anyone wishes to bring about p, he wishes to bring about q, and conversely. . . ." And so on, for other intentional attitudes.[16]

But "proposition" is also used in what may be a somewhat different sense to refer to certain entities which are rather like the things we have just been calling "propositions" but which are also such that the principles of propositional logic may be interpreted as applying to them. That is to say, it is sometimes assumed that the letters appearing in such formulae as "$\sim(p \ \& \ \sim p)$" may be interpreted as designating certain nonlinguistic entities, and the term "proposition" is then used to refer to *those* entities.

Let us restrict the term "proposition" to this second sense and let us use the term "state of affairs" for what we had introduced as the first sense of the term "proposition."

How are we to relate these three types of entity: propositions, events, and states of affairs?

5. I suggest that the simplest way of tying these entities together is to say that events and propositions are species of states of affairs. A *proposition* could be defined as any state of affairs which is necessarily such that either it or its negation does not occur, hence, by D2 above, any state of affairs which is necessarily such that either it or its negation always occurs.[17] We could now say that an event is any contingent state of affairs which is not a proposition and which is such that either it or its negation implies change, that is, it implies that there is some state of affairs p such that p occurs and not-p occurs.

Thus that state of affairs which is John walking at 3:00 P.M., E.S.T., on February 5, 1970, will be a *proposition* by our present definition, for it is a state of affairs which is necessarily such that either it or its negation does not occur. But that state of affairs which is John walking will be an *event*. For (1) John walking is contingent, inasmuch as neither it nor its negation is necessary; (2) it is not a proposition, inasmuch as it is possible for both it and its negation to occur; and (3) it implies change, inasmuch as John cannot walk unless there is some

---

[16] By similar means, incidentally, we may define a sense of *entailment* that is stronger than logical implication: "p *entails* q provided only it is necessary that (1) p implies q and (2) anyone who accepts p also accepts q." (Note that this definition allows for the possibility that p entails q even though Jones is pleased about p and not pleased about q.) Using "entails" in this restricted way, we could formulate an alternative criterion of identity: p is identical with q, if and only if, p entails q and q entails p.

[17] If we decide that some states of affairs may occur at certain places while their negations are occurring at others, we must add "anywhere" after "not" in our definition.

state of affairs p (for example, John's left foot being in front of his right foot) which is such that both p and not-p occur.

And that state of affairs which is John sitting will be neither a proposition nor an event. John sitting will not be a proposition, for it is possible that both it and its negation occur. And it will not be an event since it does not imply change. (Unfortunately there is no uniform terminology at our disposal. We might call those states of affairs that are neither events nor propositions "unchanges," or we might call them "states of affairs in the narrow sense of the term." Or we might restrict "state of affairs" to this narrow sense, which may be in accord with one of its uses, and then introduce some technical term—say, Meinong's "objective"—for the generic, undefined concept.)

We have, then, a definition of what we referred to above as the more narrow sense of the term "proposition"—that sense in which the term is taken, not as a synonym for our more general term "state of affairs," but to refer, more narrowly, to those states of affairs to which the principles of propositional logic may be interpreted as referring. Thus the principle symbolized by "$\sim(p \ \& \ \sim p)$," for example, could very plausibly be construed as telling us that, for every state of affairs p, if p is a state of affairs which is necessarily such that either p does not occur or not-p does not occur, that is, if p is a proposition, that state of affairs which is the conjunction of p and not-p does not occur. (Perhaps it is problematic whether the *only* true interpretation of the principles of propositional logic is one that takes them thus to apply to the members of a certain subset of states of affairs.[18] But they *can* be so interpreted; and since, we are assuming, there is some presumption in favor of thesis that there *are* such states of affairs, it would seem to be reasonable so to interpret them.)

We noted that there is a disanalogy between what may be said about propositions and their *truth* and about events or states of affairs and their *occurrences*. But there is a complete analogy if we restrict ourselves to those states of affairs which are necessarily such that either they or their negations do not occur, i.e., either they or their negations always occur. (If the heavenly spheres' being in motion is eternal, it is yet not a *proposition* by our definition, for it is not necessarily such that either it or its negation always occurs.)

An obvious advantage of this approach is that of enabling us to reduce the concept of the *truth* of a proposition to that of the *occurrence* of a state of affairs: p is a *true proposition* if and only if p is a

---

[18] I have discussed certain alternative possibilities, somewhat skeptically, in "Language, Logic, and States of Affairs," in Sidney Hook, ed., *Language and Philosophy* (New York: New York University Press, 1969), pp. 241–248.

proposition and p occurs or obtains, and p is a *false proposition* if and only if p is a proposition and p does not occur or obtain. If we say that a *fact* is any state of affairs that occurs or obtains, then the relation that a true proposition bears to the fact which is said to "correspond to it" is simply identity. This "theory of truth" might be called the classical theory, for it seems to be what was intended by Bolzano, Meinong, and Husserl, if not also by Frege, Moore, and Russell.

To expound and clarify this conception of events and propositions, I shall formulate and attempt to answer several objections to it.

6. (1) "Your view requires us to say that that state of affairs which is Nixon's being in Washington is not the same as that state of affairs which is Johnson's successor being in Washington. But that *event* which is Nixon's being in Washington is the same as that event which is Johnson's successor being in Washington. Therefore your view is not adequate to the concept of an event."

But *is* Nixon's being in Washington the same event as Johnson's successor being in Washington? Or, more precisely, if N is there being one and only one man who is identical with Nixon and is in Washington, and if J is there being one and only one man who succeeded Johnson and is in Washington, is N identical with J? Surely not, for we can say of N, but not of J, that had Humphrey won, it would not have occurred. (Note we are not committing the fallacy involved in arguing from "Had Humphrey won, the President would have been a Democrat" and "Nixon is the President" to "Had Humphrey won, Nixon would have been a Democrat.") And there are many other truths about N which are not also truths about J. Thus the facts which are sufficient to explain the occurrence of J are not sufficient to explain the occurrence of N. There are people who worked to bring J about who did not work to bring N about. And, in relation to what was known in 1967, the occurrence of J was considerably more probable than that of N.

Knowing Nixon to be Johnson's successor, we find it convenient to say such things as "Nixon's being in Washington is the same event as Johnson's successor being in Washington." But what we tend to *say* about sameness and identity is notoriously unreliable. As Hume observed, we have a propensity to "feign" identity in cases where, more strictly speaking, some other relation is called for. We may say, in New York tonight, "This is the same train we took yesterday," even though we realize that yesterday's train is now in Chicago. Or one trombonist may say, on introducing himself to another, "I play the same instrument that you do," without either of them supposing for a moment that they both play one and the same trombone. These loose and popular uses of "the same" may be correct enough, but they are not to be confused with the strict and philosophical sense of "identity." And they are readily reducible to a more precise terminology. (Thus to eliminate the loose and popular sense of "the same" in its application to events, we have only to apply such formulae as this: "The *F*'s being *H* is, in the loose and popular sense, *the same event* as the *G*'s being *H*, if and only if, the *F* is, in the strict and philosophical sense, identical with the *G*." [19])

(2) "(i) Every meaningful sentence has a proposition as its intensional meaning. Hence (ii) every true sentence has some other type of entity as its extensional meaning. But (iii) the extensional meaning of any expression exemplifies its intensional meaning. Hence (iv) the states of affairs to which you refer are abstract entities and some of them are exemplified in certain other concrete entities. But (v) your theory has not taken these concrete entities into account."

The premises are problematic. What is the reason for supposing that, if a true sentence has a state of affairs as its "intensional meaning," it has something else as its "extensional meaning"? Or if "intensional meaning" is to be taken in such a way that (a) only abstract objects can be said to be the intensional meaning of any expression and (b) no true sentence can be said to have an intensional meaning unless it has something else as its extensional meaning, what is the reason for saying that states of affairs *are* the intensional meaning of sentences? (Are the states of affairs we have been discussing "abstract objects"? Only if we take "abstract object" negatively, and incorrectly, to mean any object that is not a concrete individual thing, but not if we take it positively to refer to objects that may be exemplified or instantiated in other objects. Given the third view singled out in paragraph one above, the present view might be called "Platonistic," but otherwise not.)

(3) "(i) Your theory implies that, if a man believes that a storm is occurring, then that state of affairs which is the occurrence of a storm is the object of his belief. But (ii) the sentence 'He believes that a storm is occurring' is natural and clearly grammatical, whereas 'He believes the occurrence of a storm' is unnatural and not clearly grammatical. Hence (iii) if a man believes that a storm is occurring something other than the occurrence of a storm is the object of his belief." [20]

---

[19] See Jaegwon Kim, "On the Psycho-Physical Identity Theory," *American Philosophical Quarterly*, Vol. III (1966), pp. 227–235. If the views of the identity theorist are to be adequate to the fact of recurrence, then, given the distinctions made in the first section of this paper, it is not at all clear that his views have the advantage of ontological simplicity.

[20] Meinong saw this type of objection and felt it was not conclusive. He had noted that, where we may say "The existence of the leaning tower in Pisa is actual" (or, at any rate, where a German-speaking person may say "*Die Existenz des schiefen Turmes in Pisa ist tatsächlich*"), we may not say "The existence of the leaning tower in Pisa is true," this despite the fact that we may say both "It is a fact that there is a leaning

The premises of the argument are certainly true. If we wish to say of a man that he believes that a storm is occurring, we do not say "He believes the occurrence of a storm." But we may say "He *believes in,* or *suspects,* or is *counting on,* or is *mindful of* the occurrence of a storm." And where we may say of a man that he fears, regrets, hopes, or knows that a storm is occurring, we may also say, equally well, that he fears, regrets, hopes for, or is cognizant of the occurrence of a storm. Such points of usage may throw light upon our various intentional attitudes. But surely they give us no reason to suppose that "the occurrence of a storm" and "that a storm is occurring" refer to different things. The argument is simply a *non sequitur.*

(4) "(i) Your theory implies that 'Leopold met Stephen' comes to the same thing as 'Leopold's meeting with Stephen occurred'. But (ii) 'Leopold's meeting with Stephen' is a singular term. Therefore (iii) 'Leopold's meeting with Stephen occurred' implies that they met on only one occasion. But (iv) 'Leopold met Stephen' is consistent with their having met on many different occasions." [21]

"Leopold's meeting with Stephen" can be taken to designate either that event which is Leopold meeting with Stephen or that event which is Leopold's only meeting with Stephen. If we take it in the first of these two senses, we may say that (iii) is false; if we take it in the second, we may say that (i) is false.

(5) "(i) If an event recurs, then it ceases to be and at some later time comes into being again. Hence (ii) the assumption that some events recur is incompatible with the assumption that, if a thing ceases to be, then that same thing does not subsequently come into being." [22]

The premise is false. To say that there *is* a certain event p is not to say that p *occurs,* and to say that p does not occur is not to say that there is *no* such event p. (Compare: "There are a number of things he tried without success to bring about.") Hence to say that p ceases to occur is not to say that p ceases to be, and to say that p begins to occur is not to say that p comes into being. (Compare: "There is a very interesting thing that usually happens when we get to this part of the pro-

---

tower in Pisa" and "It is true that there is a leaning tower in Pisa." (In English "There being a leaning tower in Pisa is true" would seem to be as natural, or as unnatural, as "There being a leaning tower in Pisa is a fact.") For Meinong's attempt to account for these differences in usage see: *Über Annahmen,* 2nd ed. (Leipzig: Johann Ambrosius Barth, 1910), pp. 56, 95, 101; *Über Möglichkeit und Wahrscheinlichkeit* (Leipzig: Johann Ambrosius Barth, 1915), pp. 39–40; and *Uber emotionale Präsentation* (Vienna: Alfred Hölder, 1917), pp. 48–49. The latter work has since appeared in *Alexius Meinong Gesamtaugabe,* Vol. III ("Abhandlunger zur Werttheorie"), edited by Rudolf Kindinger (Graz: Akademische Druck-u. Verlagsanstalt, 1968).

[21] Donald Davidson suggests such an objection in "On Events and Event-Descriptions," in J. Margolis, ed., *Fact and Existence* (Blackwell: 1969); see p. 77.

[22] Compare Aristotle's *Physics,* Book V, Ch. 4, 228 a.

gram.") Looking at the matter this way, incidentally, we escape the following puzzle: "When did the performance of the symphony come into
being? Not with the playing of the first note, for the performance of the
symphony didn't exist *then*. Not with the playing of the final note, for
in that case, unless the performance existed only as long as the final
note existed, it existed before it came into being. Somewhere, then, toward the end of the second movement?" [23]

The theory here proposed seems to me, therefore, to be adequate
to the fact of recurrence and to withstand the obvious objections.[24]

[23] St. Augustine was troubled by one version of this puzzle. See *Confessions*, Book XI, Chapter XV.

[24] Other objections were made by Donald Davidson in "Events as Particulars," *Nous*, Vol. IV (1970). My reply is in "States of Affairs Again," *Nous*, Vol. V (1971).

Essence and Identity

ELI HIRSCH

Long Island University

I

I am concerned in this paper with questions of the following kind:
What does the identity through time of a physical object consist in?
What is it for a physical object that exists at one time to be the same
object as a physical object that exists at another time? What is it for a
physical object to continue to exist over a period of time? It is intended
that the expression "physical object" should exclude from consideration persons (and perhaps other higher forms of life) which would introduce special difficulties. More generally, let us understand the scope
of our questions about identity to be restricted to the seemingly easiest
cases. This would take in, I assume, artifacts like tables and cars, geographical features like mountains and rivers, and bits of material stuff
like pieces of paper and lumps of clay.

When we ask with regard to physical objects what their identity
through time consists in, we are asking for an account of the unity
of a physical object's career. Any physical object has a career which
stretches over a period of time. The successive parts, or stages, of an
object's career must hang together in some distinctive way; otherwise
there would be nothing to prevent us from arbitrarily combining into a
single career the early stages of one object with the later stages of a different object. If the stages of an object's career did not hang together
in some distinctive way, there could be no distinction between saying
"Some object was A at time t_1 and B at time t_2" and saying "Some object was A at time t_1, and some object was B at time t_2." Of course,

there is a very fundamental distinction between these two statements. The former statement, unlike the latter, implies that an *A* stage and a *B* stage were connected in such a way as to comprise parts of a single career. We want an account of what this connection is.

Our question may be expressed in a slightly different idiom. The career of any physical object corresponds to a certain spatiotemporal stretch of reality, to a certain portion of space-time. But if we arbitrarily combine stages of the careers of different objects we trace out a portion of space-time that does not correspond to the career of a single physical object. Our question now is this: What characteristics must a portion of space-time have in order for us to count it as corresponding to the career of a single physical object?

In trying to analyze the ordinary notion of the identity of a physical object through time we are at the same time trying to analyze a certain range of ordinary statements, namely, statements which involve the thought of a physical object persisting and having properties over a period of time. I will call any such statement a *career description*. Not every career description includes such words as "identical," "same," or "different." All of the following statements are career descriptions, since each statement evidently involves the idea of a physical object persisting and having properties over a period of time.

(1) This brown table is the same as the green table that was here at 12:00.
(2) This table was green at 12:00 and brown at 12:05.
(3) Some table was green at 12:00 and brown at 12:05.
(4) Something was a green table at 12:00 and a brown table at 12:05.

Only statement (1), which has the logical form "$x = y$," would generally be called an "identity statement." But it is clear that all of these statements are equally relevant to the problem of identity through time. So our concern is not exclusively with "identity statements," in the restricted sense that would cover only (1), but rather with career descriptions of every variety. It will in fact be helpful in what follows to focus primarily on relatively simple kinds of career descriptions like (2) through (4), statements in which an object is simply said to have a number of properties at different times.

II

The account I want to develop here is an elaboration of certain "essentialist" doctrines that have lately been expounded by, among

others, Geach[1] and Wiggins.[2] The key idea in this account is that not
all of an object's properties, not all of the general terms which are true
of an object, are logically on a par with respect to the object's identity
through time. Rather it is the case that a select few of the terms which
are true of an object play a quite special role in determining the object's identity, and these terms are, in a sense, necessary to the object's
identity. Terms which have this special capacity, I will call *E terms;*
other terms are *A terms.*[3] This terminology is meant to suggest a connection with at least some aspects of the traditional essence-accident
distinction.

The distinction between *E* terms and *A* terms initially may be explained by reference to the following criterion.

C: A general term *F* is an *E* term if and only if the statement
     "This *F* (thing) was (or will be) at place *p* at time *t*" logically
     entails "There was (or will be) an *F* (thing) at place *p* at time
     t"; a general term is an *A* term if and only if it is not an *E*
     term.[4]

The term "table" is an *E* term, since "This table was in Chicago in
1960" logically entails "There was a table in Chicago in 1960." The
term "red," on the other hand, is an *A* term, since "This red thing
was in Chicago in 1960" does not logically entail "There was a red
thing in Chicago in 1960"; the thing in question may have become
red after 1960. For the same reason "red table" is an *A* term. In general
it may be said that typical common nouns are *E* terms, whereas typical

---

[1] P. T. Geach, *Reference and Generality* (Cornell University Press, Ithaca, N.Y., 1962),
Chapter 2.
[2] David Wiggins, *Identity and Spatio-Temporal Continuity* (Basil Blackwell, Oxford,
1967).
[3] What I call an *E* term corresponds, at least roughly, to what Geach calls a "nominal
essence" (Geach, *op. cit.*, p. 44), and to what Wiggins calls a "substance-concept"
(Wiggins, *op. cit.*, p. 7).
[4] In what follows "*F*," and other capital letters, are to be understood as variables ranging
over linguistic expressions. I follow the loose convention of allowing variables which
range over expressions to operate in the intuitive way inside extended quotations.
   In formulating criterion C, I am assuming that a statement of the form "This *F* (thing)
was (or will be) at *p* at *t*" logically entails "There is an *F* (thing) here now which was
(or will be) at *p* at *t*." This assumption might be questioned by a philosopher who holds
that the referring expression "this *F*" can be used to refer to something which is not an
instance of *F*. [See Keith S. Donnellan, "Reference and Definite Descriptions," *Philosophical Review*, LXXV (1966), pp. 281–304.] For such a philosopher the criterion C
could be reformulated as follows: A term *F* is an *E* term if and only if the statement
"There is an *F* (thing) here now which was (or will be) at *p* at *t*" logically entails "There
was (or will be) an *F* (thing) at *p* at *t*."

adjectives and verbs are A terms, as are expressions which result from combining nouns with adjectives or verbs ("red table," "moving car"). But there are many exceptions to this grammatical characterization; the distinction between E terms and A terms does not exactly coincide with any simple point of grammar. For example, the noun "pet" is an A term, since "This pet was in Chicago in 1960" does not logically entail "There was a pet in Chicago in 1960"; the creature may still have been roaming wild in 1960. And the adjective "feline," in the sense of "cat," is as much an E term as the latter noun.

The upshot of criterion C might be stated as follows. A term is an E term if it cannot possibly be true of an object temporarily; if it is true of an object at all, it is necessarily true of the object throughout the object's entire career. On the other hand, an A term may (or may not) be true of an object temporarily.

Criterion C is far from airtight, and I intend it only as a preliminary introduction to the distinction between E terms and A terms. To understand the distinction properly we must understand the distinctive role that E terms play in our thought about the identity of objects. This role of E terms can only be exhibited within the context of some general account of our individuating scheme. To such an account I now turn.

III

In the present analysis our individuating scheme will be seen as constituted of two major kinds of rules: (1) *Essence Rules:* these list E terms and establish certain analytic relations between E terms and career descriptions; (2) *General Schemata of Identity:* these are rules for tracing the careers of objects (under E terms) and delimiting their temporal boundaries. I shall first introduce these rules with minimal explanation, and then I shall examine them in greater detail.

(1) *Essence Rules*

E1. Specification Rules. Here we would simply have a list of terms that are designated as E terms.

It will not matter to the ensuing theory whether or not we think of this list as containing such bare grammatical subjects as "thing," "entity," "item," "particular." But it will be more in the spirit of the discussion to stipulate now that these words are *not* to count as E terms.

E2. Ordering Rules. These are rules to the effect that one E term is subordinate to a second E term (that is, that the application of the first term logically entails, but is not logically entailed by, the application of the second term).

The result of the ordering rules is that any E term is locatable within a hierarchy of E terms ranging through varying degrees of specificity. By a *determinate* E *term* I shall mean an E term to which no E term is subordinate.

E3. *The Covering Rule.* (a) A statement of the form "Something was A at t_1 and B at t_2" is true if and only if there is some true statement of the form "Some F was A at t_1 and B at t_2," where F is a determinate E term. (b) As a special case, the statement "Something began to exist at t_1 and ceased to exist at t_2" is true if and only if there is some true statement of the form "Some F began to exist at t_1 and ceased to exist at t_2," where F is a determinate E term.

The covering rule is here stated with regard to a very restricted class of career descriptions, but it is meant to be extended to career descriptions of all forms. The general idea is that a career description cannot be true unless it applies to something which can be brought under a determinate E term. The idea in its full generality can be worked out along the following lines. Expressions like "a," "the," "some," "no," are called *applicatives*.[5] The covering rule states that a career description is true only if it is logically entailed by (covered by) a true statement every applicative within which is joined to a determinate E term.

It must be understood that the covering rule does not require that someone who utters a true career description should *know* some covering truth for that description. It is enough that there should *be* such a covering truth. For a person to use a career description correctly he must understand (be committed to) the covering rule, and be prepared to give some examples of statements which, if they were true, would serve as covering truths for his description.

(2) *General Schemata of Identity*

GS1 (*The Tracing Rule*). If F is a determinate E term, the statement "Some F was A at t_1 and B at t_2" is true if and only if there is a path P through space-time such that:

(*Te. The Essence Requirement*) F is instanced on every point of P; *and*

(*Tp. The Predicate Requirement*) A is instanced on P at t_1 and B is instanced on P at t_2; *and*

P satisfies either the T rules or the T' rule.

---

[5] Cf. Geach, *op. cit.*, p. 47.

The *T* rules are:

(*T1. The Continuity Requirement*)   *P* is spatiotemporally continuous; *and*

(*T2. The No-Choice Requirement*)   there is no path *P'* such that
F is instanced on every point of *P'*, and *P'* is spatiotemporally continuous, and *P* and *P'* partly coincide and partly diverge.

The *T'* rule is:

(*T'. The Theoretical Rule*)   By associating *P* with the career of
an instance of *F* we are able to generate a set of career descriptions
which cohere in a theoretically satisfying way with the total system
of career descriptions that are generated by the *T* rules.

GS2 (*The Duration Rule*). If *F* is a determinate *E* term, the
statement "Some *F* began to exist at t_1 and ceased to exist at t_2" is true
if and only if there is a path *P* through space-time such that *P* begins at
t_1 and ends at t_2, and (1) *F* is instanced on every point of *P*, and (2) *P*
satisfies with respect to *F* the requirements of either the *T* rules or the
T' rule, and (3) *P* is not a segment of any longer path which satisfies
(1) and (2).

Let me first explain how I am using some of the terminology that
occurs within the tracing and duration rules. A space-time path is a
series of *points,* where each point contains a place and an instant of
time (that is, each point is an ordered pair containing a place and an
instant of time). By a *place* I always mean something like a region or
volume of space, that is, something which can be said to contain an
object. In what follows, therefore, it will be understood that place
expressions like "p_1" and "p_2" always refer to extended places,
whereas time expressions like "t_1" and "t_2" always refer to instants of
time. My reason for treating of extended places, but durationless times,
is merely one of convenience; I think it makes the analysis a bit easier
to formulate.

Now, to say that the term *A* is instanced on some point (p_1, t_1) of
P is to say that *A* is instanced at p_1 at t_1. And this in turn is to be understood as meaning that there is an object *x* such that *x* is an instance of
A at t_1, and p_1 contains at t_1 all and only parts of *x*; that is, at t_1 the
outlines of *x* coincide with the outlines of p_1. For example, the term
"cat" is instanced at p_1 at t_1 if at t_1 the outlines of p_1 coincide with the
outlines of a cat. Or the term "partly red" is instanced at p_1 at t_1 if at
t_1 the outlines of p_1 coincide with the outlines of an object which is

partly red. The point to emphasize is that "cat" is *not* instanced at the part of p_1 which coincides with the cat's head; nor is it instanced at that larger region which contains the cat together with another cat.

The covering rule has already required that the career of any object must be traced under a determinate E term. The tracing rule is now supposed to tell us how to go about tracing a career under a determinate E term. We may trace a career, according to the tracing rule, in one of two ways. The first, and most basic, way is simply to associate the career of an object with any space-time path which satisfies the T rules with respect to some E term, that is, roughly, with any continuous space-time path that is traceable under an E term. The second way, countenanced by the T' rule, is to associate the career of an object with a space-time path whenever this association will help us to keep our total system of career descriptions as coherent as possible. For example, the T' rule might allow us to say that an object moved discontinuously through space, if saying this would enable us to simplify explanations. The T rules, then, provide the primary criteria for the identity of objects, while the T' rule permits the extension of these criteria in ways that are theoretically fruitful.

The T rules contain two requirements, the continuity requirement T_1 and the no-choice requirement T_2. T_1 requires that a path along which a career is traced must be spatiotemporally continuous. Very roughly this means that if (p_1, t_1) and (p_2, t_2) are points on the path, then if t_1 is very close to t_2, p_1 is very close to p_2. But I shall come back to the notion of spatiotemporal continuity later.

The no-choice requirement T_2 amounts roughly to the following stipulation. If you trace an object's path on the basis of the continuity requirement, you must not find yourself faced with the choice of following the object in two different directions, where this choice is not settled by considerations of continuity. That is, if, on the basis of considerations of continuity, the space-time path P is to be associated with the career of an instance of F, then there must be no other path P' such that P and P' partly coincide and partly diverge, and P' is, in point of continuity, as well suited as P to correspond to the career of an instance of F. Two paths partly coincide and partly diverge, in the sense here intended, if they extend over a common time interval and share some, but not all, of their points during that interval. Suppose that P and P' partly coincide and partly diverge, that both paths are spatiotemporally continuous and that the determinate E term F is instanced on every point of both paths. Then if you associated a career with both paths, you would in effect be saying that two coessential objects, two objects that satisfy exactly the same E terms, temporarily occupied the very same places. It is this which T_2 does not permit you to say. Moreover T_2 does not allow you to arbitrarily choose one of these paths and discard the other. If a choice is made, it would have to be made on some basis other than the T rules; it would have to be made by appeal to the T' rule. The kind of case in which the failure of the no-choice requirement leads to an appeal to T' will be discussed at some length later.

The duration rule is intuitively rather clear. It implies roughly that a thing cannot go out of existence just to be replaced by a coessential thing. An object's career is to be terminated when, and only when, its career can no longer be prolonged in a manner that is consonant with the tracing rule.

We may read the duration rule as a kind of quasi-technical definition of the concepts "begins to exist" and "ceases to exist." For these concepts are not exactly commonplace, at least not in all of the applications that I wish to make of them. Ordinarily an entity's beginning and end are marked by expressions that are rather specific to that kind of entity: creatures are born and then die, tables are fashioned and then destroyed, grass comes out of the ground and then is eaten, a puddle of water forms and is then dispersed, and so on. Yet we can scarcely doubt that these various expressions contain the common idea of a span of time over which a thing's career runs its course, and beyond which one could not intelligibly apply to the thing any ordinary predicates of position, composition, color, and so on. It is this very general idea of the temporal limits of a thing's career that the duration rule is meant to govern.

IV

In Section IV I discuss several aspects of these identity rules insofar as the theoretical rule T' is ignored. In the next section I will turn to a consideration of the latter rule.

(1) The question that we started with was, "What characteristics must a space-time path have in order for us to count it as corresponding to the career of an object?" The answer given by the above analysis is that a space-time path corresponds to the career of an object only if it is related in the appropriate way to an E term, the appropriate way as specified in the tracing and duration rules. The import of this answer must be clearly understood. It is not sufficient that a space-time path should be spatiotemporally continuous, nor even that it should be both spatiotemporally continuous and satisfy some general conditions of qualitative similarity. Unless the path is properly delimited by an E term, it does not qualify as corresponding to the career of an object.

The following example may serve to make this point clearer. Imagine that you are standing next to a uniformly brown table that is unchanging during the time interval from 12:00 to 12:05. Suppose that throughout that five-minute interval you move your hand haphazardly across the surface of the table. Let Q be the space-time path traced according to the following rule: At any time t between 12:00 and 12:05, Q contains just that portion of the table top that is directly below your hand at t.

Q is a spatiotemporally continuous path, all of the points of which contain qualitatively similar hand-shaped chunks of the table top. But of course Q does not trace the career of any object. If, for example, at 12:01 your hand was above a clean part of the table, and at 12:02 it was above a dirty part, you could not, on that account, say "Something was clean at 12:01 and dirty at 12:02." This is precisely what you ought to say if it were correct to associate Q with the career of an object.

Why is it not correct to associate Q with the career of an object? Why should we not say that Q corresponds to a brown object that stays constantly under your hand? The answer, according to the present analysis, is that to trace the career of an object is not merely to trace a path which satisfies some general requirements of continuity and similarity, requirements which Q amply satisfies. It is primarily to trace a path *under an* E *term;* it is to trace a path in accordance with a rule that is supplied by some E term. What is lacking in Q is that this path is not covered, in the appropriate manner, by any E term.

It emerges that our concept of identity is, at its very foundations, inextricably tied up with the role of E terms. This point has frequently been obscured in philosophical discussions of identity. C. D. Broad, for example, remarks in one place: "A thing . . . is simply a long event, throughout the course of which there is either qualitative similarity or continuous qualitative change, together with a characteristic spatio-temporal unity." [6] Broad's remark is quite typical, but it is drastically misleading. We can trace innumerable space-time paths ("events") which, like Q, perfectly preserve spatiotemporal and qualitative continuity but which, because they are not properly covered by E terms, do not correspond to any objects. Possibly we can make intelligible to ourselves a conceptual scheme within which Broad's characterization would hold. In such a conceptual scheme, the distinction between E terms and A terms would be inoperative. But this is certainly not our own conceptual scheme. In our own way of thinking the role of E terms is indispensable.

(2) I want to express the requirement of spatiotemporal continuity, as this figures in the tracing rule, a bit more precisely. For this purpose let me adopt the following conventions. Suppose that (p, t) is a point

---

[6] C. D. Broad, *Scientific Thought* (Routledge and Kegan Paul, London, 1949), p. 393.

in the space-time path P. Then I will also say that both the place p and the instant of time t are in P; and I will refer to p as $P(t)$. This functional notation is appropriate in that a space-time path P, as it is understood here, must associate a unique place $P(t)$ with every instant t in P. This much, I take it, is implicit in the notion of a path as a *series* of points. (But it should be noted that a space-time path need not associate a unique instant of time with every place in it. The path traced, for example, by a stationary object will associate different instants with the same place.)

A path P is spatiotemporally continuous in the strictest sense if, for any time t_0 in P, you can make $P(t_0)$ and $P(t)$ virtually coincide by choosing t close enough to t_0. Or, to put it another way, by choosing t close enough to t_0, you can make the difference between $P(t_0)$ and $P(t)$, the extent to which they do not overlap, as small as you like. What I have just called the "difference" between two places can be measured rather straightforwardly as follows. To arrive at the difference between p_1 and p_2, where p_1 and p_2 are two places, first measure, say in cubic inches, the amount of p_1 which is outside p_2, then measure the amount of p_2 which is outside p_1, and then add the two measures together. The strict sense of spatiotemporal continuity can now be formulated more precisely as follows.

> *Definition A:* "P is spatiotemporally continuous" means: For any time t_0 in P, and for any positive number n, there is a time interval I around t_0 such that for any t in I the difference between $P(t)$ and $P(t_0)$ is less than n.[7]

Spatiotemporal continuity in the sense of definition A seems to be quite definitely too strong as a condition of identity for objects. For a typical object can persist while having a part subtracted from it, or a part added to it. But the path that the object traces in the course of such a change cannot be coherently thought of as spatiotemporally continuous in the strict sense of definition A.

Consider, for example, a tree which has a branch chopped off between t_1 and t_2. Admittedly our ordinary thinking about the case of a tree losing a branch is too vague to permit our pinpointing the exact moment at which the branch was lost. Yet it must be possible to eliminate this vagueness coherently by deciding upon such a time. Suppose, then, that we designate t_0 as the last time that the tree included the

---

[7] This definition, and the ones which follow, would have to be slightly modified in an obvious way to take account of the end points of P.

branch.[8] If P is the space-time path traced by the tree, then for any time t after t_0, no matter how close t is to t_0, the difference between $P(t)$ and $P(t_0)$ would have to equal at least the extent of the fallen branch. In other words, we cannot make the difference between $P(t)$ and $P(t_0)$ as small as we like by taking t sufficiently close to t_0. This means that P is not spatiotemporally continuous in the sense of definition A.

The requirement of spatiotemporal continuity must then be interpreted in a sense liberal enough to accommodate typical cases of part-addition and part-subtraction. Either of the following definitions of spatiotemporal continuity would seem to accomplish this purpose.

> *Definition B:* "P is spatiotemporally continuous" means: For any time t_0 in P there is a time interval I around t_0 such that for any t in I the difference between $P(t)$ and $P(t_0)$ is less than the extent of overlap of $P(t)$ and $P(t_0)$.
>
> *Definition C:* "P is spatiotemporally continuous" means: For any time t_0 in P there is a time interval I around t_0 such that for any t in I, $P(t)$ overlaps $P(t_0)$.

Evidently the space-time path traced by an object to which a part is added or subtracted will be continuous in the very weak sense of definition C. Furthermore, the path will be continuous in the somewhat stronger sense of definition B, except in a case where the part added, or subtracted, is so large that it has the effect of at least doubling, or at least halving, the object's size. This exception does not seem to exclude any ordinary cases. It seems, then, that either definition B or definition C could provide a notion of spatiotemporal continuity that is suitable to figure as a condition of identity. And of course it would be possible to formulate senses of spatiotemporal continuity that are intermediate in strength between the senses of definitions C and B, or between the senses of definitions B and A. I think that there may in fact be some fairly cogent reasons for favoring some of these senses over others as an interpretation of the continuity requirement. For the present I want only to take away the point that the continuity requirement, as stated in the tracing rule, is to be interpreted in some sense, like B or C, which is weaker than the strict sense of definition A.

I have two more brief comments to make on the notion of spatiotemporal continuity. First, I assume that to say that a path through

---

[8] This supposition would presumably imply that there was no first time at which the tree did not include the branch. I do not think that this complication, however it might be worked out, would significantly affect the point that I am making.

space-time is spatiotemporally continuous implies that the path is *temporally* continuous; that is, that if t_1 and t_2 are any two times in the path, every time between t_1 and t_2 is also in the path. This requirement should then be added to the definitions A, B, and C.

Second, I do *not* assume that to say that a path through space-time is spatiotemporally continuous implies that every place in the path is itself continuous. I think that we certainly want to allow an object to occasionally occupy a discontinuous, or divided, place. Suppose, for example, that I take my pipe apart in order to clean it. It is surely plausible to say that the pipe persists throughout this operation. But where should we say that the pipe is when it is thus divided? The most straightforward answer seems to be that the pipe, when divided, occupies a divided place. Or, to take another example, suppose that a particular bit of water w is in a vessel at time t_1, and then is separated into two pools at time t_2. Where is w at t_2? Again, I think that the simplest answer is to say that w occupies a divided or discontinuous place at t_2. Examples like this suggest that we should not interpret the condition of spatiotemporal continuity as requiring an object to occupy only continuous places. It is sufficient that successive places occupied by an object, whether these places are continuous or not, should overlap in the manner prescribed by one of the definitions.

(3) It will be noted that the tracing rule does not include any requirement of continuity of qualitative change. My reason for ignoring this requirement is that, though it seems to be rather commonly accepted (cf. Broad's remark), when interpreted straightforwardly, it runs clearly afoul of cases in which parts are added or subtracted. Consider again the tree which lost a branch between t_1 and t_2. Suppose that the tree took up 15 cubic feet at t_1 and 14 cubic feet at t_2, the fallen branch having taken up one cubic foot. Evidently the tree suffered a discontinuous jump with respect to volume. For the tree passed from taking up 15 cubic feet at t_1 to taking up 14 cubic feet at t_2 without ever taking up 14½ cubic feet. Similar considerations show that the tree suffered a discontinuous jump with respect to shape, weight, and (probably) color distribution. And so it necessarily is for any case in which an object has a part added or subtracted.

Clearly, then, no straightforward requirement of continuity of qualitative change is tenable as a condition of identity. Nevertheless it may be argued that, just as we acknowledged a weakened requirement of spatiotemporal continuity, we ought also to acknowledge some weakened requirement of continuity of qualitative change, one which would accommodate examples in which parts are added and subtracted. This does seem plausible; however, I am at present unable to formulate, with even tolerable clarity, any such weakened requirement of continuity of qualitative change. Let it be understood, then, that this is very likely a gap in the analysis which ought ultimately to be filled in.

(4) Why did I formulate the covering rule, tracing rule, and duration rule in terms of *determinate E* terms and not in terms of *E* terms in general? I had in mind the following kind of difficulty. The criterion C would have us count "article of clothing" as an *E* term. Suppose now that you tore a shirt apart in order to use some segment of it as a scarf. Presumably you could not say "Some article of clothing was first worn as a shirt and then worn as a scarf." You could not, pointing to the scarf, say "That article of clothing once had buttons on it." But if we allowed ourselves to trace a career under the *E* term "article of clothing" we might be led to just these statements. This suggests that careers should be traced only under more determinate *E* terms like "shirt" and "scarf."

Or consider the following more-general difficulty. The criterion C would trivially accord an *E* term status to any disjunctive term "*F* or *G*" where both *F* and *G* are *E* terms. But certainly you could not legitimately trace a career, for example, under the term "table or pile of ashes." Again the expedient suggests itself of allowing career tracings only under determinate *E* terms.

But we must not extend the application of this expedient beyond reasonable limits. Typically we will have a vaguely defined series of *E* terms, each more determinate than its predecessor, and such that we could safely trace careers under any term in the series. Consider, for example, the series "animal," "dog," "terrier." I would count each of these as *E* terms on the grounds that there are no conceivable circumstances in which it would be *clearly right* to apply the term to an object temporarily. On the other hand, I can think of no conceivable circumstances in which it would be *clearly wrong* to trace a career under "dog," or even "animal." In other words, the only kind of case in which a conflict could arise between tracing under "terrier" and tracing under "dog" or "animal" would be a borderline case. Consequently there could be no point in insisting that one trace only under "terrier" (or, for that matter, that one trace only under "schnauzer," "fox terrier," and so on).

The general point is this. The identity rules are not to be construed as closing gaps of vagueness which ordinary usage leaves open. The rules merely express that structure of thought within which all career descriptions, whether clear-cut or borderline, must find a place. We may picture the ordering rule as assigning to "terrier" the status of a determinate *E* term; or, perhaps better, we may picture the ordering rule as assigning to the whole set, "terrier," "dog," "animal," the status of "determinate enough to trace under." The crucial point is that if a conflict situation should ever arise, if, for example, scientists should learn how to change terriers into spaniels, then we should have to make a decision within the structure of our identity rules. We may decide to treat "terrier" as an *A* term; or to stop treating "terrier" as subordinate to "dog"; or even to overhaul in more radical ways our total scheme for classifying animals. But so long as we are to bring the situation under the logical form of a career description, under the concept of identity through time, the basic structure of our individuating scheme, as expressed in the various rules, must remain intact.

V

I have already alluded to one possible application of the theoretical rule *T'*. Suppose that a table vanishes into thin air at time *t*, and that immediately after *t* a very similar table, bearing all of the distinctive marks of the vanished table, appears at a different place. In such a case it might seem plausible to say that the second table is the same as the first and to forego the continuity requirement. If we did describe the situation in this way, we should not be appealing to any logically sufficient conditions of identity that are a priori built into the concept "same table." Instead our judgment of identity would have to be based on some argument to the effect that, given everything that we have learned about tables, the simplest hypothesis in the present case is that a table moved discontinuously. The clause "given everything that we have learned about tables" must be emphasized. Unless we had a backlog of information about how tables ordinarily behave, we should have no way at all of approaching the present anomalous case. For we should not know whether tables are generally expected to vanish into thin air, or what counts as a "distinctive mark" on a table. It is only insofar as we have already built up an extensive body of knowledge, by applying the criteria stated in the *T* rules, that we can meaningfully consider extending these criteria, and possibly foregoing the continuity requirement in exceptional cases.

This application of *T'* is purely hypothetical. We do not, in point of fact, have any occasion to describe tables, or other ordinary objects, as moving discontinuously through space. If we confine ourselves to actual cases (as opposed to cases which are merely logically possible), it seems correct to say that the criteria of identity which we apply to tables and many other ordinary objects can be adequately explained without bringing in anything more complicated than the *T* rules.

There is, however, an important range of objects for which the *T* rules are thoroughly inadequate. I am referring to such items as a pint of water, the dirt in the yard, the snow on the roof. These are items which strike us as being securely entrenched in the most ordinary thought. Nevertheless, as I now want to show, the career descriptions of such items unquestionably require an appeal to rules well beyond the simple T rules, and almost certainly an appeal to the theoretical rule T'. Indeed it was primarily for the sake of these items that I formulated the T' rule.

In order to develop this point, let me introduce some additional terminology. Goodman calls a term F *dissective* if the application of F to an object guarantees the application of F to every part of the object.[9] An example might be "red all over" (if we ignore, as I want to, microscopic parts). A term is *nondissective* if it is not dissective, that is, if its application to an object does not guarantee its application to all of the object's parts. An example would be "spherical."

If a term is both nondissective and an E term, I will call it an *articulative* E *term*. Examples are "table," "mountain," "cat." If a term is both dissective and an E term, I will call it a *mass* E *term*.[10] I am concerned with mass E terms which apply to bits or quantities of material stuff. Examples are "(bit of) water," "(bit of) dirt," "(bit of) snow."

The term "water" is a mass E term since every (macroscopic) part of water is water. "Water" seems to function as a proper covering concept for such a career description as "Some water was first in New York and then in Chicago." But the T rules fail to explain how this concept operates. The reason for this failure is precisely the dissectiveness of "water." Since every part of a bit of water is a bit of water, we can pass from any bit of water to any one of its parts, or from any one of its parts to any other part, over continuous paths on which "water" is constantly instanced. Consequently, if P is the space-time path traced by some water, there will be innumerable paths P' such that P' is continuous, and "water" is instanced on every point of P', and P and P' partly coincide and partly diverge. This means that the path traced by any bit of water will necessarily violate the no-choice requirement T_2, and an appeal must always be made to something beyond the T rules.

Suppose, for example, that we have a full glass of water which sits intact and unchanging during the time interval from 12:00 to 12:05. The glass is, let us say, five inches tall. Let P be the space-time path traced throughout the five-minute interval by the water which occupies the bottom three inches of the glass. And let P' be a path traced ac-

---

[9] Nelson Goodman, *The Structure of Appearance,* 2nd ed. (Bobbs-Merrill, 1966), p. 53.

[10] My use of "articulative E term" and "mass E term" is related to, but not the same as, Quine's use of "articulative term" and "mass term." See W. V. Quine, *Word and Object* (The M.I.T. Press, Cambridge, Mass., 1960), p. 90, note 1, and p. 91. I make no use of the "E" less expressions.

cording to the following rule: For any time t between 12:00 and 12:05, if t is n (whole or fractional) minutes after 12:00, then at t the path P' contains the water which occupies the bottom n inches of the glass. That is, at a half-minute after 12:00, P' contains the water which occupies the bottom one-half inch of the glass; at 12:01, P' contains the water which occupies the bottom inch of the glass; and so on.

Both P and P' are continuous paths, and the term "water" is instanced on every point of each path. P and P' partly coincide (at 12:03) and partly diverge (at every other time in the interval). Whereas P corresponds to five minutes in the career of a single bit of water, P' corresponds not to the career of a single bit of water, but rather to successive stages of different bits of water. Why does P' fail to qualify as corresponding to the career of a single bit of water? Why should we not say that P' corresponds to the career of a bit of water which becomes larger throughout the five minute interval? The answer must be that, though P' is a continuous path and is traceable under the E term "water," it violates the no-choice requirement, in that it partly coincides with P (and innumerable other continuous and "water"-traceable paths). But, by the same token, P also violates the no-choice requirement. Therefore our criteria for favoring P over P', and for counting only P as corresponding to the career of a bit of water, must take us beyond the simple T rules. And this conclusion evidently holds for any path, like P, which traces the career of some water.

There is, then, a fundamental difference between articulative E terms and mass E terms. If you consider an articulative E term like "table," you can say that a concept of identity is associated with it that operates in a perfectly definite and rule-governed manner, at least for ordinary cases. For these cases the identity concept is adequately explained by appealing to the relatively simple T rules. The fact that no part of a table is a table insures that the no-choice requirement, as well as the continuity requirement, can ordinarily be satisfied by the path of a table. The overall identity concept for "table" is thereby seen to be firmly anchored by rule to experience. That the concept has a residual aspect of "open texture" may then be readily conceded without depriving the concept of its straightforwardly experiential character.

The situation seems to be quite different with regard to mass E terms like "water." Even if you isolate a quantity of water, and it sits intact and unchanging for a period of time, you cannot base your judgment of its identity through time on any relatively simple rules like the T rules. For the dissectiveness of "water" guarantees the failure of the no-choice requirement even in optimal cases. Still less can the T rules adjudicate more difficult cases, where the water splits in two, or merges with other water, or is mixed with a different substance.

Before pursuing this point further I want to introduce another category of terms. These are terms which provide a kind of bridge between ordinary articulative E terms and mass E terms. I refer to such terms as "puddle of water," "pile of dirt," "drift of snow." These are to be adjudged as E terms since they properly cover career descriptions. The decisive test is that the duration rule can be appropriately applied on their bases. If a puddle of water is swept into the sewer, or a pile of dirt levelled, or a drift of snow shovelled away, then the puddle, the pile, the drift, no longer exist; their careers are brought to an end.

These E terms are articulative; that is, they are nondissective. The simple proof of this is that if the parts of a pile of dirt were piles of dirt, it would make no sense to say, for example, that there are exactly two piles of dirt in the backyard. In general, a logically sufficient condition for an E term's being nondissective, and therefore articulative, is that it should make sense to count how many instances of the term are located in a designated area. Conversely, mass E terms have the important property that they are not in this sense "count nouns."

Words like "puddle," "pile," and "drift" I will call *articulators*. And the result of conjoining an articulator to a mass E term I call an *articulated-mass* E term. These latter, as we just saw, are peculiar specimens of articulative E terms and are not specimens of mass E terms. Indeed there seems to be a quite negligible difference between "puddle of water," "pile of dirt," "drift of snow" and such straightforward articulative E terms as "lake," "mountain," "snowball."

Questions like "Is the same water still there?" may frequently be ambiguous, in that it can mean either "Is the same puddle (pool, expanse, and so on) of water still there?" or "Is the same water, the same material stuff, still there?" Interpreted in the first way, as involving an articulated-mass E term, the question can apparently be answered by a straightforward appeal to the T rules. What I have tried to show, however, is that when the question is interpreted in the second way, as involving a mass E term, it cannot be answered by an appeal to the T rules.

We have, then, two major classes of physical objects. In the first class there are objects whose careers are traced under articulative E terms (both ordinary articulative E terms and articulated-mass E terms). These objects we may call "articulated objects." The second class consists of objects, quantities of matter, whose careers are traced under mass E terms. These we may call "mass objects." We have seen that the identity through time of an articulated object can be elucidated by reference to the *T* rules but that the identity through time of a mass object cannot be thus elucidated. The question that remains is what the identity through time of a mass object consists in.

I do not have a very clear idea of what the answer to this question is, but let me suggest, very briefly, the general lines along which I think the answer ought to be sought.[11] Suppose that we tried to give up all discourse about mass objects, and confined ourselves to describing the world in terms exclusively of articulated objects. What would we lose? Plainly we would lose a good deal of our ability to explain why articulated objects behave the way that they do. I am not now referring to any relatively sophisticated scientific explanations, but rather to explanations that occur at even the most rudimentary level of common sense. Think, for example, of how common sense would explain why it is that when a pool of water (an articulated object) is divided into three pools of water (articulated objects) the sum of the volumes of the three new pools appears to equal the volume of the original pool. The explanation is that though the original pool was dispersed, and three new pools were formed, we still have the *same water,* the same mass of stuff. Here we see how employing the mass *E* term "water" helps us to explain, to render more coherent, the careers of articulated objects. And this suggests numerous similar examples in which discourse about mass objects helps, at even a common-sense level, to explain what happens when articulated objects are divided up, or merged together. The explanatory role of mass *E* terms becomes even more apparent if we pass beyond the level of simple common sense and consider scientific levels of discourse, where, for example, laws of chemistry may be formulated in terms of different kinds of mass objects (different kinds of matter).

The incorporation of mass objects into our conceptual scheme helps us to explain the behavior of articulated objects. And I want to suggest that ultimately the only rule of identity for mass objects is just this: Reidentify mass objects in such a way as to simplify explanations. That is, the identity through time of a mass object is not governed by any clear-cut rules of the same general sort as the *T* rules. The only general rule which may be said to provide logically sufficient constraints on procedures for tracing the careers of mass objects is the rule that these procedures must somehow fill out the world of articulated objects in a theoretically satisfying way. From this very general rule there emerges, both at the level of common sense and at scientific levels, various subsidiary principles which specify how the careers of mass

---

[11] A view on the identity of matter similar to the one which I am about to suggest is to be found in Bertrand Russell's "The Relation of Sense-Data to Physics," in *Mysticism And Logic* (London: George Allen & Unwin Ltd., 1917), pp. 169–173.

objects may be presumed to unfold under different circumstances. But these principles are both partial and provisional, and may, within broad limits, be supplemented or revised in the light of scientific progress.

To put this in slightly different terms, I am suggesting that even a very rudimentary form of common sense embraces an incipient *theory* of mass objects, a theory which relates, in a partial and open-ended way, the careers of mass objects to the careers of articulated objects. One such open-ended relation is the principle that, other things being equal, an articulated object is presumed to remain composed of the same mass object. (For example, the same puddle of water is presumed to remain composed of the same water, unless there is a stream running through the puddle, or somebody took a glass of water out of the puddle, or something else happened.)

Another principle seems to be something like this: Other things being equal, the same portion of an articulated object is presumed to remain composed of the same mass object. (For example, the bottom three inches of a glass of water is, other things being equal, presumed to remain composed of the same water.) It is such principles as these, continually reviewed and revised by scientific advance, which give sense to discourse about mass objects.

Let me remark, in closing, that one of my purposes for belaboring the distinction between mass objects and articulated objects was to separate the very difficult from the not so difficult. The identity of mass objects remains in need of a great deal of further explanation. But I hope to have shown that the core idea of the identity of an articulated object is simply the idea of a continuous space-time path that is traced under an articulative E term. Therefore, at least with regard to articulated objects, there should be no mystery about what it might mean to say that an object has an essence, and that its essence determines its identity.

Identity and Spatiotemporal Continuity

ROBERT C. COBURN

University of Chicago

1. "This is the same rock we used yesterday as a doorstop." "The Volvo I bought last February is now in the shop." "Our piano is older, but none the worse for wear." "This is the cat you held in one hand just five years ago last month." Such statements, which assert or imply that some material object has persisted, has retained its identity through time, are as common as any we make. This fact is sometimes expressed by saying that central to the "conceptual scheme" we operate, to the system of general notions which finds near-constant expression in everyday thought and speech, is the idea of persisting material things. In what follows I want to consider a certain view which bears on the question as to what it is for a material thing, such as a rock or a cat, to have a history or to retain its identity over a stretch of time.

The view in question is as familiar as it is natural. Here are some characteristic expressions of it.

> In the case of ordinary "material things," e.g., tables and stones, we can speak of spatiotemporal continuity . . . as a logically necessary . . . condition, of identity.[1]

> One of the requirements for the identity of a material thing is that its existence, as well as being continuous in time, should be continuous in space.[2]

[1] Sydney Shoemaker, *Self-Knowledge and Self-Identity* (Ithaca, N.Y.: Cornell University Press, 1963), pp. 4–5.

[2] P. F. Strawson, *Individuals* (London: Methuen & Co., 1959), p. 37.

51

In the case of material objects, we can draw a distinction between identity and exact similarity. . . . This notion of identity is given to us primarily, though not completely, by the notion of spatio-temporal continuity.[3]

It is part of our common-sense concept of a thing that its existence is spatio-temporally continuous. It never leaps gaps in either time or space.[4]

For convenience of reference I shall label this doctrine that spatio-temporal continuity is a logically necessary condition of material object identity through time "*Icn.*"

2. Though *Icn* is rarely argued, it is not difficult to see what some of the main considerations are which make it attractive when it is construed in a natural way. Here I have in mind the construction which results when the notion of spatiotemporal continuity is understood as involving both "temporal continuity" and "spatial continuity," where (1) a material object exhibits the former through an interval K provided that there are no intervals within K, however short, throughout which it does not exist; and (2) a material object exhibits the latter through an interval K provided that it never occupies two distinct places at different instants within K (say t_1 and t_5) without having successively occupied all of the places on one of the logically possible spatial paths connecting the places in question between t_1 and t_5. (This "natural" way of understanding the notion of spatiotemporal continuity is, to be sure, an exceedingly rough way—for reasons I shall detail later.)

Suppose, to begin with, that a material object such as a rock or a cat could be temporally discontinuous. This means, given the rough analysis of temporal continuity just noted, that there could be an interval—say K—during which some cat—say Beau Soleil—did not exist. But if Beau Soleil does not exist during K, she must have ceased to exist before K. But if she ceased to exist before K, then how could she be identical with any cat which begins to exist after K? After all, as Locke said: "One thing cannot have two beginnings of existence."[5]

---

[3] B. A. O. Williams, "Personal Identity and Individuation," *Proceedings of the Aristotelian Society*, LVII (1956–57), p. 230.

[4] D. Armstrong, "Absolute and Relative Motion," *Mind*, LXII (1963), p. 220. See also D. Gasking, "Clusters," *Australasian Journal of Philosophy*, XXXVIII (May, 1960), p. 25; G. C. Nerlich, "Sameness, Difference, and Continuity," *Analysis*, XVIII (June, 1958), p. 147; G. C. Nerlich, "On Evidence for Identity," *Australasian Journal of Philosophy*, XXXVII (December, 1959), p. 201; B. A. Brody, "Natural Kinds and Real Essences," *Journal of Philosophy*, LXIV (July 20, 1967), pp. 444–45; A. J. Ayer, *Philosophical Essays* (London: Macmillan & Co., Ltd., 1954), p. 14.

[5] John Locke, *Essay Concerning Human Understanding* (New York: Dover Publications, Inc., 1959), Bk. II, Chap. 27, Sec. 1. Presumably his point was that if some cat, a say, ceases to exist at t, it necessarily does not exist after t; and if some cat, b say, begins to exist at some later time t', then it necessarily did not exist prior to t'.

Also, if there could be a temporal gap in Beau Soleil's existence, then we should have to say that there was a time between her birth and her death when she was not located anywhere in the universe. But surely the idea that a material object such as a cat should, on some occasion during its career, be nowhere is in the same category with such notions as that $\sqrt{2}$ might be lonely and the sides of a chiliagon nondenumerable.

Even if cogent, these considerations against the possibility of temporal gaps in the history of a material object do not rule out the possibility of spatial gaps of course. A tempting argument for excluding this possibility is the following. (This argument, incidentally, can obviously be adapted so as to buttress the reasoning of the preceding paragraph too.) Suppose that there could be a case of a material object's exhibiting spatial discontinuity. Such a situation is depicted schematically in Diagram 1. Then it would seem that there could (logically) be three qualitatively indistinguishable marbles each of which undergoes a discontinuous translation in space at the same instant. (Here I define two objects as *qualitatively indistinguishable* provided that any property which one has and which it is logically possible for the other also to have, the other has too.) Such a situation is depicted in Diagram 2. But in order for this situation to be logically possible, it must make sense to say, for example, that $a = d$ and that $a \neq d$, and similarly for the other possible pairings of marbles on the left side of the gap with those on the right side of the gap. That it does, however, this line of thought continues, is very doubtful. For given the qualitative indistinguishability of the marbles involved, there seems to be no way of pairing the left-hand marbles with the right-hand ones which has more to commend it than has any alternative way of pairing them. But if nothing whatever could justify identifying a with d (say) as opposed to e or f, then it does not make clear sense to maintain that each left-hand marble is identical with one of the right-hand marbles: The notions of correctness and incorrectness simply have no application to such pairings.

A slightly different version of the same argument might be expressed as follows. Given the possibility of a material object's having a spatially discontinuous career, it is difficult to see what could rule out

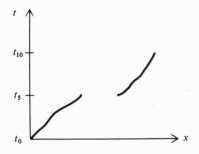

t

t_{10}

t_5

t_0

x

Diagram 1. The broken line represents the spatio-temporal path of a material object from t_0 to t_{10}. Here and throughout I represent only one component of the object's spatial path.

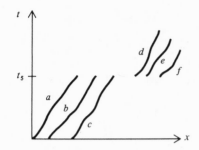

Diagram 2. The left-hand lines represent the spatiotemporal paths of the three marbles before the jump; the right-hand lines represent their paths after the jump.

the possibility of a situation of the type depicted in Diagram 3. This latter possibility, however, is not a genuine one, for it would be a genuine possibility only if there were (in principle at least) some way of deciding which of *b* and *c* was (identical with) *a*. But the "qualitative indistinguishability" of *b* and *c* rules out any conceivable basis for picking one rather than the other as being *a* in a later phase of its career. Hence, once again, it seems that no clear sense can be attached to the words which describe this putative possibility, with the result that the notion of a spatially discontinuous material object is logically defective.[6]

3. Attractive as *Icn* at first may appear, especially when buttressed by considerations of the kind presented in the preceding three paragraphs, it is liable to a number of objections. However, before turning to an examination of these objections, it will be helpful to look more closely at the crucial notion of spatiotemporal continuity. For so long as we do not have at hand a clear understanding of this concept, we will be poorly placed for determining the status of any doctrine, such as *Icn*, which involves it.

It might be thought that an adequate account is readily available in the writings of advocates of *Icn*. This unfortunately is not so — as a rapid survey of some of the things several recent advocates have said about the notion of spatiotemporal continuity makes evident. Consider, to begin with, the following account which Shoemaker gives after making the remark quoted above: "Roughly speaking, the identity of Φ's involves spatiotemporal continuity if and only if the positions occupied by a Φ during any interval during which it exists must form a continuous line (or, in the special case in which the Φ remains motionless, a single point)."[7] This account is much too rough, however. A cow is not a Boscovitchian mass point. Hence the position occupied by a cow during some interval through which it is motionless is not a

[6] Cf. B. A. O. Williams, "Bodily Continuity and Personal Identity," *Analysis*, XXI (December, 1960); G. C. Nerlich, "Sameness, Difference, and Continuity"; and B. A. Brody, "Natural Kinds and Real Essences."

[7] Shoemaker, *Self-Knowledge and Self-Identity*, p. 5, n. 3.

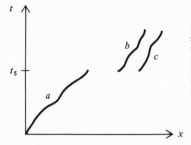

Diagram 3. Here the left-hand line represents the spatiotemporal path of an object prior to its "jump"; the right-hand lines represent the spatiotemporal paths of two material objects, one of which is identical with a and the other of which is an object that is qualitatively indistinguishable from the first and that comes into existence at t_5.

single point; nor, when it moves, do the positions it occupies form a line. Moreover, we are not told exactly what it is for the members of a set of punctual positions, each of which is occupied by some moving object, to "form a continuous line."

Strawson makes a somewhat more adequate attempt to clarify the idea of spatiotemporal continuity which Icn involves. After saying that continuity in both time and space is "one of the requirements for the identity of a material thing," he goes on thus:

> That is to say, for many kinds of thing,[8] it counts against saying that a thing, x, at one place at one time is the same as a thing, y, at another place at another time, if we think there is not some continuous set of places between these two places such that x was at each successive member of the set of places at successive times between these two times and y was at the same member of the set of places at the same time.[9]

If we assume, as I have been assuming, that when Strawson speaks of "one of the requirements for the identity of a material thing" he is talking of a logically necessary condition of identity, then what this elucidatory passage comes to might be restated as follows: A logically necessary condition of the spatiotemporal continuity of a material thing, x, which occupies place p_1 at time t_1, with a material thing, y, which occupies place p_2 ($p_1 \neq p_2$) at some later time t_{10}, is that (1) there is some "continuous set of places"—say S—between p_1 and p_2; (2) x occupies each successive member of S at successive times between t_1 and t_{10}; and (3) y occupies the same member of S at the same time x occupies it.

Upon reflection, however, this attempt at clarifying the notion of spatiotemporal continuity appears little better than the admittedly

---

[8] Apparently material things count as a kind of thing for Strawson. For otherwise this sentence contradicts its predecessor in virtue of implying that there are some material things whose identity does not require spatiotemporal continuity.

[9] Strawson, *Individuals*, p. 37.

rough account provided by Shoemaker. In the first place, the idea of a
"continuous set of places" is as much in need of explication as the notion it is invoked to explain. This becomes especially clear when we
recall that most material things change their shapes and sizes through
time. Nor is it clear, for all Strawson says, whether the "successive
members of S" and the "successive times between t_1 and t_{10}" constitute,
for example, discrete series, merely dense series, or continuous series
in the Cantorian sense. It may be, of course, that the notion he is at-
tempting to elucidate is too gross to permit an answer to this question.
But no reason is provided to think so. And in the absence of any such
reason the account can, I think, justifiably be faulted for its lack of ex-
plicitness at this point. Finally, the account is defective both because
it fails to give a sufficient condition for the spatiotemporal continuity of
a material thing x (at t_1) and a material thing y (at t_{10}; $t_1 < t_{10}$) [10] and
because it does not even give a logically necessary condition in the
general case, which subsumes stationary things as well as things which
move.

4. Perhaps the most detailed attempt to elucidate the notion in
question is the account recently presented by Richard Swinburne. To
say that "a material object M' at temporal instant t' " is spatiotemporally continuous with a material object M "previously identified at
t" ($t < t'$) is, Swinburne writes, to say

> that there was a material object M'' approximately similar . . . to
> both M and M' at every temporal instant t'' between t and t', such
> that each M'' at each t'' occupies a place contiguous with the place
> occupied by the M'' at the prior and succeeding instants, however
> precisely temporal instants are identified, the series beginning with
> M at t and ending with M' at t'.[11]

Moreover, he continues,

> Most parts of the M'' of equal volume at each t'' must also occupy
> places contiguous with a place occupied by a part of the M'' at the
> prior and succeeding instants.[12]

"What counts as 'approximately similar' will vary," Swinburne says,
with the "type of object" in question.[13] Also, an instant, we are told, is

---

[10] I use throughout expressions of the form '$t < t'$' to mean: t is earlier than t'; and expressions of the form '$t \leq t'$' to mean: t is either earlier than or identical with t'.
[11] R. Swinburne, *Space and Time* (New York: St. Martin's Press, 1968), pp. 22–23.
[12] *Ibid.*, p. 23.
[13] *Ibid.*, p. 22.

"a very, very small period of time, such as could be occupied by an event very, very short compared with the period of time separating it from other events with which we are concerned." [14]

Unfortunately, Swinburne's words are less than pellucid. However, one plausible way of construing the analysans of his account is as follows:

> No matter how short we make our "instants," [15] i.e., the intervals of time over which the time variables 't_1', 't_2', etc. range, it is true that $(t_1)(t < t_1 < t' \supset (\exists t_2)(\exists t_3\{[(t_2 \underset{\tilde{}}{<} t_1 \underset{\tilde{}}{<} t_3)$ & $(t \leq t_2)$ & $(t_3 \leq t')]$ & $(\exists x_1)(\exists x_2)(\exists x_3)$ $[(x_1$ exists through t_1 & x_2 exists through t_2 & x_3 exists through $t_3)$ & $(x_1$ occupies a place contiguous with the place occupied by x_2 and $x_3)$ & $(x_1$ is approximately similar to M and to $M')$ & (most equal-volume parts of x_1 are such as to occupy places contiguous with a place occupied by a part of x_2 and with a place occupied by a part of $x_3)$ & $(t_2 = t. \supset x_2 = M)$ & $(t_3 = t'. \supset x_3 = M')$ & (x_4) $(x_4$ exists at t_1 & x_4 occupies a place contiguous with the place occupied by x_2 and x_3 & x_4 is approximately similar to M and to M' & most equal-volume parts of x_4 are such as to occupy places contiguous with a place occupied by a part of x_2 and with a place occupied by a part of $x_3. \supset x_4 = x_1)]\})$.

(Here the 'x_i' are variables which range over material objects and the predicate '① $\underset{\tilde{}}{<}$ ②' is short for '① is immediately prior to ②'.)[16]

Even this more detailed account of the notion of spatiotemporal continuity which *Icn* involves, however, falls considerably short of what we need. To begin with, the explication Swinburne gives of the notion of "approximate similarity" is such as to insure that if the object in your car yesterday is spatiotemporally continuous with the thing now in the basket, then the former is the same "type of object" as the latter. But this is an unhappy consequence. Surely we do not want to rule out the (logical) possibility of Proteus's having exhibited spatiotemporal continuity despite the kind-traversing character of the changes he allegedly underwent from time to time. ("Then, with a shout, we leapt upon him and flung our arms round his back. But the old man's

---

[14] *Ibid.*, p. 157. It should be noted that Swinburne modifies this account slightly in the light of his discussion of a problem I consider later. The modification does not free it of the difficulties I mention below, however.

[15] That is, for any choice of "instant" lengths, no matter how short. . . .

[16] Throughout I use the symbolism for English predicates devised by W. Quine and used by B. Mates. See W. V. O. Quine, *Methods of Logic*, 2nd ed. (New York: Holt, Rinehart and Winston, 1959), pp. 131 ff., and B. Mates, *Elementary Logic* (New York: Oxford University Press, 1965), pp. 73 f.

skill and cunning had not deserted him. He began by turning into a
bearded lion and then into a snake, and after that a panther and a giant
boar.") [17] It may be, to be sure, that the notion of an object's retaining
its identity through such radical changes is incoherent. But it is not
plausible to suppose that any such incoherence stems from the im-
possibility of spatiotemporal continuity in cases of radical, kind-traversing change. Secondly, the account — as I have construed it — implies
that there are limits on the velocities which bodies can attain so long
as their motions exhibit spatiotemporal continuity. This is so because,
according to this account, a logically necessary condition of M's being
spatiotemporally continuous with M' is that, for any choice of "instant"
lengths, "each M'' at each t''" occupy "a place contiguous with the
place occupied by the M'' at the prior and succeeding instants," as
Swinburne puts it. (The equal-volume parts requirement has the same
consequence, of course.) But again, to build a limit of this kind into the
very notion of spatiotemporal continuity seems quite inappropriate.
Though there is strong evidence for thinking that bodies cannot exceed
the speed of light, it is far from clear that we cannot conceive of possible worlds which are not under the constraints of special relativity. A
third defect stems from the lack of clarity of the notion of "a place
contiguous with [another] place." It does not seem right, for example,
to suppose that p_1 and p_2 are contiguous provided they partially overlap, for then continuity would be compatible with very jerky motion.
But if the notion of partial overlap will not serve, we have a right to ask
what will, it seems to me. Finally, the account in question implies that
every moving object occupies one and only one place during an "instant." Thus in my restatement of Swinburne's analysans x_1, which
exists through t_1, occupies a place contiguous with . . . and so on. But
if this is so, even the most continuous motions will have a staccato
character since they will be made up of as many periods of rest as
there are "instants" in the temporal stretch under consideration. Surely
this also is an unacceptable consequence.

5. Despite the difficulties which the foregoing accounts suggest
are involved in providing a satisfactory elucidation of the notion of the
spatiotemporal continuity of a body which exists at one time with a
body which exists at some later time, an account which is at least a
considerable improvement on the foregoing is not hard to find. We only
need to remember the definitions of a limit and a continuous function

[17] Homer, *The Odyssey*, trans. E. V. Rieu (Baltimore, Md.: Penquin Books, 1946), p.
76. My attention was drawn to this passage by D. Wiggins' essay "The Individuation
of Things and Places," *Proceedings of the Aristotelian Society*, Suppl. vol. XXXVII
(1963), p. 191.

which are generally adopted in contemporary mathematical analysis.[18] These definitions more or less immediately suggest an account like the following. To assert ⌜α is spatiotemporally continuous with β⌝, where α identifies a material thing as existing at t_i and β identifies a material thing as existing at t_j[19] ($t_i < t_j$), is to say that the bearer of α moves continuously throughout the interval $[t_i, t_j]$[20] and that it coincides with the bearer of β at t_j, where

D1. x *moves continuously throughout interval* K = (t) (t is in K ⊃ x moves continuously at t),

D2. x *moves continuously at instant* t = (y) [y is a spatial volume which contains the primary place of x at t ⊃ (∃z) (z is an open temporal interval containing t & y contains the primary place of x throughout z)] & (y) [y is a spatial volume contained by the primary place of x at t ⊃ (∃z) (z is an open temporal interval containing t & the primary place of x contains y throughout z)].

D3. *Spatial volume* V *contains the primary place of* x (or simply x) = the surface defining the primary place of x is wholly enclosed by and nowhere in contact with the surface defining the boundary of V,[21] and

D4. x *coincides with* w *at* t = (the primary place of x at t = the primary place of w at t).

Also, the primary place of a body is understood, following Swinburne, to be the spatial volume defined by a surface which fits snugly around the body, completely enclosing it; [22] the variable 't' ranges over instants where instants are now understood in such a way that those making up any open temporal interval constitute a linear continuum in the classi-

---

[18] See, for example, A. K. Aleksandrov, A. N. Kolmogorov, and M. A. Lavrent'ev (eds.), *Mathematics: Its Content, Methods, and Meaning* (Cambridge, Mass.: Massachusetts Institute of Technology Press, 1963), Vol. 1, Chap. II, Secs. 3 and 4.

[19] Here and hereafter when I say that a singular term α "identifies an object as existing at t," I shall mean that either α is a definite description containing a temporal reference (such as, for example, 'the apple which was in the bowl at noon yesterday') which accurately characterizes the object it designates, or α is a singular term of some other kind which in the context of its use conveys similar temporal information about its referent.

[20] The interval $[t_1, t_{10}]$ is the set of instants whose coordinates satisfy the inequality $t_1 \leqslant t_i \leqslant t_{10}$. Such an interval is called a closed interval.

[21] I shall say that the points making up the surface which "defines" a certain volume are included in the volume so defined.

[22] Swinburne, *Space and Time*, p. 12.

cal sense; [23] and the variables 'x' and 'w' range over material objects.

I say that the analysis given above is an improvement on the fore-going accounts for the following reasons. To begin with, the analysis insures that there is no chunk of space V such that, for any instant within $[t_i, t_j]$ at which the bearer of α is within V, it is false that there exist neighboring instants at which the bearer of α is also within V. And reflection makes it very tempting to suppose that such an exclusion is among those which a proper analysis of the notion of spatiotemporal continuity requires. After all, if that apple (say) traversed a continuous path through both space and time yesterday, surely we want it to be the case that, however fast the apple was moving at (say) t, we could (in principle) find an instant, later than t, at which the apple was still within any previously chosen spatial volume which contained it at t. Moreover, the analysis takes fully into account the fact that spatio-temporal continuity is compatible with a thing's changing its size and shape through time, and it insures that such changes are also continu-ous in a way which squares with what readily appear to be our intuitive requirements. It does this because the definition of 'x moves continu-ously at t' (D2) appears to serve equally well as a definition of 'x changes its size/shape at t continuously'. No less important, the anal-ysis is clearly free of the myriad difficulties which beset the foregoing abortive accounts. Thus, it does not require us to think of ordinary bodies as Boscovitchian mass points. Superficial appearances to the contrary, it permits spatiotemporal continuity to obtain in cases of rest. To see that this is so, we need merely note that 'moves continuously' is a technical expression the definition of which is such that an object's moving continuously does not entail that it is moving. It does not in-volve any such unexplicated notions as *continuous line, continuous set of places*, and *contiguous places*. It allows spatiotemporal continuity to hold despite radical, Proteus-like, changes — or, at any rate, it does if such a Protean object can (in logic) survive such changes. It puts no a priori limit on the speeds of objects following spatiotemporally con-tinuous paths. And it avoids the result that material things which move along spatiotemporally continuous paths necessarily move jerkily in virtue of remaining stationary for (nearly countless) short stretches during the periods of their motion.

6. In addition there are ready replies to various objections — sev-eral that are obvious and one that is not — that might be raised to this analysis. Thus it might be objected that those who advocate doctrines like *Icn* need not have in mind the ideas which enter into this account's analysans, since it is quite possible to urge and argue for doctrines like

[23] See, for example, R. Wilder, *Introduction to the Foundations of Mathematics*, 2nd ed. (New York: John Wiley & Sons, Inc., 1965), Chap. VI, especially definition 1.4.1.1.

Icn without having any acquaintance, for example, with the set-theoretical concept of the linear continuum. Such an objection is beside the point. Obviously a person can implicitly have in mind technical notions he has never heard of. For example, he might be disposed to respond affirmatively to a certain sequence of questions, knowing that his answers are correct. And the result might be his coming to see the truth of a certain doctrine which he had never explicitly entertained and which involved quite complicated notions which he had never previously had explicitly in mind. Moreover, I see no reason why such a doctrine might not be a correct analysis of some notion the person had previously employed.[24]

Another obvious objection might be made as follows. The intuitive notion of spatiotemporal continuity with which philosophers operate when they discourse upon the identity through time of material objects is one whose sense is conveyed and acquired ostensively. That is, a spatiotemporally continuous path is essentially the sort of path which ordinary, everyday examples of material objects — things like apples, rocks, and cats — follow as they move about or rest quietly in a bowl, on a mountain, or under a tree; and it is by reference to examples like these that the notion of a path of this kind is both explained and acquired. Since this is so, the objection continues, any analysis which makes even the density of time, much less the "strong continuity" of time, a necessary condition for the truth of claims about the spatiotemporal continuity of the path followed by such objects as Towzer, clearly departs from the analysandum in an unacceptable way.

Though perhaps more persuasive at first glance than the first, this second objection is also unconvincing. To begin with, it is not at all obvious that there is *a* notion of spatiotemporal continuity. Putting this matter aside, however, the claim that *the* notion of spatiotemporal continuity is connected in the ways indicated with everyday examples of moving and stationary material objects obviously needs considerable backing to be convincing. Paul Grice has recently noted that there is "nothing absurd in the idea that a non-specialist concept should contain, so to speak, a blank space to be filled by the specialist." [25] We might add that there seems also to be nothing absurd in the idea that such a concept should typically be explained and acquired ostensively — or at least that appeals to (alleged) examples should often play a key role in the teaching and learning of such a concept. Indeed, having

---

[24] See in this connection M. Misner, *Chomsky's Concept of Implicit Knowledge* (unpublished Ph.D. dissertation, Department of Philosophy, University of Chicago, 1969), Chap. 3.

[25] H. P. Grice, "The Causal Theory of Perception," *Proceedings of the Aristotelian Society*, Suppl. Vol. XXXV (1961), p. 144. Reprinted in R. J. Swartz (ed.), *Perceiving, Sensing, and Knowing* (Garden City, N.Y.: Anchor Books, 1965).

made the remark quoted, Grice goes on to give reason for thinking that the concept of seeing may very well possess such a "blank space," and we can certainly imagine a person's explaining and/or acquiring this concept by appeal — at least in part — to (alleged) instances of the concept. But now if these points are correct, it seems quite possible that the notion of spatiotemporal continuity with which advocates of *Icn* operate contains such a "blank space," and this despite the fact, if it is a fact, that the notion is (typically) explained and acquired by reference to everyday cases of moving and stationary objects. But this is tantamount to saying that it is quite possible that details about the density or Cantorian continuity of time should have just the place in a correct analysis of the notion which the account in question provides.

Moreover, it is quite implausible to maintain that there is as close a connection between the notion in question and its (alleged) instances as this objection seems to require. For even if it is true that often philosophers, for example, explain the idea of a spatiotemporally continuous path by referring to the movements of cats and rocks, it is surely also true that they seek to convey the idea in the way we have seen that Shoemaker and Strawson among others do. That is, they try to state necessary and/or sufficient conditions for its being the case that an object which exists at one time is spatiotemporally continuous with an object which exists at some prior or subsequent time, and in doing so they invoke the general notion of the continuous understood (presumably) as simply the opposite of the interrupted, the gappy, the staccato. In view of this fact, it seems quite unreasonable to suppose that the notion so conveyed is as removed from that expressed in the analysans in question as the objection implies. After all, if any argument could be provided that some ostensible case of spatiotemporal continuity were in fact gappy, on a natural understanding of the expression 'gappy', surely it would be quite natural for someone operating with a notion of continuity which had been conveyed by a definition like (say) Shoemaker's to question whether the case under consideration were really a case of spatiotemporal continuity. These considerations suffice, I think, to answer the present objection in the form in which I have stated it.

7. The unobvious objection alluded to earlier is that an argument of the kind which makes accounts of spatiotemporal continuity that employ the notion of a merely dense series of instants unacceptable can also be constructed to criticize any account, such as the one in question, which uses the idea of a series of instants which satisfies the standard axioms of linear continuity. A typical argument against accounts of the former type might run as follows. A body exhibits spatiotemporal continuity through interval K only if it possesses uninter-

rupted existence during K. But our intuitive notion of the continuity of time cannot be adequately expressed by the notion of a merely dense order. For suppose (1) there is a body b which weighs π pounds during the interval $[t_1, t_{10}]$. That is, suppose it is true that were b to be placed on one pan of an equal-arm balance at any point during $[t_1, t_{10}]$ (a) it would ascend if any body were placed in the other whose weight in pounds could be given by a rational number which is greater than π and (b) it would descend if any body were placed in the other whose weight in pounds could be given by a rational number which is less than π. Suppose further (2) that there is some process P which, when it is applied to a body, makes it grow continuously heavier over a continuous stretch of time. Finally suppose (3) that body a is subjected to P through the interval $[t_1, t_{10}]$ with the result that at t_{10}, a weighs twice what it did at t_1 — say 4 pounds. On these suppositions, a must weigh the same as b at some point within $[t_1, t_{10}]$. Otherwise P would not have the effect indicated, given our intuitive understanding of continuity. But this means that there must be instants in $[t_1, t_{10}]$ which correspond to the irrational numbers between 2 and 4 as well as instants which correspond to the rational numbers between 2 and 4. Hence, if the above suppositions represent a conceivable state of affairs — as it seems reasonable to think — our intuitive notion of temporal continuity cannot be adequately expressed by supposing the temporal order is merely dense.[26]

But now, this objection continues, an analogous argument can be constructed to show that our intuitive notion of temporally continuous existence also excludes the possibility that an open temporal interval satisfies the standard axioms of linear continuity. Let us add to the suppositions made above the following: (4) that there exists a body c which weighs exactly ϵ pounds, where to say this is to say that when c is placed in one pan of an equal-arm balance (a) it ascends when any body is placed in the other pan whose weight in pounds can be given by a positive rational number, and (b) it descends when no body is placed in the opposite pan;[27] (5) that there is a body d which weighs exactly 3 pounds. On this expanded set of suppositions, it would seem that a must weigh the same as d plus c at some point within $[t_1, t_{10}]$. That is, there must be an instant within $[t_1, t_{10}]$ at which a's weight is such that, if it were then placed opposite both c and d, it would neither ascend nor descend — at any rate, given our intuitive notion of the continuous and a fortiori our intuitive idea of what it would be for

[26] This argument is an adaptation of the argument José Benardete gives in his paper "Continuity and the Theory of Measurement," *Journal of Philosophy,* LXV (July 18, 1968), pp. 417 f.
[27] Cf. *ibid.,* p. 414.

something to "grow continuously heavier over a continuous stretch of time." But if this is so, then given the coherence of the set of suppositions (1)–(5), it follows that our intuitive notion of temporal continuity is no better expressed by the axioms of linear continuity than by the notion of mere density, for the suppositions imply that not only must there be instants in K which correspond to each weight in pounds expressed by the real numbers between 2 and 4 (inclusive), but also (and in addition) instants which correspond to each of these weights $\pm$ a weight equal to that of c — weights which clearly cannot be expressed by the use of the real numbers alone.

There are at least three things which can be said in reply to this last objection. The first is that it is by no means clear that supposition (4) is intelligible. What we are asked to suppose is that there exists a body which does weigh something, that is, is subject to gravitational attraction (presumably),[28] and yet weighs less than any object whose weight in pounds can be given by a rational number. This supposition is surely suspect. And our suspicions are only strengthened when we recognize that if we accept this supposition as intelligible, it opens the way to an endless succession of such queerly ponderable bodies. Second, even if the argument in question or some variant of it proves acceptable, it would not follow that time is not continuous in the classical sense, but only that our intuitive notion of the continuity of time is not adequately expressed by the axioms of the linear continuum. Hence, if there is reason to believe — as there seems to be[29] — that time is continuous in the classical sense, no significant basis for rejecting the account of spatiotemporal continuity in question would be provided by such an argument. Finally, even if it should someday happen that there was as good reason for thinking time to be continuous in some sense other than (and stronger than) the sense in which the real numbers constitute a continuum as there is today for believing time to be continuous in the classical sense, the modification of the analysis of spatiotemporal continuity given above which this development would suggest would be quite minor, affecting only the range of the variable 't'.

8. Starting in Section 5, I have been giving the reason for saying that the analysis of material object-spatiotemporal continuity, stated at the outset of Section 5, is an improvement on certain accounts (or partial accounts) in the recent literature. I have not argued either that this analysis is the only, the best, or even an adequate analysis of the

---

[28] The movements of the equal-arm balance alluded to in stating the supposition are presumably to be understood as a function of the action of gravity upon the objects put in its pans.

[29] Cf. A. Grünbaum, *Modern Science and Zeno's Paradoxes* (Middletown, Conn.: Wesleyan University Press, 1967), Chap. II.

notion in question. However, since it is in many ways a moderately clear account and since it is in many respects more satisfactory than the others I have mentioned, I shall begin the examination of Icn on the construction which results when the notion of spatiotemporal continuity is understood in accordance with this account. I shall proceed by considering *seriatim* a number of objections to which the doctrine so construed appears, at least *prima facie*, to be liable.

The first objection I want to take up can be expressed by the following line of argument. If Icn holds, a condition of someone's knowing that a sentence of the sort exemplified by 'the apple which was in the bowl yesterday at noon = the apple which is now in his hand' (hereafter abbreviated as '$a = b$') holds in some situation is that he have established the corresponding continuity statement — such as 'aCb', where 'C' is short for the predicate '① is spatiotemporally continuous with ②'. But a condition of a person's having done this, in turn, is that he have determined the truth of some statements of the form $\ulcorner\delta = \gamma\urcorner$, where here and below the values of 'δ' and 'γ' are singular terms which designate places which exist at different times. This is so because a sentence like 'aCb' holds (in some situation) only if a moved continuously at, say, 1:00 P.M., that is, that (*inter alia*) (y) [y is a spatial volume containing the primary place of a at 1:00 P.M. ⊃ $(\exists z)$ (z is an open temporal interval containing 1:00 P.M. and y contains the primary place of a throughout z)]. But this condition can obtain only if there is a spatial volume — V say — at 1:00 P.M. which contains the primary place of a and also a spatial volume — V' say — at 1:00 P.M. plus ϵ such that $V = V'$, where '1:00 P.M. plus ϵ' designates a later instant within one of the z-intervals containing 1:00 P.M. However, determining the truth-value of a statement of the form $\ulcorner\delta = \gamma\urcorner$ clearly requires having picked out some frame of reference relative to which the statement in question is to be assessed; and since, as Strawson puts it, "the identification and distinction of places turn on the identification and distinction of things," [30] a person can do this only if he already knows some truths of the type exemplified by '$a = b$'. Hence, this argument concludes, if Icn holds, a necessary condition of someone's knowing that his judgment concerning the identity through time of a material object is true is that he already knows some judgments of this kind to be true. Since the apodosis of the foregoing statement must be false, Icn must also be false. [31]

The objection which this line of reasoning poses to Icn, however, is patently spurious. Suppose, to begin with, that we read the argument

[30] Strawson, *Individuals*, p. 37.
[31] Cf. Swinburne, *Space and Time*, pp. 23 ff.

as asserting that, given *Icn,* various things must temporally precede a person's coming to know true such a statement as '*a* = *b*'. Then it is clear that the truth of the premises of the argument does lead to the absurdity that every bit of knowledge of a certain kind which a person has is such that prior to his coming to have it he had another bit of the same kind. But this reading makes various of these premises highly implausible. Why, for example, given *Icn,* must it be the case that every justified judgment of the form exemplified by '*a* = *b*' is preceded by a successful inquiry concerning spatiotemporal continuity? Presumably because if *p* entails *q,* then we cannot be certain that *p* without first checking out *q.* This principle can be tempting if we restrict our attention to certain cases and keep it focused only briefly. Thus we might reflect: "We can hardly be sure that another knows that *p* without first finding out whether *p* is true; nor can we feel justifiably confident that someone remembers seeing such and such take place until after we have acquired good reason for thinking that he was in a position to witness the event(s) in question," and so on. But the principle's falsity becomes evident as soon as we recall that most proofs in quantification theory are not obvious, or notice, for example, that ' 'Snow is white' is true' can plausibly be held to entail 'If God exists, then He believes that snow is white'.[32] In view of facts like these, it is quite clear that it is *not* a requirement of a person's knowing the entailing proposition that he first have discovered the truth of the entailed proposition.

Suppose, to the contrary, we read the argument as asserting (or rewrite it so that it asserts) merely that, given *Icn,* someone knows that a sentence like '*a* = *b*' is true ⊃ he knows the truth of the corresponding continuity sentence, a person knows that a sentence like '*aCb*' is true ⊃ he knows to be true some statement of the form ⌜δ = γ⌝, and so on. Then the argument will also fail, though for different reasons. One reason why it fails on this construction is the obvious falsity of the principle ⌜If *p* entails *q,* then if α knows that *p,* α knows that *q*⌝ (where 'α' ranges over names of persons). Thus we need not deny that

(1) The number of the stars is even and greater than four.

entails

(2) The number of the stars is the sum of two primes.

---

[32] On one natural understanding of 'God' and its cognates. See, for example, N. Pike, "Divine Omniscience and Voluntary Action," *Philosophical Review,* LXXIV (January, 1965), Sec. I.

merely because, though we know (1) holds, we do not know whether
(2) holds.[33] Another reason it fails is that, so construed, the absurdity
upon which it turns fails to materialize. Thus not only is it quite conceivable that a sentence like 'Jones knows that $a = b$' should materially
imply that there is some statement concerning the identity through time
of a material object, the truth of which Jones knows, it is obviously unavoidable. But such a result is not an absurdity, but a truism.

9. The next objection I want to consider is both more complex and
more serious. Consider the following argument (hereafter Ω). Given
the analysis of Section 5, a logically necessary condition of the spatiotemporal continuity of a body a identified as existing at t_1[34] with a body
b identified as existing at t_{10} is that a moves continuously at t_5 ($t_1 < t_5 <
t_{10}$), that is, that (inter alia) (y) [y is a spatial volume containing the
primary place of a at $t_5 \supset (\exists z)$ (z is an open temporal interval containing t_5 and y contains the primary place of a throughout z)]. If this condition holds, however, it will be true that there is a spatial volume V at
t_5 which contains the primary place of a and a spatial volume V' at
$t_5 + \epsilon$ such that $V = V'$, where '$t_5 + \epsilon$' designates a later instant
within one of the z intervals containing t_5 relative to V. But now whether
a place at one time is identical with (the same place as) a place at some
later time is relative to a frame of reference, for example, some (more
or less) rigid body which persists through the interval in question, or
some group of such bodies which retain the same spatial relations to
one another through the interval in question.[35] Hence, the identity of
V and V' is a relative matter, a matter which depends on the spatial
relations of V and V' to the item or items constituting some frame of
reference. If this is so, however, it follows that the spatiotemporal
continuity of a and b is also relative to a frame of reference. Generalizing, the conclusion might be put thus: Just as statements of the forms
⌜δ is the same place as γ⌝ and ⌜α moved during interval K⌝ are "incomplete" statements, statements of which the truth conditions are indeterminate until it is clear what the frame of reference is relative to
which the identity of the bearer of δ and the bearer of γ, or the motion
of the bearer of α, is to be assessed; so statements of the form ⌜α is
spatiotemporally continuous with β⌝ (where α is a term which identifies
a body as existing at one time and β a term which identifies a body as

---

[33] This example I take from B. Mates, *Elementary Logic*, p. 2.
[34] Here and throughout I intend certain verbs to carry their tenseless sense. It should be
clear from the context when this is so; hence I shall not employ a special convention
to indicate tenselessness. (I shall leave it an open question whether the tenseless sense
of a verb is to be analyzed by the use of the tensed sense of the verb when the instances
of the property the verb expresses are temporal existents.)
[35] Cf. Swinburne, *Space and Time*, p. 13.

existing at some different time) are similarly incomplete in the absence
of a specification (by context or otherwise) of a frame of reference.

As a way of seeing the intuitive plausibility of this conclusion
(hereafter Cr), imagine a Newtonian world containing two solar systems, G and H, such that relative to G, H appears at regular intervals
to traverse a spatially discontinuous path, and relatively to H, G
appears likewise at the same intervals. Now suppose that there is a
book d located in a study in a house on the surface of planet J in G. And
suppose further that to normal observers in G d appears at some point
to jump through space without covering the intermediate places. We
can, it seems, perfectly well imagine that d's ostensible discontinuity
relative to system G disappears relative to H because d's ostensible
jump coincides both spatially and temporally with the jump of H (relative to G); that is, it takes place at the same time and covers the same
distance. Hence we can, it seems, perfectly well imagine a body's being
spatiotemporally continuous relative to one frame of reference (in
this case H) and discontinuous relative to another (in this case G).

Given argument Ω and its conclusion Cr, we can now state the
objection as follows. *Icn* and Cr in conjunction yield a number of
consequences. One (hereafter R_1) is that any statement of the form
$\ulcorner\alpha_{(t_i)} = \beta_{(t_j)}\urcorner$ (where here and below $\alpha_{(t_i)}$ is a singular term which identifies a body as existing at t_i and $\beta_{(t_j)}$ is a singular term which identifies
a body as existing at some different time t_j) will be incomplete in the
absence of reference (explicit or implicit) to a frame of reference relative to which it is to be assessed. That this is so follows directly, given the
relativity of spatiotemporal continuity together with the essential role
of continuity in the identity through time of material objects. A second
and less obvious consequence (hereafter R_2) is that statements of the
form $\ulcorner\alpha$ is a (an) $\Phi\urcorner$ (where here and below α is a term which designates
a body and Φ is any common noun which expresses a sortal concept
the instances of which necessarily have histories) [36] are likewise incomplete. Here the argument rests upon the idea that bodies can
instantiate such sortals — for example, the concept expressed by 'horse'
and 'Pferd' — only provided they persist through time for some period,
in conjunction with the thought that the persistence or identity through
time of bodies is a relative matter. Thus a thing will not count as a
horse, for example, unless it lasts a bit; but whether a thing endures is,

---

[36] By a sortal concept the instances of which necessarily have histories I shall mean (for
present purposes) a concept such that its possession by a person involves his understanding and knowing how to apply criteria of distinctness and identity-over-time for
the items falling under it. Thus if C is a sortal concept of this kind, then anyone who
has C knows what would show that there are, say, three instances in the house, and
also that, say, instance a now before us is the same C thing as the one we saw yesterday.

given R_1, relative to a frame of reference. Hence whether a thing counts as a horse will also be a relative matter. Two further and deeper consequences are that, appearances to the contrary notwithstanding, statements of the form $\ulcorner \alpha_{(t_i)} = \beta_{(t_j)} \urcorner$ make no clear sense (hereafter S_1); similarly statements of the form $\ulcorner \alpha$ is a (an) $\Phi \urcorner$ (hereafter S_2) also make no clear sense. Thus suppose B is some statement of the form $\ulcorner \alpha_{(t_i)} = \beta_{(t_j)} \urcorner$. Then, the argument runs, B is not only incomplete but incapable of completion. For if we add to B 'relative to frame J' (where 'J' is a singular term which designates some frame of reference constituted of various bodies which endure throughout the interval — say K — spanned by B), we still fail to render B's truth conditions fully determinate since, given R_1, the items making up J are material objects which persist through K only relative to some frame of reference J'. And similarly for J'. But the regress thus begun is endless. Hence B is incompletable and so ineluctably lacks a clear sense. Obviously a parallel argument can be constructed for a statement of the form $\ulcorner \alpha$ is a (an) $\Phi \urcorner$. But now, the objection concludes, since these consequences are clearly unpalatable, one or both of Icn and Cr must be false. But there is a sound argument in support of Cr, namely Ω; hence Icn must be false.[37]

10. It might be thought that the objection presented above could be answered by making the following argument against Cr, the doctrine that spatiotemporal continuity is relative, and hence against the soundness of argument Ω which purports to establish Cr. If spatiotemporal continuity were relative, this argument begins, then a situation of the following type (call it S) is conceivable — anyhow, given a Newtonian world, for example. A body a is spatiotemporally continuous through interval K relative to frame F_1 but is spatially discontinuous relative to frame F_2 because it jumps across a spatial gap at t within K relative to F_2; and a body b is spatiotemporally continuous through K relative to F_2 but is similarly discontinuous at t relative to F_1. This situation might be schematically portrayed as in Diagrams 4 through 7. (Obviously S requires the discontinuity of F_2 at t_5 relative to F_1, and conversely. For, only if this is so, could a be spatiotemporally continuous relative to F_1 and discontinuous relative to F_2 in the way indicated; the same holds for b.) But now, the argument continues, situations like S are logically impossible due to the incoherence of the account defining this kind of situation. Thus suppose the question is raised, for example, where b

---

[37] Versions of Ω appear in the literature in several places. See, for example, D. Armstrong, "Absolute and Relative Motion," and R. Swinburne, *Space and Time*, Chap. 1. Though both Armstrong and Swinburne note that their versions of Ω seem to imply that the identity through time of a material object is relative, they do not draw the further ostensible consequences noted.

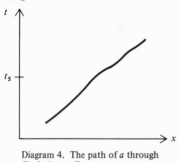

Diagram 4. The path of *a* through *K* relative to F_1.

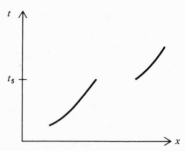

Diagram 5. The path of *a* through *K* relative to F_2.

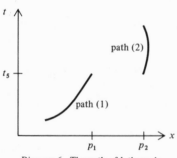

Diagram 6. The path of *b* through *K* relative to F_1.

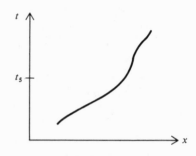

Diagram 7. The path of *b* through *K* relative to F_2.

is at instant t_5 relative to F_1. It would seem that there are only three possibilities: (1) *b* is at both p_1 and p_2 (see Diagram 6), (2) *b* is at neither p_1 nor p_2 (nor anywhere else), or (3) *b* is on path (1) and the first moment it is on path (2) is separated from t_5 by a short temporal interval, or *b* is on path (2) and the last moment it is on path (1) is separated from t_5 by a short temporal interval. After all, path (1) ends at p_1, and path (2) begins with p_2. Hence there must be a last moment at which *b* is on path (1) and a first moment it is on path (2). But time is continuous. Hence every cut [*M*, *N*] of *K* is such that either *M* has a last member or *N* has a first member, where 'or' carries its exclusive sense.[38] Accordingly, if [*M*, *N*] is a cut of *K* and t_5 is the last member of *M*, then *N* has no first member; and if [*M*, *N*] is a cut of *K* and t_5 is the first member of *N*, then *M* has no last member. But this means that if t_5 is the last moment at which *b* is on path (1) there is no first moment

[38] Where [*M*, *N*] is a *cut* of $K =_{df} [(K = M \cup N) \ \& \ M <' N]$, where $M <' N = df[M \neq \Lambda \ \& \ N \neq \Lambda \ \& \ (x)(y) \ (x \in M \ \& \ y \in N. \supset x < y)]$. See R. Wilder, *Introduction to the Foundations of Mathematics*, Chap. V, Sec. 2.

it is on path (2), unless (1) or (3) holds. And similarly if t_5 is the first moment at which b is on path (2). Hence, if there must be a last moment at which b is on path (1) and a first moment it is on (2), then either (1) holds, or (3) holds, or there is a temporal gap between its occupation of p_1 and p_2 which contains t_5 and during which it is not on either path — which is to say that (2) holds. But surely, this argument then concludes, (1) is ruled out by the fact that a body cannot be at two noncontiguous places at one time, and (2) and (3) are ruled out by the *ex hypothesi* spatiotemporal continuity of b relative to F_2. Thus situations like S are impossible — even in Newtonian worlds. And since their conceivability is entailed by Cr, Cr must be false and argument Ω, which purports to establish Cr, unsound.[39]

The reply which the foregoing argument provides to the objection under consideration, however, will not do. For this argument rests (*inter alia*) upon the claim that, given a situation such as S, there must be an instant which is the last instant b is on path (1) and an instant which is the first instant it is on path (2), in the sense of these words required for the argument to proceed. But this claim does not appear, on further examination, to be coercive. Let us take K to be the closed interval $[t_1, t_{10}]$. Now suppose that (t) $\{t_1 \leqslant t \leqslant t_5 \supset b$ is on path (1)$\}$ and (t) $\{t_5 < t \leqslant t_{10} \supset b$ is on path (2)$\}$. Clearly, I think, b could still be spatiotemporally continuous relative to F_2, given the analysis of Section 5, for F_2 might, relative to F_1, jump "at the same time" and in the same way as b — that is, in such a way that F_2 is on its left-hand path for all t_i in K earlier than or identical with t_5 and on its right-hand path for t_i in K later than t_5. Moreover, even on the supposition indicated, it could still be true in a sense that path (2) of b "begins with" p_2 — namely, in the sense that however fast b is moving at any point in K, the closer we get to t_5 as we approach it from a later time, the nearer b's position approximates to p_2. And why, we may add, should path (2) "begin with" p_2 in any other sense? Indeed, if we mark the point where a is at t_5 in Diagram 4 as p_1 and divide a's path into two, path (1) including p_1; then path (2) "begins with" p_1 only in the sense indicated. Hence if the argument under consideration raises a problem for the 'gappy' case, it would seem to raise the same problem for the continuous case — a fact which clearly reduces the argument to absurdity.

11. A rather different reply to the objection under consideration is suggested by Armstrong in the paper cited above (see note 4). Suppose we adopt the following (stipulative) definitions:

---

[39] The general form (though not the details) of this argument was suggested to me by a remark in an unpublished paper by Gareth Matthews.

D5.   *x* is a *frame of reference during interval* K = x is composed of a group of material objects which retain the same spatial relations to one another throughout *K*.

D6.   *x* is an MO-*invariant set of frames* = each member of *x* exhibits spatiotemporal continuity relatively to all the other members of *x*.

D7.   *The* E-*group of frames* = the largest *MO*-invariant set which includes the Earth.

D8.   *x* is an E-*frame* = x is a member of the *E*-group of frames.[40]

Then what Armstrong claims, in effect, is (*inter alia*) that (1) as a matter of fact there simply are no non-*E*-frames, that is, frames of reference which exhibit spatiotemporal discontinuity relative to the Earth;[41] and (2) "our ordinary notion of [spatiotemporal] continuity builds into itself the admittedly contingent fact that no such awkward points of reference present themselves."[42] Presumably what he means when he makes this last remark is that the alleged fact concerning the absence of non-*E*-frames from the world is so related to our concept of spatiotemporal continuity that the applicability of this concept entails that this (alleged) fact holds, and this because (perhaps) if there were any non-*E*-frames the notion of spatiotemporal continuity would cease to be a viable concept just as, in Wittgenstein's words, "if there were . . . no characteristic expressions of pain, of fear, of joy; if rule became exception and exception rule; or if both became phenomena of roughly equal frequency—this would make our normal language-games lose their point."[43] In any case, when he is so interpreted, the reply his paper suggests is that the objection at issue rests upon a faulty under-

---

[40] The terminology employed in these definitions is Swinburne's. Also, D6 through D8 are quite close to the definitions he presents. Thus he writes: "A group of frames, measurements relative to which yield the same judgments of spatio-temporal continuity and thus the same judgments of 'same material object', I shall term as *MO*-invariant groups. The *MO*-invariant group which includes the Earth will be called the *E*-group, and any member of it an *E*-frame" (*Space and Time*, pp. 26–27). Swinburne omits 'largest' in his definition of "the *E*-group of frames" but he clearly needs it since his definition of '*MO*-invariant group' makes it nonsensical to speak, as he does, of *the MO*-invariant group which includes the Earth.

Definition 7 might appear to involve the fiction that one can count material objects as such; but it needn't: one can measure size by appeal to the number of nucleons, for example.

[41] See Armstrong, "Absolute and Relative Motion," p. 221. It should perhaps be noted for accuracy's sake, that the claim is qualified so as to apply only at the macroscopic level.

[42] *Ibid.*

[43] L. Wittgenstein, *Philosophical Investigations* (Oxford: Basil Blackwell, 1953), Sec. 142.

standing of the common-sense concept of spatiotemporal continuity and that, when this concept is properly understood, it is clear that no such argument as Ω can be constructed in support of Cr, the doctrine that the notion of spatiotemporal continuity is a relative one, since the relativity of the identity through time of place will not, given (2), yield the relativity of continuity.

Is a reply along these lines adequate? I think not. In the first place, Armstrong's basis for holding that, as a matter of contingent fact, there simply are no non-E-frames is apparently that it is just obvious once we understand that non-E-frames are discontinuous relative to E-frames. Thus, speaking of the claim in question, he says:

> This may be seen to be true when we reflect that a point of reference from which ordinary objects seemed to lack spatial continuity would itself seem to lack spatial continuity when ordinary objects were taken as point of reference.[44]

But surely the claim is not at all obvious. Perhaps we have just never had the good or bad fortune to run into any non-E-frames. At any rate, the mere fact that such frames would be discontinuous relative to any and all E frames does not by itself insure that if there were any such frames we should have encountered them by now. But worse, even if we were to agree that as a matter of contingent fact there are no non-E-frames, why should we then also agree that this fact is "built into" the ordinary notion of spatiotemporal continuity? Oddly enough Armstrong offers no reason at all for thinking this conceptual doctrine true. Having argued in the unconvincing way indicated for the claim that the fact in question holds, all he says is that "it might then be said our ordinary notion of spatiotemporal continuity builds into itself the admittedly contingent fact that no such awkward points of reference present themselves." That is, I take it, someone might then hold the conceptual doctrine in question. "This," he then concludes, "seems a sufficient reply." [45]

Moreover and more importantly, it is hard to see exactly how this doctrine might be cogently supported. We naturally suppose that an advocate of the doctrine would, if pushed, have to say something like this: "Well, suppose we discovered a non-E-frame — imagine a spatially gappy hunk of granite one-quarter the size of the Moon getting trapped by the Earth's gravitational field. Could we operate with the notion of spatiotemporal continuity, and the notion of an enduring physical object which includes it, as though nothing had happened? Surely not.

[44] Armstrong, "Absolute and Relative Motion," p. 221.
[45] *Ibid.*

Surely we'd be in the same position vis-à-vis these notions as Wittgenstein says we'd be in vis-à-vis the concept of personal identity if 'ordinary circumstances' changed in the way he describes at one point in the *Blue Book*[46] or vis-à-vis the concept of pain 'if there were no characteristic expressions of pain . . . ; if rule became exception and exception rule; or if both became phenomena of roughly equal frequency.'[47] That is, the words expressing these notions would no longer be 'clearly prescribed'; [48] we would not be in a position to apply them with confidence in the new circumstances." Such remarks would not I think persuade — and this even if we find attractive the views alluded to concerning the notions of personal identity and pain. Why, we want to ask, would the circumstances presented by the spatially gappy rock have the kind of effect claimed for the disappearance, say, of characteristic expressions of pain or the bizarre memory phenomena-cum-personality-changes described in the *Blue Book?* The answer is far from obvious. What is worse, even if a serious argument could be provided for the doctrine in question, it would have to be very strong to avoid being subject to reversal in view of the following argument against the doctrine. We do unquestionably know that some objects maintain their identity through time. Thus I know, for example, that the human body which I now see at my desk is the same material thing as the human body which was located behind the steering wheel of my car at noon yesterday — anyhow I know this if I know any of the things I ordinarily think and say I know. But if, as Armstrong maintains, we also know that spatiotemporal continuity is a logically necessary condition of the identity through time of a material object, then we know that some objects exhibit spatiotemporal continuity. But clearly we do not know that, as a matter of contingent fact, there are no non-*E*-frames. Therefore, the existence of a non-*E*-frame does not entail that no objects exhibit spatiotemporal continuity — anyhow assuming, what seems plausible, that if the entailment held we would, or readily could upon reflection, know it did.

12. Swinburne, in his book *Space and Time,* suggests a way of handling the objection we have been considering which, in its general structure, is very close to that adumbrated by Armstrong. For he too in effect argues that the notion of spatiotemporal continuity, properly understood, is nonrelative, and hence that the objection is harmless since it rests upon a seriously defective way of construing *Icn.* For Swinburne, however, the nonrelativity of the notion of spatiotemporal continuity does not derive from its "containing" the (alleged) fact that no

[46] L. Wittgenstein, *The Blue and Brown Books* (Oxford: Basil Blackwell, 1958), p. 62.
[47] Wittgenstein, *Philosophical Investigations*, Sec. 142.
[48] *Ibid.*

non-*E*-frames exist; rather it derives according to Swinburne from the fact that, properly understood, the notion is such that $\ulcorner \alpha \ C \ \beta \urcorner$ holds (where α is a term which identifies a body as existing at one time and β is a term which identifies a body as existing at some earlier or later time) provided either of two conditions is satisfied: namely, (1) that the bearer of α and the bearer of β are spatiotemporally continuous in the sense stated in Section 4 above relative to an *E*-frame, and (2) that the bearer of α and the bearer of β are spatiotemporally continuous in this latter sense relatively to a non-*E*-frame that can be identified and/or shown to be such a frame by appeal solely to the kinds of similarity which the "objects" making up the frame exhibit through time.[49] To adapt this view so as to make it more immediately relevant to the objection at issue merely requires substituting our improved analysis of spatiotemporal continuity for the more obviously defective one to which reference is made in (1) and (2).

Unfortunately, this treatment of the objection is no better than its immediate predecessor. In the first place, Swinburne offers no other support for his revised analysis of spatiotemporal continuity than that it enables us to avoid having to say that the identity through time of a material object is relative, that is, having to hold R_1 (see p. 68). But this is hardly an adequate support. We do not solve the mind-body problem by analyzing the whole battery of mental concepts in a Rylean way if we have nothing to commend the analyses beyond the fact that the problem dissolves on the assumption of their correctness. Nor do we escape the difficulties surrounding the notions of "passage" and "becoming" by offering Smart-type analyses [50] of statements containing tenses and/or temporal indicator words, if all we can say in support of these analyses is that, should they be sound, the difficulties in question do not arise. Second, it is difficult to see how there could be adequate ground for Swinburne's proffered analysis. What, for example, could conceivably justify the line the analysis draws between cases where it could be shown on the basis of considerations of similarity alone that some "objects" retain their identity through time (and hence satisfy one of the conditions of there being a non-*E*-frame of reference) and cases where this could not be shown? After all, if some "thing" is spatiotemporally continuous relative to non-*E*-frame *J*, then the "objects" constituting *J* are continuous relative to it, too; hence the claim that, in the absence of (1), spatiotemporal continuity requires that (2) be satisfied as opposed to the condition that the bearer(s) of α and β be

---

[49] This statement of his view involves a bit of interpretation since his words are somewhat unclear (see *Space and Time*, p. 29).

[50] See, for example, J. J. C. Smart, *Philosophy and Scientific Realism* (London: Routledge and Kegan Paul, 1963), Chap. 7.

continuous (in the previous sense) relative to a non-E-frame *tout court,* seems quite gratuitous.

13. So far I have examined three replies to the objection under consideration, two of which have been suggested by approaches taken in the recent literature. There are, however, a number of further possibilities to explore. Two of these consist of arguments, like that of the first paragraph of Section 10, which are designed to show that the conclusion of argument Ω, namely Cr, leads to absurdity. The first such argument runs thus. If it were true that the notion of spatiotemporal continuity is relative, then the existence of one or more non-E-frames would be at least logically possible. For obviously if it were a necessary truth that all frames of reference are E-frames, it would make no sense to speak of the concept of spatiotemporal continuity as relative. Only the general character of the spatiotemporal path followed by a body could be genuinely relative to a frame of reference. But it is very doubtful that the existence of non-E-frames is logically possible. A non-E-frame, after all, is by definition a material object (or group of material objects) which exhibits spatial discontinuity relative to the Earth (see Section 11 above). Imagine the following situation: (1) we sight in June a heavenly body a we have not noticed before; (2) we see an object b through our telescope in September which we have excellent reason to believe is spatiotemporally discontinuous with a (relative to the Earth). Could we plausibly suppose, given (1) and (2), that $a = b$, that is, that the first heavenly body is the very same object as the one sighted in September? It seems not, and this fact, the argument concludes, makes it very questionable that the necessary condition of the truth of Cr which was mentioned really holds.

This argument is, I think, quite unconvincing. In the first place, it assumes — what has not as yet been shown — that, given Cr, the spatiotemporal continuity of a and b (say) could (logically) fail only relative to a frame of reference as defined in Section 11 — in other words, that the frames of reference in relation to which questions about the identity of places through time can be answered must be constituted of bodies. But even apart from this unargued assumption, the argument fails because when the kinds of consideration argument Ω involves are brought to mind, it is no longer clear that it is right, *tout court,* to take discontinuity relative to the Earth as a sufficient condition of diversity, even in an astronomical case such as the one just described. It certainly is not adequate merely to report what we would be inclined to say as regards the relation of a to b under conditions (1) and (2). For, as the history of the paradox of Galileo makes luminously clear, what we would say in a state of relative innocence is often very different from what we would say after our innocence has been removed.

The second *reductio* against Cr, alluded to above, goes as follows. The truth of Cr rules out as inconceivable a situation we can readily conceive to have existed in the past or to come into existence at some future time, namely, a situation in which the only thing which exists is a large, green, mint-flavored mothball. After all, it might be said, we can perfectly well imagine a company producing such things; and we can with no less difficulty imagine everything's being destroyed except for one of these items.[51] But if at some time (past or future) only one such object is in existence, then given that the identity through time of a material object entails spatiotemporal continuity (Icn), it would follow that spatiotemporal continuity is nonrelative, since the object at one moment would be spatiotemporally continuous with the object at a later moment even though not spatiotemporally continuous relative to a frame of reference - whether frames are conceived narrowly (as in Section 11) or more broadly.

Unfortunately, this argument is no better than its predecessor. The main difficulty lies with the premise that it is perfectly conceivable that there should have once been or should someday be a situation in which there exists just one, solitary, but nonetheless spatiotemporally continuous object. For in view of argument Ω, it is unclear what the difference would be between there being a situation of the kind described and a situation in which "the object" in question, though temporally continuous, was spatially gappy. And merely repeating the different descriptions of the two situations does not provide the desiderated difference because, in view of the incompleteness of propositions asserting the identity of places through time, we simply do not understand these descriptions.

14. So far, all the replies which have been examined to the objections under consideration involve, in effect, criticism of Cr. Since these have failed, it might seem that there is no alternative to the rejection of Icn. This is not, I think, true. But, before saying why, I want first to mention the difficulties which it seems to me attend the two most obvious candidates for replacements of Icn by way of adding additional force to the way of meeting the objection that I shall commend below. The two candidates in question are the following:

Icn': $\ulcorner\alpha_{(t_i)} = \beta_{(t_j)}\urcorner$ entails $\ulcorner\alpha$ is spatiotemporally continuous with β relative to the E-group of frames$\urcorner$.

Icn'': $\ulcorner\alpha_{(t_i)} = \beta_{(t_j)}\urcorner$ entails $\ulcorner$there exists some frame relative to which α is spatiotemporally continuous with $\beta\urcorner$.

[51] R. Taylor, among contemporary philosophers, finds no difficulty here, for example. See his *Metaphysics* (Englewood Cliffs, N.J.: Prentice-Hall, Inc., 1963), pp. 87 f.

Either would be a possible replacement for *Icn,* given the cogency of
the objection under consideration, inasmuch as neither leads in conjunction with *Cr* to the worrisome consequences R_1, R_2, S_1, and S_2.
And both are obviously attractive possibilities, given *Cr;* the *prima
facie* plausibility of *Icn,* and the need to avoid R_1-S_2.

There are, however, good reasons to reject both of these alterna-
tives to *Icn.* Suppose that some material object — *a* say — exists at t_1
and is spatiotemporally discontinuous (relative to the Earth) with body
b which exists at some later time t_{10} and which is the same kind of
thing as *a.* Acceptance of *Icn″* in place of *Icn* would mean that whether
a is identical with *b* will (under certain circumstances)[52] depend upon
whether, as a matter of contingent fact, there exists a frame of reference[53] somewhere in the universe relative to which *a* and *b* are spatiotemporally continuous. But this is very implausible. Imagine two pos-
ible worlds W_1 and W_2 which differ only in the respect that W_2 contains
one and only one non-*E*-frame (understood now as simply a frame which
yields different judgments of continuity from any *E*-frame) relative to
which *a* and *b* are spatiotemporally continuous, and W_1 lacks this
frame.[54] Is it reasonable to maintain, on the assumption that *a* and *b* are
members of both W_1 and W_2 and that *a* and *b* are related in both in the
way described (see note 52), that *a* = *b* in W_2, but *a* ≠ *b* in W_1? How
could the identity or diversity of *a* and *b* be dependent upon whether
God included in the world he created a certain contemporaneous non-*E*-
frame — perhaps millions of light years from both? Further, since we may
be in the position of not knowing whether our world is W_1 or W_2, acceptance of *Icn″* would mean, under certain circumstances, not only that
we would not know whether *a* was the same object as *b,* but, what is
worse I think, that we could settle the question in the negative only by
a thorough exploration of the world's contents. *Icn″* thus seems to involve a very serious departure from the conceptual facts.

Icn′ is no improvement, as the following line of thought demon-
strates. Suppose we imagine ourselves removed from the Earth one
night by some bizarre extraterrestrial visitors. When we awaken —
perhaps fifty or so years after our departure — our surroundings seem
fairly like those of the Earth, though there is a slightly *Yellow Sub-
marine*-look about both flora and fauna. Now if *Icn′* were true, we
simply would have no idea whether any of the "bodies" we ostensibly

---

[52] I have in mind circumstances in which there is a situation of the sort that would be
schematically depicted by Diagram 1 above.
[53] I here lean upon the possibility of a broader construction of 'frame of reference' than
that given in Section 11 above.
[54] W_1 and W_2 will, of course, have to differ in every way which is entailed by the difference noted.

perceive in our new habitat are the same from moment to moment or hour to hour. Indeed, we would not be in a position to tell whether our own bodies lasted through our first (ostensible) yawns. Moreover, our epistemological position would be the same if we were merely convinced by diabolical "friends" that we had suffered such a journey. But again, these are consequences which we should want to avoid, in my judgment.

15. I turn now to what I think is a more acceptable answer to the objection to Icn that we have been considering. The objection, it will be recalled, turned upon three propositions: (1) that Cr is true; (2) that the conjunction of Icn and Cr entails certain consequences which I labelled R_1, R_2, S_1, and S_2; and (3) that these consequences are quite unacceptable. Thus far I have noted that a number of criticisms of Cr are unconvincing and that the most attractive replacements for Icn are, upon reflection, inadequate. I shall now argue that (a) R_1 and R_2 are not as unpalatable upon reflection as they at first appear, and then that (b) S_1 and S_2 do not really follow from the conjunction of Icn and Cr.

R_1 says, it will be recalled, that the truth of statements of the form $\ulcorner \alpha = \beta \urcorner$ (where α identifies a material object as existing at some time t_i and β identifies a material object as existing at some later time t_j) are relative to a frame of reference, and hence that such statements are incomplete (possess indeterminate truth conditions) pending implicit or explicit specification of a frame of reference. Now R_1 is certainly an odd-sounding doctrine — perhaps even counterintuitive; but this fact does not mean it is false. After all, the Leidenfrost phenomenon is also very strange and very surprising; it too conflicts starkly with what our "intuitions" tell us must be so. I refer to the fact that if a metal plate is heated to several hundred degrees centigrade, a drop of water placed on the plate will not evaporate with an explosive hiss (as it would if the plate had been heated to only 100° C); rather it will oscillate to and fro for about five minutes, gradually getting smaller during this period and finally disappear.[55] Similarly counterintuitive is the fact that if an imaginary sheet of paper .001 inch thick is torn in half, one half being put on top of the other; and the two pieces torn in half, the one pile of two being again put on top of the other pile of two; and so on for a total of 50 times; the upshot will be a stack that is over 17 million miles high.[56]

---

[55] See Hannes Alfén, *Worlds-Antiworlds* (San Francisco: W. H. Freeman and Co., 1966), Chap. V.

[56] See E. Northrop, *Riddles in Mathematics* (New York: D. Van Nostrand Co., Inc., 1944), p. 25. Cf. also the following passage from A. A. Fraenkel, *Abstract Set Theory* (Amsterdam: North-Holland Publishing Co., 1961), p. 6:

1000 different types for consonants, vowels, digits, punctuation marks, etc. as well as for the empty space may serve as the raw material for printing books. Considering

Accordingly, the question we must ask is, "Are there any reasons for thinking R_1 false besides its odd ring, reasons adequate (in Mill's phrase) to 'influence the intellect'?" I do not know of any, and none are provided by those, like Armstrong and Swinburne, who find R_1 unacceptable. It might, of course, be thought that the fact that we never do need to specify any frame of reference, when we make judgments of the form in question, by way of assuring completeness and/or audience comprehension, counts as such a reason. The fact may be conceded. But obviously there is a ready explanation of it other than that judgments of the form $\ulcorner \alpha_{(t_i)} = \beta_{(t_j)} \urcorner$ are not incomplete pending specification of a frame of reference, namely, the *de facto* nonexistence, so far as we know, of any non-E-frames — in the broad sense of this expression suggested in Section 14 (p. 78) above. Suppose the world were such that with one exception each body maintained fixed spatial relations to all the others. In such a world there would be no need for the telepathically communicating angels to specify a frame of reference when "talking" with one another about the movement of the exceptional body. Our world is, as regards spatiotemporal continuity, rather like this — so far as we know anyway.

As regards R_2, which says that statements of the form $\ulcorner \alpha$ is a (an) $\Phi \urcorner$ (where α designates a body and Φ is a common noun which expresses a sortal concept the instances of which necessarily have histories) are also incomplete when they are viewed as having been made without implicit or explicit specification of a frame of reference, it might be thought that the argument allegedly showing it to follow from the conjunction of *Icn* and *Cr* is harmless since there are no sortal concepts which are applicable to material things and which are such that their instances necessarily have histories, however short. Thus it might be said that if a material object of some kind, say a cow, exists during interval K, then it exists at t_1, where K includes instant t_1; and if this is so, then it could have existed *only* at t_1 since the "contents" of a moment are logically independent of the "contents" of any other moment. However, this line of reasoning is patently unsound. We might as well say that if a person remembers at t_{10} that he did action x at t_1 ($t_1 < t_{10}$),

that "short" books can be extended by adding spaces and "long" books decomposed into several volumes, we may define as a *book* any distribution (with repetitions) of the types among, say, a million available spots on paper. Though most of such books are just meaningless accumulations of types and spaces, also all real books, poems, advertisements, menus, etc. published in the past or to be published in any future — among them the Bible, Euclid, Shakespeare's dramas, logarithmic tables, reports on the first manned flight to the Moon — constitute each a "book." The Universal Library of all such books, even if printed on the thinnest paper available, would fill the universe beyond the farthest visible stars; nevertheless the Library constitutes a finite set of books, containing exactly $1000^{1,000,000}$ volumes.

he could have performed (or undergone) this "mental act" no matter what the "contents" of all previous moments. The "contents" principle, as it might be called, is simply false in the sense it must have for the argument in question to be sound.[57] However, what has been said of R_1 also holds for R_2, so far as I can see — namely, that there are no good reasons for rejecting it. Hence, if the argument for thinking that R_2 follows is both sound and not "harmless"; and if we have reason for accepting both Cr and Icn; then we ought to accept R_2, despite its "counterintuitiveness."

The same cannot be said for S_1 and S_2, however. If they follow from Cr and Icn, then one or both of the latter doctrines must give way: for that statements of the forms $\ulcorner \alpha_{(t_i)} = \beta_{(t_j)} \urcorner$ and $\ulcorner \alpha$ is a (an) $\Phi \urcorner$ (where $\beta_{(t_j)}$, α, and Φ are understood as before) are senseless is as obviously false as any views in philosophy ever get. Fortunately, S_1 and S_2 are not unavoidable, given Cr and Icn. The argument that led to S_1 and S_2 was, it will be recalled, that statements of the forms in question are not only incomplete, when viewed as made in the absence of any specification (explicit or implicit) of a frame of reference, but also incompletable. And this because, if we supplement a statement of one of these forms — say Q — by adding a phrase like 'relative to F' (where 'F' is a singular term which designates some frame of reference in relation to which Q's truth value could in principle be assessed), we still do not render our initial statement's truth conditions determinate owing to the fact that, given R_1, the items which make up F count as enduring material things only relative to some other frame F'. Hence we need to supplement Q further, and this need arises again at each stage. Hence, Q can never be "completed." This line of argument, however, is clearly deficient. Suppose Q is 'the car now in back of the house is the car you drove last Thursday'. In ordinary circumstances it is always understood what things might be employed as a frame of reference for deciding when this car is spatiotemporally continuous with that one; hence in ordinary circumstances we need say nothing by way of "completing" a statement like Q. So much is obvious. But now imagine our situation to be different in ways which put at least some of our judgments of the identity through time of a material object in the same boat with statements like 'the book is where it was yesterday'. Would we then be required to talk *ad indefinitum* in order to secure both determinateness of sense and audience understanding? Surely not — and this even if we assume that frames of reference must be constituted of persisting material things. In ordinary cases of motion and rest, it suffices,

[57] Cf. J. M. E. McTaggart, *The Nature of Existence* (Cambridge: Cambridge University Press, 1927), Chap. 33, Secs. 337–38.

if the context does not make things clear, to add something like 'I mean, relative to the house, not to the Earth'. As regards Q, it might similarly suffice, depending upon the circumstances envisaged, to say 'I mean, relative to the E-group of frames or any members of it you wish to pick'. To be sure, the objects making up these frames, or any one of them, constitute objects which persist through a given interval K only relative to other objects in this group. But this causes no difficulty. There is no reason at all why a speaker should need, under any circumstances, to specify explicitly some frame relative to which any given E-frame persists through K. For if he says 'I mean, relative to the E-group of frames' by way of clarifying his intent in uttering Q in certain imaginable circumstances, he has *ipso facto* made clear what the frames are relative to which any E-frame his audience wishes to pick maintains spatiotemporal continuity through K. In short, the regress upon which the argument leading from Icn and Cr to S_1 and S_2 turns is spurious.

16. Thus the objection stated in Section 9 fails. This objection, as well as the first one considered, took the form of an argument purporting to show that Icn leads to patent falsehoods when conjoined with certain other seemingly innocuous propositions. I turn next to a series of objections which consist in putative counterexamples (or specifications of classes of such) to the doctrine in question, that is, actual or conceivable cases in which it is allegedly true both (1) that a material object which is identified as existing at t_i is the same as some material object which is identified as existing at some later time t_j, and yet (2) that the first is not spatiotemporally continuous with the second.

It might be said, to begin with, that an ordinary case of amoeba fission constitutes a counterexample to Icn, that is, a case in which, say amoeba a divides into two, b and c. After all, this reasoning might continue, there seems to be no less justification for saying that a is identical with both b and c than there is for saying that a would have been the same as a' if there had been no fission and 'a'' designated the amoeba that would have existed at the time b and c exist; [58] yet one can hardly maintain that a is spatiotemporally continuous with both b and c. This is so because spatiotemporal continuity is obviously a relation which is both transitive and symmetrical; hence if a were spatiotemporally continuous with both b and c, then b and c would have to be spatiotemporally continuous with each other — which they clearly are not.[59]

---

[58] C. B. Martin takes this view in "Identity and Exact Similarity," *Analysis,* XVIII (March, 1958), p. 84.

[59] Bernard Williams comes close to this last line of argument. He says at one point that "in a case of fission, such as that of an amoeba the resultant items are not, in the strict sense, spatiotemporally continuous with the original. The justification for saying this

The obvious reply to this objection, of course, is that a could not be identical with both b and c since this fact would entail the falsity of the principle that one material object cannot be in two noncontiguous places at the same time,[60] the falsity of Leibniz' Law, and the falsity of the Law of Contradiction. The first entailment holds because the relation of identity, as classically understood, is both symmetrical and transitive. Hence, if a were identical with both b and c, b and c would be identical, with the result that an amoeba would occupy two places at the same time. The second and third follow from the first. Thus if '$b = c$' holds and b is at p_1 and c at p_2 ($p_1 \neq p_2$), then b has a property which c lacks, and both the ascription of this property to b and its denial of b will both be true. It may be that those, like C. B. Martin, who insist that b is identical with c have — as Bernard Williams suggests — confused the relation of identity with the relation expressed by the predicate '① has the same life history as ②'.[61] To the contrary, it may be that a philosophical doctrine lurks in the background to the effect that claims concerning the identity through time of objects do not involve the classical concept of identity at all, that is, the concept according to which identity is an equivalence relation for which Leibniz' Law holds.[62] If this is so, however, no adequate justification has yet been provided for thinking this background doctrine true. And in any case, I have been implicitly understanding $I cn$ throughout by reference to the classical notion; hence any genuine counterexample must also employ this notion.

17. A quite different type of counterexample to $I cn$ is suggested by the following passage from an essay of Norwood Hanson's. Hanson writes that "when an orbital electron is excited in the H-atom, it jumps out to a wider orbit; yet one has no way of speaking of it as having ever been between the orbits."[63] Now, it might be said, if this remark is correct, then whenever we have a case of a hydrogen atom's being put into an excited state, we have a case in which a material thing retains its identity through time without traversing a spatiotemporally continuous path.

---

would be that the normal application of the concept of continuity is interfered with by the fact of fission, a fact which would itself be discovered by the verification procedure tied to the application of the concept. There would be a motive for saying this moreover, in that we might want to insist that spatiotemporal continuity, in the strict sense, was transitive." ("Bodily Continuity and Personal Identity," p. 48.)

[60] Bernard Williams has often stressed this point. See, e.g., his "Personal Identity and Individuation" and "Bodily Continuity and Personal Identity."

[61] Cf. Williams, "Bodily Continuity and Personal Identity," p. 47, n. 1. He writes: "To say that (putatively) two amoeba are identical is to say that *pro tanto* I have only one amoeba; to say that they share the same life-history is not."

[62] There is much to be said on this matter. However, I shall not pursue it here.

[63] N. Hanson, "The Dematerialization of Matter," *The Concept of Matter,* ed. E. McMullin (Notre Dame, Indiana: University of Notre Dame Press, 1963), p. 556.

There are several ways in which we might deal with this class of putative counterexamples. We might, first, simply deny that electrons count as material things. In support of this tack, we could point out that electrons, as conceived in classical quantum mechanics, are logically precluded from simultaneously possessing both position and velocity; that there are no workable concepts of an electron's shape, density, or solidity; that " 'being in contact with an electron' has the same null status"; [64] and that electrons do not have "material" parts. Such a reply would not, however, be decisive. To be sure, the facts noted do show that electrons fail to count as "bodies" in the sense of this expression which descends from Locke. For on the Lockean account, the so-called "primary qualities" — size, shape, position, and so on — are "internal properties" of bodies, that is, properties which enter into the correct analysis of the concept of body.[65] Also, these facts make it clear that electrons lack materiality in the broad sense in which nothing counts as a "material thing" unless it is "decomposable into matter." [66] Nonetheless, it is not implausible to say that an item counts as a material thing if it is of a kind the instances of which go into the composition of paradigm material objects such as cats, rocks, and clocks.[67] And on this criterion electrons evidently do count as material things. A different reply is suggested by the view, held at least by some physicists, that it is "more appropriate" to think of all interactions at the level of elementary particles as consisting of the annihilation and/or creation of particles at definite points in space and time. That is, given a situation such as that depicted in Diagram 8, one ought to think of electron *a* as ceasing to exist at *B* and electron *b* as beginning to exist at *B*. The reason that it is allegedly "more appropriate" to think along these lines is, as Kenneth Ford puts it, that this way of viewing the matter "corresponds more closely to the mathematical theory of the fundamental interactions," and "also leads to a simple, unified description of particle events and antiparticle events." [68]

I do not know if this view is cogent; hence I cannot evaluate the reply it suggests, namely, that the putative counterexamples are not really cases in which a material thing persists over a spatiotemporal gap. Accordingly, I shall leave the matter thus. If the reply in question cannot be sustained, then *Icn* perhaps needs to be restricted so as to

[64] *Ibid.*, p. 556.
[65] See Locke, *Essay Concerning Human Understanding*, Bk. II, Chap. VIII, Sec. 9.
[66] See D. Wiggins, *Identity and Spatio-temporal Continuity* (Oxford: Basil Blackwell, 1967), p. 61.
[67] Cf. Swinburne, *Space and Time*, p. 15.
[68] K. Ford, *The World of Elementary Particles* (New York: Blaisdell Publishing Co., 1963), p. 199.

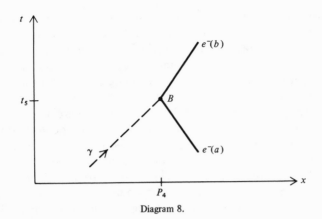

Diagram 8.

apply only to Lockean-type material objects – or, in more contemporary terms, enduring material objects which are either atoms or decomposable into atoms. It should be noted, however, that such a restriction, if necessary, is not a very serious one in view of the fact that electrons and the other elementary particles are at best rather borderline cases of "material things."

18. A considerably more bizarre class of putative counterexamples to Icn arises from the alleged possibility that material things should occasionally "travel backwards in time." There are two sorts of cases to consider here: One involves elementary particles again, and the other involves everyday material things of the kind which are ordinarily thought of as composed of elementary particles. Thus it might be said first that, confronted with a process of photon-electron scattering such as that depicted in Diagram 9, we can describe what happens thus: electron a moves to point B, where it emits a photon; then it moves

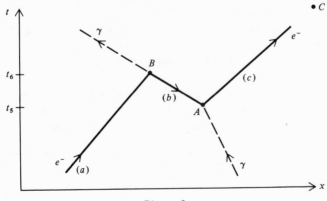

Diagram 9.

backward in time to point A, where it absorbs a photon; following this, it once again moves forward in time, in the direction of C. But, the argument would continue, if this description fits the facts, then it sometimes happens that a material thing exists at three places at the same time (at t_5 in the situation depicted in Diagram 9). But this is clearly incompatible with Icn, since it is incompatible with such an object's maintaining spatiotemporal continuity during its career.

In response to this line of criticism, we could of course simply repeat the approach taken in the previous section. However, we do not have to, since a considerably stronger reply is also available here, namely the following. It is not at all necessary to describe the situation depicted in the way indicated, even if we allow (*contra* Ford) that elementary particles can survive their interactions with others. For the situation can also be described by saying that at B, a collides with a positron (b) and ceases to exist, where b is viewed as having been born at A as a result of a photon's having given birth to an electron-positron pair (b and c).[69] Thus, if there are good reasons for accepting Icn, even when it is construed to be applicable to elementary particles, then the description which has a moving backwards in time "after" emitting a photon at B is ruled out. Hence the line of criticism in question fails because, in assuming that the description in question is a possible one, it *ipso facto* assumes that Icn is false and thereby begs the question at issue.

The second kind of case involving backward time travel is the kind presented by Hilary Putnam in his contribution to the 1962 American Philosophical Association Symposium on "Necessary Truth." [70] Putnam envisages the possibility, which he claims to be even in harmony with natural law as currently understood,[71] of a man's having a world line like that indicated in Diagram 10. In this case, the counterpart of the description of a forward-moving positron of the last paragraph would run (roughly) thus: Oscar ceases to exist at B' (t_{10}) where he coalesces with an object which begins to exist at A' (t_3) and which is such that, if a movie were taken of it during the stretch from t_3 to t_{10}, it would look like a film of Oscar doing and undergoing "normal" actions and processes only if it were run backwards.[72] Also, another object begins to exist at t_3, which resembles Oscar and which lives a normal life from t_3 on—though he has some queer memories perhaps. Once again, the mere possibility of such a situation, which could be described

[69] See *ibid.*, p. 201.
[70] H. Putnam, "It Ain't Necessarily So," *Journal of Philosophy*, LIX (October 25, 1962).
[71] See *ibid.*, Sec. IV.
[72] See *ibid.*, p. 666.

by saying (*inter alia*) that a man travelled backwards in time, destroys *Icn* since it means that the identity through time of an object is compatible with the absence of spatiotemporal continuity.

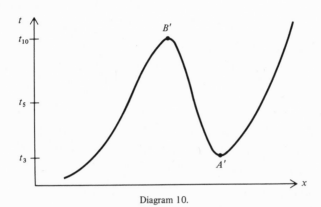

Diagram 10.

Cases of the second kind fare no better than those of the first, however, for not only is the argument based upon it liable to a *petitio* charge for the same reason adduced two paragraphs back, but it is defective in addition on the following grounds. If we could correctly describe the situation depicted in Diagram 10 in the way Putnam says we could, we seem to be forced to admit the conceivability of (1) a man's seeing himself from a distance (a) with awareness that he is doing so and (b) without any awareness that he is doing so, and (2) a man's being in three noncontiguous places at the same time. Indeed we seem compelled even to admit the logical possibility of a man's having dinner with himself—in a nonordinary sense of these words. These admissions, however, are clearly ones we should not like to make.

19. Still another kind of (putative) counterexample to *Icn* forms the basis of the following argument against *Icn*. Persons are obviously among the things which possess such properties as relative position, size, shape, weight, mass, and density. It follows that persons are a kind of material object, since it is the possession of just such properties which entails material objecthood. It is equally obvious, however, this line of thought continues, that it could (logically) be that $a = b$, where 'a' identifies a person as existing at t_i and 'b' identifies a person as existing at t_j ($t_i < t_j$), even though the body which constitutes a at t_i is not spatiotemporally continuous with the body which constitutes b at t_j. Hence, it is possible, *contra Icn,* that a material thing should main-

tain its identity through time though it does not maintain spatiotemporal continuity.[73]

Presumably the second premise of this argument would be supported by such familiar considerations as these. Suppose a person — George, say — were suddenly to vanish. We all saw him and heard him chatting on the sofa with Mrs. Jones a moment before. Then he was gone — before our very eyes. Next suppose that two days later a person just as suddenly "appears" at a table in a busy restaurant in the same city at noon. This person is dressed as George was; he has the same (ostensible) "memories," knowledge, skills, and personality traits that George had; and his body bears the same scars as did George's and is in every other way exactly similar to George's. Moreover, this person — George*, say — does not know how he got to the restaurant or what he is doing there. When questioned, he says things like this: "Good grief! Where am I? A moment ago I was sitting on a couch talking to Mrs. Jones — in fact I was in the middle of a sentence, as I recall. Then all of a sudden, I find myself here. What's going on?" Finally, suppose that George cannot be found between the time of his strange disappearance and the equally strange appearance of George*, that is, suppose not only that exploration fails to turn him up, but that it could not, since he just is not to be found. This set of suppositions represents an imaginable sequence of occurrences — in an easily understandable sense of the phrase. But now if such a sequence of occurrences were actually to take place, clearly there would be no more doubt that it was George who had turned up at the restaurant than there would be if there had been no "gap" and that, for example, George had been alone (and hence unobserved) between leaving the party (in a normal way) and heading to the restaurant two days later, or that he had suffered loss of consciousness for forty-eight hours prior to his turning up at the restaurant, owing to a crack on the head delivered (perhaps) by Mrs. Jones. After all, "he" says he is George; his wife says, "It's George all right"; his friends, enemies, relatives, and dog concur in this judgment; and, though these events give some reason to suspect there is more in heaven and earth than is dreamt of in our philosophy, there is no more reason to believe that substitutionary tricks (by God or any other agent from heaven, hell, or a galaxy in *Coma Berenices*) have been played in the George-George* case than in any normal, nongappy case.

Whatever judgment we form about arguments like that of the last paragraph, however, the argument they are designed to buttress fails in any case. Using standard notation plus the modal operators '◊' and

---

[73] A philosopher who asserts both premises of this argument is R. Swinburne. See his *Space and Time*, p. 23.

'□', presumably the argument is to be understood in one or the other of the following ways.

A. (1) $(x)(Px \supset Mx)$
    (2) $\lozenge\ (\exists x)(Px\ \&\ \sim Cx)$
    (3) $\therefore\ \lozenge\ (\exists x)(Mx\ \&\ \sim Cx)$

B. (1) $\square\ (x)(Px \supset Mx)$
    (2) $\lozenge\ (\exists x)(Px\ \&\ \sim Cx)$
    (3) $\therefore\ \lozenge\ (\exists x)(Mx\ \&\ \sim Cx),$

where 'Px' is short for 'x is a person', 'Mx' for 'x is a material object of the kind we point to when we point at persons or weigh when we weigh persons' and 'Cx' for 'x traces a spatiotemporally continuous path during its career'; and where the diamond is read: *it is conceivable that,* and the square: *it is a necessary truth that.* However, if A is a correct representation of the argument in question, the argument will be invalid on any remotely plausible semantics for alethic modal propositional logic. That this is so can be perhaps most perspicuously brought out by considering the argument which results when we read 'Px' as 'x is an object in my pocket', 'Mx' as 'x is spherical', and 'Cx' as 'x is non-cubical'. In English it might be put thus:

A'. (1) Whatever is an object in my pocket is spherical.
     (2) It is conceivable that something is in my pocket and is cubical.
     (3) Therefore, it is conceivable that something is both spherical and cubical.

To the contrary, if B correctly represents the argument in question, the argument can plausibly be viewed as valid. After all, how could it be true, for example, that (1) uncles are necessarily males and that (2) it is conceivable that there is an uncle who is unmarried, without its also being true that (3) there could be something which was both a male and unmarried? But on this construction of the argument, it is difficult to see how premise (1) – namely, $\square\ (x)(Px \supset Mx)$ – could be defended. It obviously will not do merely to note that persons have position and weight, for example, as is done in the third paragraph back, for this does not establish at all what needs to be shown, namely, that persons are necessarily material objects of the kind in question. Moreover, there are at least two persuasive arguments for doubting that the latter can be shown.

The first of these arguments runs thus. If persons were necessarily material objects of the kind in question, then in the absence of bodily identity, personal identity would be impossible. But it quite clearly is not. At Western Reserve University a team of scientists have developed techniques which enable them to remove the brain of a monkey from its body and keep it alive and functioning for as long as twenty-four hours. "Bare except for two bits of bone to help support it," Dean Wooldridge writes,

> the nerves and blood vessels that once connected it to the monkey's body severed, the brain is suspended above a laboratory table. Attached to it are the tubes of a mechanical heart to maintain its blood supply; from it run wires to recording instruments. Their measurements of its electrical activity not only show that it remains alive but even suggest that sometimes this isolated brain is conscious.[74]

These facts make it easy to imagine scientists of the not too distant future doing the same with the brain of a man whose body is being consumed by cancer. And it is only a slightly larger step to imagine this brain's being replanted, so to speak, in a healthy body the brain of which has recently "died."[75] Suppose such a transplantation of a living brain were successful. The result would be a healthy organism with (say) *a*'s brain and *b*'s body. But now if this organism possessed all of *a*'s (ostensible) "memories," knowledge, skills, personality traits, and so on, then, despite the fact that all but its brain was the body of *b*, it would clearly be correct to hold that, though *b* was gone, *a* was still very much with us. Though a nonstandard case of re-identification, in view of its quite anomalous features, such a case would not be a borderline case.[76] Thus, personal identity does not necessarily involve bodily identity; *a fortiori* it is false that the concept of a person is the concept of a kind of material object of the sort we weigh when we

---

[74] Dean Wooldridge, "How the Machine Called the Brain Feels and Thinks," *New York Times Magazine* (October 4, 1964), p. 24. See also Dean Wooldridge, *Mechanical Man: The Physical Basis of Intelligent Life* (New York: McGraw-Hill Book Co., 1968), pp. 137 and 173.

[75] In a recent paper Roland Puccetti offers some further considerations which can aid the reluctant imaginer in making this larger step. Specifically he points out some scientific developments which yield some hope of enabling us to overcome a few of the more obvious obstacles in the way of successful brain transplantation. See his "Brain Transplantation and Personal Identity," *Analysis*, XXIX (January, 1969), especially pp. 66 f.

[76] Cf. *ibid.*, Sec. 1. Cf. also D. Wiggins, *Identity and Spatio-temporal Continuity*, Pt. IV.

weigh a person — and this even if it is true that persons necessarily have a material constitution at every moment during their existence.[77]

The second argument against the view that persons are necessarily material objects of the kind in question — that is, $\Box\,(x)(Px \supset Mx)$ — rests on the following principle:

(P) If Φ's are necessarily Ψ's, then the Ψ thing which some Φ thing is cannot survive the destruction of that Φ thing.

The argument is this. If the concept of a person were the concept of a certain kind of material object, then the destruction of a person would necessarily involve the destruction of a material object of the relevant kind. But obviously a person can cease to be, even though his body continues in existence — either as a corpse or as a living human body whose "owner" has suffered "brain death." Hence, '$\Box\,(x)(Px \supset Mx)$' is false. So far as I can see, this argument, like the last, is sound. (P) may not seem obvious when stated as above. However, when we consider cases, its power is soon felt. Thus suppose that cats are necessarily animals, as is usually thought. Then surely if Beau Soleil is killed, some animal is killed. Again, brothers are necessarily siblings. Does it not follow that if my brother is drowned, some sibling dies? Hence the force of the first premise. The second needs no buttressing at all, I believe. And the conclusion follows as surely as do those of any informal arguments.

20. Imagine next an objector saying the following: "Two weeks ago Thursday my son took his bicycle apart. For two and one-half days the parts were scattered all over the basement floor. Then on Sunday he reassembled it. Now surely the bicycle he rode to school on the following Monday was the same bicycle as the one he rode to school on the preceding Monday — assuming, of course, that the latter (*a*) is the one he took apart on Thursday and the former (*b*) is the one which he put together out of the parts on the basement floor on Sunday morning. Yet *b* was not spatiotemporally continuous with *a*; one could not say, for example, that *a* was 'moving continuously' at noon on Friday: it did not even have a 'primary place' then. Hence *Icn* is false."

---

[77] To say that person *a* is constituted of material object *m* is not to say that $a = m$. This is so because persons and the material objects constituting them have different persistence conditions (for example, the one can be in existence after the other has ceased to exist). Hence it can be false that $\Box\,(x)(Px \supset Mx)$, which is equivalent to: $\Box\,(x)\{Px \supset (\exists y)(My\ \&\ y = x)\}$, even if it were true that $\Box\,(x)\{Px \supset (\exists y)(My\ \&\ x$ is constituted of $y)\}$.

The only plausible way of countering this objection would be to show that $a \neq b$, appearances (as reflected in common speech) to the contrary notwithstanding. One argument to this conclusion might go thus. Suppose that a bicycle (a') was brand new (and unused) when disassembled; and that its parts were widely distributed and used in many different bicycles for many years of hard riding before being recollected and put together to make bicycle b'. Then if we could correctly identify b' with a', we could say with truth that b' was worn out even though it had never been ridden. Since it is absurd to suppose that any bicycle could satisfy this description, it is false that b' could be correctly identified with a'. But if $b' \neq a'$, it is hard to see how b could be identical with a.

This argument, however, is hardly persuasive. In the first place, it is not at all obvious that it would be absurd to describe b' as worn out even though never ridden. It would be an odd thing to say perhaps; but the oddity would result only from the unusual circumstances of the case, not from unintelligibility of the description. Second, even if we were to agree that $b' \neq a'$, this would not compel us also to hold that $a \neq b$. There is no reason at all why the different histories of the respective parts of a and a' should not make a difference as regards the question whether the results of reassembling those different collections of parts are identical with the objects from which the parts originally came.

A rather different argument for denying that $a = b$ which might tempt us runs as follows. If $a = b$, then either the object both terms designate existed when it was disassembled (during K, say) or it did not exist during K. If it existed during K, then a material object (or, more specifically, a bicycle) can exist at t even though it has no primary place at t. But that is absurd. In contrast, if it did not exist during K, it must have ceased to exist at some point prior to K and have come into existence again at some point subsequent to K. But that too is absurd: If a material thing (or, more specifically, a bicycle) comes into existence at t, then it could not have existed prior to t; and if such a thing ceases to exist at t, then it could not exist at any point subsequent to t. Hence, it is false that $a = b$.

Though this argument perhaps appears to be more attractive at first glance than the first, it appears to be little better upon reflection. The reason is that cases like the one in question concerning a and b provide plausible counterexamples to the absurdity claims upon which this argument turns. Thus it seems quite reasonable to say in the case of a, I submit, that it did exist when disassembled. To be sure, it would be natural to add, ". . . in a disassembled state." ("Yes, my son has a bicycle—though at the moment it is not ridable, since he just took it apart and it's now lying all over the basement floor.") Insofar a material thing can exist at t, even though it then lacks a primary place, absurd as this may sound at first hearing. (It may be useful here to recall that it also sounds absurd at first hearing to be told that the set of natural numbers, the set of rational numbers between 0 and 1, and the set of real numbers between 0 and 1 are all infinite sets; but that though the number of natural numbers and the number of rationals between 0 and 1 are the same, the number of reals between 0 and 1 is a distinct and larger number.) Similarly, it is plausible to hold in the case of a', for example, that it did not exist when disassembled. At any rate it strikes me as highly questionable that someone could say at some point after a' has been disassembled and scattered about, that a certain bicycle exists — namely a' — which is the bicycle that he owns. On the other hand, it does not seem obviously wrong to maintain that $b' = a'$ — especially if the interval during which a''s parts were used in other bicycles was not too long. Hence it seems reasonable to question the Lockean dictum that a body cannot have two beginnings of existence.[78]

A third line of argument against the identification of a and b begins with the premise that the legitimacy of their identification entails that if one were to take his car apart and distribute the parts to his auto-mechanically minded friends, then he wouldn't know whether his car has ceased to exist until he has become sure that no one will ever collect the parts together and reassemble the car. But surely, this line of thought continues, one can know that one has destroyed one's car when one has disassembled and dispersed it in the way described.

This argument is also defective. It is not at all clear that a person knows his car is no more once he has given its parts to his friends. Perhaps thirty minutes later he will have a change of heart, go out and retrieve the parts, and put his car back together.

A final argument for denying the identity upon which the counter-example of the beginning of this section depends is this. Suppose that a ship gradually has its parts replaced, that someone keeps the replaced parts as they are discarded, and that after all the ship's parts have been replaced the scavenger puts his collection together and thereby makes a ship out of the used parts.[79] Then, if $a = b$, the scavenger's product (b_1'') would be identical with the original ship (a''). But this conflicts with the obvious fact that the ship with the new parts (b_2'') is identical

---

[78] See p. 52 above. There may be, admittedly, some tendency to deny the identity judgment in cases where one wants to make the nonexistence judgment.

[79] The case was originally set forth by Hobbes. See *The English Works of St. Thomas Hobbes*, ed. Sir William Molesworth (London: John Bohn, 1889), Vol. I, pp. 136–137. The relevant passage is quoted in Wiggins, *Identity and Spatio-temporal Continuity*, p. 37

with a'', since granting both identity judgments would be tantamount to granting the identity of b_2'' and b_1'' — that is, of two distinct, simultaneously existing ships. Hence, it must be false that $a = b$.

Once again, however, the argument fails. This is so because it simply does not follow from the fact that $a = b$ that the scavenger's product is identical with the original ship. To hold it does is to hold that the circumstances surrounding a case where an object undergoes decomposition do not matter as regards the question whether the object which results from putting certain parts together is identical with the object from which the parts came. But that the circumstances do matter is clearly brought out by the case at hand. For in this case it seems evident that $a'' = b_2''$. After all, if someone were to steal b_1'', it can hardly be maintained that a'' has been stolen. But it is equally evident that $b_1'' \neq b_2''$. Hence, the circumstances do matter and the argument is unsound.

It seems then that there is no escape from the objection under consideration, and accordingly that *Icn* is false. However, it is not difficult to see how *Icn* can be modified so as to escape destruction by counterexamples of the kind to which this objection appeals. All that is required is that the scope of the doctrine be restricted to cases in which there has been no decomposition of the object in question during the period the identity judgment spans. One way of stating such a revised version of *Icn* is as follows:

I*cn: ⌜If $\alpha = \beta$ (where α identifies a body as existing at t_i and β identifies a body as existing at some later time t_j) then, provided the body both terms designate does not undergo decomposition during $[t_i, t_j]$, it will necessarily be the case that $\alpha \subset \beta$⌝.

(Here I shall understand 'undergoes decomposition' to cover any case in which a material thing is broken down into (its) parts, either through intentional action(s) or other causes. I shall exclude cases where we should want to say merely that some part or parts had been removed from the thing while it remained more or less intact.) This restricted doctrine, it may be noted, still gives to spatiotemporal continuity a quite central place within the notion of the identity through time of material objects. For even though it leaves room for cases in which there is identity through time of material objects in the absence of spatiotemporal continuity, it clearly entails a counterfactual continuity principle even for these cases, namely the following:

⌐If $\alpha = \beta$ and if, contrary to fact α had not undergone decomposition during $[t_i, t_j]$, then α would have been spatiotemporally continuous with β (where α and β are understood as above)⌐.

21. I want to consider now an objection which appears applicable to I^*cn, the revised doctrine to which the last objection led, as well as to Icn. Suppose, this objection begins, that 'a' identifies an apple as existing at t_1, that 'b' identifies an apple as existing at t_{10}, and that to all appearances a moves continuously throughout $[t_1, t_{10}]$ (hereafter K) and coincides with b at t_{10}. But suppose further that it is false that a in fact moves continuously throughout K because there are one or several intervals of less than (say) 10^{-90} seconds in duration during which a does not exist or fails to move continuously. In such a case, the objection would conclude, a would not be spatiotemporally continuous with b, given the analysis of continuity presented in Section 5 above; yet clearly we would have as good grounds for asserting '$a = b$' as we ever have. Hence, the falsity not only of Icn, but also its restricted analogue I^*cn.

There are two ways in which we might be tempted to reply to this objection. We might, first, question the intelligibility of the description defining the putative counterexample on the ground that it is impossible to specify any empirical findings which would count in favor of saying that, for example, some object failed to move continuously during some interval of less than 10^{-90} seconds.[80] Such a reply would obviously be quite weak. For even if the reason for worry mentioned were true — and that it is is not obvious to me — I know of no cogent argument which effectively ties the intelligibility of a description to the notion of verifiability in a way which would give this reply force.

A second reply that might also tempt us would question the legitimacy of identifying a and b, given their lack of continuity. Unfortunately, it is equally difficult to see how this worry could be justified. The argumentation of Section 2 (first half of second paragraph) would not suffice for this purpose, for it turned on the idea that the possibility of a temporal gap in a thing's existence conflicts with the Lockean dictum that "one thing cannot have two beginnings of existence," and this dictum we have just seen reason to believe is less than obvious. Nor will it do to rest such a worry on the alleged absurdity of the thought that a material object should, on some occasion during its

[80] Kenneth Ford writes (in 1963) that "since the shortest distance probed experimentally is about 10^{-14} cm, it is fair to say that the shortest known time interval is 10^{-24} sec (although direct time measurements are still far from reaching this short an interval)" (*The World of Elementary Particles*, p. 36).

career, be nowhere (see Section 2, second half of second paragraph), for the possibility that a thing should exist "in a disassembled state" refutes that principle. And if the principle's scope is restricted to items which do not "undergo decomposition" (in the sense of this expression specified above) it appears suspect, it seems to me, as soon as we contemplate putative counterexamples of the kind upon which the objection under consideration rests. Finally, the argumentation of the latter half of Section 2 above cannot be deployed in support of the present worry either. For that line of thought rested on the premise that if it were conceivable that there should be a case of a material object's maintaining identity through time where spatiotemporal continuity was not present, then cases like the marble case would also be conceivable. But this premise is falsified by the counterexample of the bicycle given in Section 20. And if it is restricted so as to render the argument applicable to $I*cn$, it also loses its plausibility when viewed in the light of possible interval gaps of less than 10^{-90} seconds in length.

Moreover, even if a cogent reply to the objection at hand were forthcoming, there are other difficulties we must deal with. One is that the notion of the "primary place" of a body at a time has not been given an adequately precise definition. And, further, it is by no means evident that it can be, since it is not at all clear that there *is* a chunk of space which any given object exactly fills at an instant in the sense 'exactly' must carry if the other definitions upon which the analysis of spatiotemporal continuity in question turns are to be applicable. Another difficulty is that even if an acceptable analysis of the notion of a thing's primary place at an instant could be provided, it would seem that, on the analysis of spatiotemporal continuity in question, a thing could follow a spatiotemporally continuous path through an interval only provided it neither gains nor loses any parts during this interval. This becomes evident as soon as we reflect on the definition provided above for the idea of a body's moving continuously at an instant.[81]

Accordingly there is reason to reject $I*cn$ as well. Once again, however, it is not difficult to see how $I*cn$ might be revised so as to be rendered immune to difficulties of the kinds just mentioned. It would suffice to construe what it is for a material object a to trace a spatiotemporally continuous path through an interval K as follows: (1) a exists throughout every subinterval of K; (2) a occupies some place or other at each instant within K; and (3) if a occupies two distinct and spatially separated places between two distinct times within K, then it occupies places that are adjacent to or that overlap those places between the times in question, where the notions of a body's occupying a

---

[81] I am indebted for this observation to John Nelson.

place, of a body's occupying spatially separated places at different times, of a place's being adjacent to a place occupied by a body, and so on, are understood in a fairly rough and intuitive way. I shall refer to the resulting doctrine as $I**cn$.

22. The last objection I wish to examine is an objection which bears even upon $I**cn$, our doubly revised version of Icn. Since $I**cn$ asserts that spatiotemporal continuity in the crude sense just indicated is a logically necessary condition for a material object's maintaining identity through a period during which it does not undergo decomposition, it in effect claims that there is no "possible world" [82] containing a body which persists through some stretch K, which fails to exhibit spatiotemporal continuity in our new sense through K, and which does not undergo decomposition during K. Now the objection in question can be framed as either a denial of this claim, or an assertion that there is no good reason to accept it. Thus it might be urged that we obviously can conceive of a possible world in which, for example, an apple undergoes a spatial discontinuity at some point during its career, or a possible world in which, for example, each of the eighty-five rotating, sphere-shaped objects which exist jumps through space a distance equal to exactly three times its diameter after each complete rotation. Alternatively, it might merely be urged that no basis is at all evident for denying that there are such possible worlds, that is, that the actual world might have satisfied such descriptions as the above.

I suspect that the strongest reply which might be made to this objection would involve an adaptation of the argument which was presented in the third and fourth paragraphs of Section 2 above. That argument ran in outline thus: [83]

(1) If it were conceivable that there should be a case of material object identity through time in which the object in question failed to exhibit spatiotemporal continuity, then cases of type Φ would also be conceivable.

(2) Cases of the latter kind, however, are not conceivable.

(3) Therefore, it is not conceivable that there should be a case of material object identity through time in which the object in question failed to exhibit spatiotemporal continuity,

---

[82] Where a possible world is understood, following Jaakko Hintikka, as what a "complete novel" describes, where CN is a *complete novel* provided that it is composed of a set of sentences (in some language) such that addition of any further sentence (of that language) to the set renders it inconsistent. See J. Hintikka, "Individuals, Possible Worlds, and Epistemic Logic," *Nous*, I (March, 1967), p. 40.

[83] I have changed the argument slightly by generalizing premise (1).

where cases of type Φ include cases such as my marble case (see page 53), my reduplication case (see pages 53–4 ff.), and the variants of them which involve (1) temporal discontinuity but no spatial discontinuity and (2) both temporal and spatial discontinuity. The reason this argument requires adaptation is obvious in view of the objections which have led us to reject both *Icn* and *I*cn*. Moreover, these objections make evident what needs to be done in order to make the argument attractive in connection with the objection presently under consideration. We need to understand spatiotemporal continuity in the way indicated at the end of Section 21, and we need to restate the protasis of (1) (and also the conclusion) so that cases of objects which fail of continuity owing to decomposition are excluded from consideration. For convenience of reference I shall speak of the resulting argument as the Vacuity Argument and I shall label its first premise and conclusion (1*) and (3*) respectively. What I want to do next is to ask whether it provides a satisfactory reply to the objection of the preceding paragraph.

A possible objection to premise (1*) of the Vacuity Argument might run thus: "This premise is false since it could be true both that cases of type Φ are impossible and that gross discontinuities in the careers of bodies which do not undergo decomposition occur. For it might be the case that identifications across spatial and/or temporal gaps are legitimate only when there is but a single candidate on the other side of the gap for the position of being (identical with) the object which existed and exhibited continuity up to t_i. At any rate, until this possibility is ruled out the truth of premise (1*) is not evident."

When so phrased this difficulty is not, I think, persuasive. After all, it certainly appears *prima facie* clear that if identifications across gaps are ever legitimate, then cases like my marble and reduplication cases are possible. For if a single marble could jump in space, what could preclude another's jumping at the same time, where this second marble is "qualitatively indistinguishable" from the first? Or another's coming into existence on the other side of the gap, where again this second one is "qualitatively indistinguishable" from the first? Also, if the possibility in question were genuine, then we could never be in a position to know that the object on one side of an ostensible gap was identical with the object on the other side, unless we could somehow know that there was no other candidate somewhere in the universe. And, of course, it would follow that judgments of the identity through time of material objects in gappy cases entail negative existentials. These additional consequences make the doctrine in question appear quite suspect at the least.

There are several objections which might be raised in connection with premise (2). The argument in support of this premise was, in brief, that, since there is no way of pairing the object(s) on the earlier side of a gap with those on the later side which has more to commend it than any alternative pairing, it lacks clear sense to maintain that one (or some) of the pairings are correct and the other(s) incorrect. The first objection to (2) I want to consider can be expressed as follows. Suppose we have a reduplication situation involving qualitatively indistinguishable objects of the sort that can be depicted schematically as in Diagram 11. Then the following counterfactual statements would seem to make sense:

S_1:   If a's world line had continued unbroken through and beyond $[t_1, t_{10}]$, then a would have coincided with b at t_{10}.

S_2:   If a's world line had continued unbroken through and beyond $[t_1, t_{10}]$, then a would have coincided with c at t_{10}.

S_3:   If a's world line had continued unbroken through and beyond $[t_1, t_{10}]$, then a would have coincided with neither b nor c.

But if this is so, then the statements '$a = b$', '$a = c$', and 'a is distinct from both b and c' must also make sense. For obviously S_1 entails '$a = b$', S_2 entails '$a = c$', and S_3 entails '$(a \neq b)$ & $(a \neq c)$'; and surely it is true that if a statement makes sense, then any statement it entails makes sense. But now, the objection concludes, since the identity statements noted make sense, the situation in question could be a Φ-type situation, and since this situation is plainly conceivable, premise (2) fails.[84]

This difficulty, however, is no more decisive than the objection to premise (1*) we have just examined. For an advocate of the Vacuity Argument could obviously cite his own argument for (2) as a reason for reversing the argument made above. More specifically, he could use his argument as a basis for claiming that the apparent senselessness of statements like '$a = b$' throws in question the premise that the counterfactuals $S_1 - S_3$ make clear sense and/or the premise that these counterfactuals have the entailments indicated. Indeed, he might even urge that it is (inter alia) the lack of any clear understanding of the truth conditions and entailments of counterfactual statements like these which the argument for premise (2) brings into the open. It is difficult to see, I submit, that were an advocate of the Vacuity Argument to so

[84] The objection was suggested to me by remarks in G. C. Nerlich's paper " 'Continuity' Continued," *Analysis*, XXI (October, 1960).

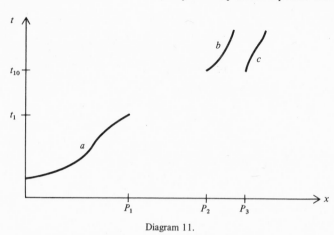

Diagram 11.

respond to the objection in question, he would have less reason on his side than is on the side of the objector.

A second objection to premise (2) is that we can perfectly well imagine the existence of a being sufficiently powerful and sufficiently capricious (a) to create and destroy material objects of any description, in any place, and at any time he chose, and (b) to cause occasional discontinuities in the spatiotemporal paths of material objects. But, this objection would continue, if we can conceive of such a being, we can *ipso facto* conceive of their being Φ-type situations.

The trouble with this objection is that it rests upon an equivocation which, when removed, turns the argument into either a *non sequitur* or a *petitio*. The equivocation is between (a) being able to imagine some state of affairs and (b) being able to conceive this state of affairs, where the conceivability of a state of affairs is understood to involve the logical possibility of its holding. That these notions are distinct is evident from the fact that it is obviously imaginable (at least in one familiar use of the word), though hardly conceivable, that someone should climb into a machine, turn some dials in accordance with a book of instructions, and then travel back to eighteenth-century Paris; or take a drug which enabled him to "move at will" back and forth between our spatiotemporal system and a spatiotemporal system the denizens of which are at no distance from, and in no temporal relations to, the denizens of our system; or discover a prime number than which no greater exists. Thus suppose we construe the first premise of the argument in accordance with (a). Then the argument will in no way guarantee the *conceivability* of Φ-type situations. On the other hand, if we read (or revise) the first premise in accordance with (b), the argument simply begs the question at issue.

Still another objection to premise (2) might be put thus. The argument adduced in support of (2) presupposes the principle that if under certain circumstances there is no basis for a judgment of identity which justifies going beyond a weaker judgment which is compatible with diversity, then in these circumstances a judgment of identity lacks sense. But this principle is not self-evident. Indeed it seems clear, this objection might continue, that it would be equally or more reasonable to maintain instead merely that if under certain circumstances there is no basis for a judgment of identity which justifies going beyond a weaker judgment which is compatible with diversity, then in these circumstances a judgment of identity would be unwarranted — that is, we could not know whether the judgment of identity was true or whether some weaker judgment compatible with diversity was true. After all, there are lots of statements the truth value of which we cannot find out, but which nonetheless make perfectly good sense. We cannot, for example, find out the dying thoughts of Dag Hammarskjöld; or what Jesus had to eat on his fourth birthday; or what is happening on the planets of stars in remote galaxies; or whether Goldbach's conjecture is true.

This objection overlooks some important distinctions. In the marble case, for example, there is a difficulty in saying merely that we can not know whether $a = d$ which does not afflict cases of the sort alluded to in the last sentence of the preceding paragraph. For in the marble case, unlike these others, there is nothing more to know that is relevant to the question whether $a = d$. But this is tantamount to saying that we can form no conception of what it would be for anyone to know that $a = d$. However, the notion that an intelligible statement should be a garden variety empirical one and yet that we should be able to form no conception of what it would be for anyone to know that it is true (or false) is most dubious. And this dubiety is obviously in no way mitigated, as the objection suggests, either by appeal to statements such that though we cannot know their truth value, others better placed could; or by appeal to statements which cannot be described as of the garden variety empirical kind.

23. I conclude, then, that the Vacuity Argument is quite attractive, and hence that the objection stated at the outset of Section 22 is not obviously a telling one — at least in the form in which I have presented it. Unfortunately, there are some additional objections to the Vacuity Argument which I remain unclear about at present. So whether we are justified in accepting even the doubly revised version of *Icn* seems to me also unclear.[85]

[85] Work on this paper was supported in part by the National Science Foundation (GS-2064). I am also indebted to Gareth Matthews, Ian Mueller, and Sydney Shoemaker for helpful comments on various parts of the paper.

Wiggins on Identity[1]

SYDNEY SHOEMAKER

Cornell University

The topic of identity, and especially the problem of the application of the logicians' notion of identity to the empirical world, has not received the attention it deserves from philosophers. The topic of *personal* identity has of course been extensively discussed, but this has too often been, in discussions of identity, the tail that wags the dog. Fortunately there is now available a study of the topic of identity which is more comprehensive and up-to-date than anything hitherto available and which attempts to put its various aspects (including the problem of personal identity) in proper perspective. Although it is not an easy book to read, Professor David Wiggins' *Identity and Spatio-Temporal Continuity* is an impressive and stimulating work. In what follows I discuss critically, but I hope not unsympathetically, several of Wiggins' central claims and arguments. There is much of great interest in his book that I do not discuss.

The book is divided into four parts, but one of these, Part III, is purely transitional. Part I is a criticism of the thesis, which Wiggins calls R, that identity is relative in such a way that a and b can be the same f and different g's, where "f" and "g" represent different "sortal" concepts. (I shall follow Wiggins in using "f," "g," and "h" to represent sortal predicates and concepts, and in using ordinary predicate variables ϕ, ψ, etc. to represent predicates in general. I shall italicize "f," "g," etc. when they are used as dummy names of sortal concepts, but

[1] This was originally written as a discussion-review of David Wiggins' *Identity and Spatio-Temporal Continuity* (Oxford: Basil Blackwell, 1967) for *The Philosophical Review*, where it appeared in slightly different form in the October, 1970 issue.

not when they are used as dummy predicates or predicate variables.) Wiggins insists that R is distinct from the thesis, which he calls D, that (as he initially formulates it) "if someone tells you that $a = b$, then you should always ask them 'the same what as b?' " (p. 1), and holds that while R is false, D is true. In Part II Wiggins attempts to give an explication and defense of D, and in so doing he attempts to give a formal characterization of the notion of a sortal, and so of a substance (in particular, a material substance). Part IV applies the analysis of the earlier parts to the topic of personal identity, and is primarily concerned to show that "no correct spatio-temporal criterion of personal identity can conflict with any correct memory-criterion or character-continuity criterion of personal identity" (p. 41).

Wiggins' case against R is a formidable one. He starts by giving a very simple formal argument to show that R is incompatible with Leibniz' Law. What the argument shows is that if identity relations such as "is the same f as" are reflexive, and if they confer substitutivity *a la* Leibniz' Law, then if a is both an f and a g it cannot be the same f as b without being the same g as b. After arguing briefly for the indispensability of Leibniz' Law (which, he says, "marks off what is peculiar to identity and differentiates it in a way in which transitivity, symmetry and reflexivity . . . do not," and which he is inclined to regard as being "as obvious as the Law of Non-Contradiction" [p. 3], he goes on to consider a number of putative examples of relativity of identity. He tries, with considerable success, to show that each example is spurious.

Rather surprisingly, in constructing putative cases of relativity Wiggins overlooks what seems to me the most plausible sort of case. But his discussion provides the materials for handling cases of this sort, and a brief consideration of one of them may help to illuminate some of his points — and will perhaps have some intrinsic interest as well. Suppose that I say (A) "That piece of bronze, the one on the table there, is the statue I told you about." The truth of this is compatible with its being the case both that (1) the one and only bronze statue now on my table is not identical with (is not the same statue as) the one that was on my table a month ago, and (2) the one and only piece of bronze on my table is identical with (is the same piece of bronze as) the one that was on my table a month ago. For I may have destroyed the statue I had a month ago and hammered the bronze of which it had been composed into a different statue. If we take the "is" in (A) as expressing identity, we seem to have here a case of relativity. And there is some plausibility in so taking it, for there are circumstances in which I might naturally say (B) "The statue on my table and the piece of bronze on my table are one and the same thing" (for example, I might say this in order to straighten out the confusion of someone who has asked me, "Which shall I bring, the statue or the piece of bronze?"). If we reject R, as I do, we cannot take the "is" in (A) and the "are" in (B) as expressing identity. How then are we to take them?

Wiggins distinguishes the "is" of identity, and also what he calls the "predicative 'is' " (which is such that "*a* is [predicatively] an f" is equivalent to "*a* is (numerically) identical with some f"), from what he calls the "constitutive 'is'," which is what he takes the "is" in "The jug is a collection of china bits" to be. But the latter, if it can be glossed "is composed of" (or "is constituted of," as Wiggins has it on p. 13), is not what we have in (A) and (B). Nor do we have an "is" that means "constitutes" or "makes up." While the statue is composed of bronze, and of a particular portion or quantity of bronze, it does not seem right to say that it is composed of a *piece* of bronze—and still less is it correct to say that the piece of bronze is composed of a statue. The relationship asserted in (A) and (B) to hold between the statue and the piece of bronze is, unlike the relationships "composed of" and "constitutes," a symmetrical one. But having noticed the constitutive "is" we need not look far in order to discover what the relationship is. While neither is composed of the other, the statue and the piece of bronze are both composed of the very same bronze, or, more generally, of the very same matter. It would appear from this example that this relationship—*being composed of the same matter as*—can be expressed both by "is" and by "are one and the same thing." And it is a relationship that is especially easy to confuse with identity; for if *a* and *b* are, at time *t*, composed of exactly the same matter, then they will necessarily be indiscernible at *t* with respect to a large range of properties—their position, shape, weight, and so on at *t* will necessarily be the same. But this relationship is nevertheless not identity, since it is compatible with *a* and *b* being composed of the same matter at *t* that *a* should have come into existence before or after *b*, that *a* should cease to exist before or after *b* does, and that at some time other than *t*, *a* and *b* should differ in location.

Wiggins does not discuss precisely this relationship in connection with R, but it is in fact this relationship, rather than identity, which he believes to hold, at any given time, between a person and that person's body. This view has the great merit of reconciling two highly plausible doctrines that may seem on the face of them to be incompatible, namely (1) the doctrine (recently associated with Strawson) that physical properties belong to persons in a nonderivative way (that is, they belong to the same subject as do states of consciousness) and (2) the view that it is logically possible for a person to have different bodies at different times. Doctrine (1) may seem to imply [what is contradicted by (2)] that a person is identical with his body, but Wiggins holds, quite rightly I think, that it does not imply this.

Part II, in which Wiggins defends thesis D, is far and away the most difficult part of the book. It is difficult, first of all, to make out just what thesis D comes to. Wiggins enunciates some relatively clear theses in Part II, some of which, the thesis (Dii) for example, for which he gives his most extended argument, are characterized as "forms" of D. What is difficult is to see how these theses, plausible as they may be in their own right, amount to explications of D, given Wiggins' initial formulations of D and some of the things he says about it. But in addition to this, Wiggins' argument for thesis (Dii), which appears to be central to Part II, is obscure and full of unargued steps and apparent confusions.

At the beginning of Part II, D is characterized as the view that "on pain of indefiniteness, every identity statement stands in radical need of the answer to the question *same what?*" This resembles remarks of P. T. Geach's and suggests that Wiggins accepts Geach's view that "When one says 'x is identical with y,' this . . . is an incomplete expression; it is short for 'x is the same A as y,' where 'A' represents some count noun understood from the context of utterance—or else, it is just a vague expression of a half-formed thought." [2] Geach holds that the proposition "x is the same A as y" does not "split up into" the propositions "x is an A (and y is an A)" and "x is the same as y." [3] And Wiggins would seem to be expressing a similar thought when he says that "*a* is the same f as *b*" is "logically prior" to "*a* is an f, *b* is an f, and *a* = *b*" (p. 28). Throughout the book Wiggins favors a notation in which the identity sign does not occur by itself as a self-contained relational predicate but always occurs as part of a complex predicate expression, for example, "$\underset{f}{=}$", which has a sortal term built into it. This certainly suggests that he holds the Geachian view. Further evidence that D is meant to be the Geachian view is the fact that Wiggins takes Quine to have been opposing D in his review of Geach's *Reference and Generality*, where Quine deplored "the doctrine that 'x = y' is meaningless except as relative to some general term as parameter: 'x and y are the same F.' " [4]

Yet it is difficult to reconcile Wiggins' apparent advocacy of the Geachian view with his rejection of R and his staunch advocacy of

[2] P. T. Geach, "Identity," *Review of Metaphysics,* XXI (1967–1968), 3.

[3] P. T. Geach, *Reference and Generality* (Ithaca: Cornell University Press, 1962), p. 152.

[4] Quine's review appeared in the *Philosophical Review,* LXXII (January, 1964), 100–104; see esp. p. 101. See Wiggins, note 1, p. 65.

Leibniz' Law. It is true that if we say something of the form "a is the same as b" there is sometimes an indefiniteness, or indeterminacy, that can be removed by inserting a sortal expression after "same." [5] But will this be an indefiniteness in the sense of the predicate, as the Geachian position implies, or will it be rather an indefiniteness in the reference of the terms? [6] It seems to me that it will be the latter, and that this *ought* to be Wiggins' position. If you and I have an obstructed view of a building, and you remark "This [pointing right] is the same as that [pointing left]," I might have an unclarity about your meaning that could be resolved by your saying "I mean the same building, not the same wing." But this is clearly not a case in which I know what the terms of the asserted identity are, but am initially unclear as to which of several relations (*same building as, same wing as,* and so on) you are asserting to hold between them; it is a case in which I am initially unclear as to whether your "this" and "that" refer to (one or more) buildings or whether they refer to (one or more) wings of buildings. (Compare Quine's discussion, in "Identity, Ostension and Hypostasis," of rivers, river stages, and so on.[7]) And it is a consequence of Wiggins' own views, in particular his rejection of R, that if the references of "a" and "b" are fixed and determinate, and if a and b are g's as well as f's, then we cannot change the truth value of "$a =_f b$" by replacing "f" with "g." Thus it would seem that if there is an indefiniteness in the sense of "a is the same as b" which is due to the alleged incompleteness in the sense of "is the same as," rather than to indeterminacy of reference, this is an indefiniteness that does not lead to an indeterminacy of truth value. And how is that possible?

All of the discussion above suggests that we should interpret Wiggins' D, not as the Geachian thesis, but as a thesis about the conditions for determinacy or definiteness of reference. And there is much to support this. The last third or so of Part II is devoted to an explication and elaboration of the claim that "To trace a I must know what a is," and that what is needed to specify what a is, which involves specifying what *sort* of thing a is, "is precisely the same kind of thing as what is needed to make the command 'Trace a and trace b and see whether they turn out to coincide with one another' a comprehensible and obeyable command" (p. 35). To put the point briefly, and in a way

---

[5] This is true quite aside from the fact that these words can be used to assert similarity in some respect; in the present discussion "same" and "identical" will always be used to express "numerical" identity.

[6] The importance of pressing this question was impressed on me by the excellent discussion of Geach's views in John Perry's unpublished doctoral dissertation on identity (Cornell, 1968). The present discussion is indebted to Perry's at a number of points. See also Perry's paper "The Same F," *Philosophical Review*, LXXIX (1970), 181–200.

[7] *From a Logical Point of View* (Cambridge: Harvard University Press, 1953), Essay IV.

that does not do justice to the subtlety and complexity of Wiggins' discussion, reference involves "locating" the referent under a sortal concept, either named or unnamed, which determines a criterion of identity for the things that satisfy it.

But while all of this is plausible, it does not seem to give us D as originally formulated. It implies that if "$a = b$" is to express a determinate judgment then a and b must both be located under sortals, but it does not imply that they must be located under *one and the same* sortal—and it is the latter that seems to be implied by saying that "on pain of indefiniteness" there must be an answer to the question "same what?" Now Wiggins does argue that where a and b are located under different sortals f and g, it is a condition of "$a = b$" being true that f and g "restrict" (or "qualify") a single sortal, in the way in which the sortals *girl* and *woman* restrict (qualify) the single sortal *human being*. This is a consequence of things he says in arguing for his thesis (Dii), which tells us that for any substance there must be some sortal, a "substance sortal," which it satisfies throughout its existence (where "a satisfies f at t" is equivalent to "a is an f at t"). Or as Wiggins expresses it, $(x)(\exists g)(t) [(x \text{ exists at } t) \supset (g(x) \text{ at } t)]$. A sortal f is a substance sortal only if "x is no longer an f" entails "x is no longer," and Wiggins holds that "phase sortals," that is, sortals (like *girl*) of which this is not so, are "of their very nature" qualifications or restrictions of underlying substance sortals. It is a consequence of all this that it is a necessary condition of "$a = b$" being *true* that there be an answer to the question "same what?", that is, that there be a substance sortal under which both a and b are ultimately "placed." But surely, conditions for truth cannot in general be regarded as conditions for definiteness of sense (or of truth value, or of anything else). Perhaps Wiggins does hold that this particular condition for an identity sentence expressing a truth—let us call it the "common underlying sortal condition"—is also a condition of its expressing a determinate judgment. But this does not follow from his argument for (Dii) (which at best establishes that this is a condition for the truth of an identity judgment), or from any other argument that he gives. And it would commit him to something I find implausible, namely that such putative identity statements as "I am identical with my body" and "My typewriter is identical with the number Two," that is, those that fail to satisfy the common underlying sortal condition but do not suffer from indeterminacy of reference, are senseless (or at least suffer from indefiniteness of sense) rather than being straightforwardly (though conceptually) false.

Nevertheless, it does seem possible to give thesis D a rationale of sorts if we assume (Dii), that is, assume that the common underlying sortal condition must be satisfied if an identity statement is to be true. Suppose that we have an identity statement "$a = b$" in which a is placed under sortal concept f and b is placed under sortal concept g. If f and g are not "of their very nature" restrictions of a common sortal, then either (1) they will be determinate sortal concepts which "of their very nature" are *not* restrictions of a common sortal, that is, the nature of the concepts will exclude the possibility that they restrict a common sortal, or (2) they will be what Wiggins at one point calls "porous or indeterminate sortal concepts," that is, "concepts which enable us to pick out f's during some stretch of their existence and which leave quite open the character of f's during other periods of their life history" (p. 59). In the latter case the identity statement may be genuinely indeterminate in truth value because of an indeterminacy in the reference of its terms. But in the former case the statement will be, on our assumptions, not only false but conceptually false, and will be such that it can be seen to be false a priori by anyone for whom concepts f and g are determinate in the way envisaged. Since we can assume that people generally have no motive for asserting what they can see a priori to be false, and do not deliberately assert what is indeterminate in truth value, if someone tells us that a is identical with b, we can normally assume that the common underlying sortal condition is satisfied, or at least that the speaker thinks it is — and then we will want to ask, if we do not already know, what the underlying sortal is, for we must know this in order to know what a and b are and under what conditions "$a = b$" will be true. This suggests the following modification of the formulation of D that Wiggins gives at the beginning of Part II: ". . . on pain of indefiniteness [of reference, *or* of conceptual falsity], every identity statement stands in radical need of the answer to the question *same what?*" (The words in brackets are my suggested addition.) But I am at a loss to see how this interpretation of his thesis, or anything else his arguments can plausibly be said to establish, supports his claim that "a is the same f as b" is logically prior to "a is an f, b is an f, and a = b." In my opinion Wiggins "$=\!\!\!\!\!=_f$" notation is a breeder of confusion.

Wiggins' argument for thesis (Dii) falls into two parts. As I understand it, the first part has the conclusion

(I) If two sortals f and f' are (or can be) successively satisfied by the same thing in such a way that the f phase and f' phase of the thing's existence are temporally adjacent but not overlapping, then f and f' must be restrictions of some common sortal.

What Wiggins then goes on to argue is that the relation "f restricts the same sortal as f'" is transitive, and (being obviously symmetrical and reflexive) is thus an equivalence relation, from which, along with (I), it follows that "some one underlying sortal extends from any adjacent pair of phases throughout the whole chain" (p. 31).

One is immediately inclined to object that this illicitly assumes that the history of a thing can be divided into a "chain" of adjacent and non-overlapping sortal phases, and fails to take account of the case in which sortal phases overlap, that is, in which something is first an f but not an f', is then both an f and an f', and is then an f' but not an f. This is a defect in the way Wiggins sets up the argument, but in the end it is not important. What Wiggins has to show, in order to establish (Dii), is that any two sortals that can be satisfied by a single thing, either at the same time or at different times, must restrict a common sortal. (For the sake of simplicity I am assuming that, as a limiting case, every sortal restricts itself.) He can establish part of this by establishing (I), and the rest by establishing

(II) If two sortals f and f' are (or can be) simultaneously satisfied by a single thing, that is, are (or can be) satisfied by it in such a way that the f-phase and the f'-phase of the thing's existence wholly or partially coincide, then f and f' must be restrictions of some common sortal.

It follows from (II) that if two sortals are restricted by a common sortal they restrict a common sortal, and from this in turn, and from the fact that the relation "restricts" is transitive, it follows that the relationship "restricts the same sortal as" is transitive and thus an equivalence relationship. And while, *contra* Wiggins, (Dii) does not follow from (I) and the transitivity of "restricts the same sortal as" (since this does not take account of the case in which different sortal phases are overlapping rather than adjacent), it does follow from these together with (II) [for (II) does take account of the case of overlapping phases]. Indeed, it follows from (I) and (II) by themselves.

Let us now consider the argument for (I). Suppose that an f ceases to be an f and that immediately thereafter there is an f' where the f was. That is, an f'-phase of something is spatiotemporally contiguous with an earlier f-phase of something. We must distinguish here between the f's being replaced by an f' and its continuing to exist, having changed into an f'. So the question is, what conditions must be satisfied if the f' is to be identical with the former f? To sharpen the issue, we can suppose that there is also a g-phase of something which is spatiotemporally contiguous with the f-phase and which coincides with the f'-

phase at its beginning but diverges from it later on. The g cannot be identical with the f′, so it is impossible that both the g-phase and the f′-phase should continue the former f in existence. So on what basis could it be claimed that the f′-phase, and not the g-phase, continues the f in existence? It is clear, I think, that we would have a basis for this if we knew that $f′$ does, while g does not, restrict a common sortal with f [by the argument for (II) it is impossible that both $f′$ and g should restrict a common sortal with f]. And Wiggins claims, without further argument, that this is the *only* possible basis for such a claim.

Can we supply the argument that Wiggins does not provide, that is, the argument to show that an f′-phase can continue a former f in existence *only* if f and $f′$ are restrictions of a common sortal? I think that there is an argument for this that is plausible, though hardly conclusive. If it is true that an f′-phase can, and given the appropriate spatiotemporal relationships will, continue a former f in existence, presumably this must be a conceptual truth, and presumably it must be true in virtue of the nature of the sortal concepts f and $f′$ and their relationship to one another. It is relatively easy to see how this would be a conceptual truth if f and $f′$ were restrictions of a common sortal h, for then f and $f′$ would share a common criterion of identity; the principle for tracing f's through time would be the same as the principle for tracing f′'s through time, for both would be the principle for tracing h's through time. But it is difficult to see how any other relationship between f and $f′$ could make it a conceptual truth that an f′-phase can, and in appropriate circumstances will, continue a former f in existence. And I suppose it might be said with some plausibility that if f and $f′$ are so related as to make this a conceptual truth, this *amounts to* there being a sortal, possibly unnamed, which both f and $f′$ restrict.

The second part of Wiggins' argument, which attempts to show that the relation "restricts the same sortal as" is transitive, is the most puzzling passage in the book. Wiggins envisages a situation in which sortals $f′$ and $f″$ both restrict a sortal g_1 and in which $f″$ and h both restrict a sortal h_1. What is to be shown is that in such a case g_1 and h_1 must restrict a common sortal; for if this is so, then because "restricts" is a transitive relationship the sortal restricted by g_1 and h_1 will also be restricted by $f′$, $f″$ and h. And to show that this will be so is to show that the relation "restricts the same sortal as" is transitive and hence an equivalence relationship.

Wiggins begins his argument by saying that "To be an f″ is on present suppositions to be a g_1 that is ϕ or an h_1 that is ψ, for some ϕ and ψ or other." This is puzzling; one wonders why Wiggins writes "or" instead of "and." To say that f_i restricts f_j is to say that "f$_i$(x)" entails f$_j$(x), so if $f″$ restricts both g_1 and h_1 (as Wiggins supposes) then "f″(x)" entails the conjunction, and not merely the disjunction, of "$g_1(x)$" and "$h_1(x)$." This may seem hardly worth mentioning (since what Wiggins says is not *false*)—but it is symptomatic of a confusion that becomes important later in the argument.

Wiggins goes on to say that either the sortals g_1 and h_1 are, or they are not, so related that

$$(x)(y) [((g_1(x)) \& (h_1(x)))) \supset [(x_{g_1} = y) \equiv (x_{h_1} = y)]]$$

Again one is puzzled, for given the falsity of R, this formula [call it (A)] will hold no matter what sortal terms we substitute for "g_1" and "h_1." Wiggins comes close to recognizing this in his Appendix, in which he points out that (A) will be vacuously satisfied if g_1 and h_1 are so related that nothing can be both a g_1 and an h_1, but he never points out that this renders the remainder of his argument incoherent. For what he goes on to do is to consider what the consequences are if g_1 and h_1 are such that (A) does not hold. Instead of saying that this is impossible, he says that it would have the consequence that f'', though it could be a "perfectly legitimate concept," would not be a legitimate sortal; referring us to his later discussion of Hobbes's example of the ship of Theseus, he implies that f'' would have the status of the pseudosortal *ship or plank collection*. But this is a confusion. What is obviously suggested is that the disjunctive pseudosortal *ship or plank-collection* restricts the sortals *ship* and *plank-collection* (just as f'' restricts g_1 and h_1). But it does not. What does restrict them is the *conjunctive* pseudosortal *ship and plank collection*. And the latter, since nothing can be (predicatively) both a ship and a plank-collection, is hardly a "perfectly legitimate concept."

Wiggins apparently equates g_1 and h_1 being so related that (A) holds with their "being so related that their disjunction cannot give rise to branching." It is wholly unclear what the latter means (branching having been ruled out as logically impossible by the argument against R), but Wiggins goes on to claim, without further argument, that if g_1 and h_1 are so related, then there is a common sortal which both restrict—which is what he set out to show. I suppose that the idea is that if g_1, and h_1 are so related, then their disjunction, which both obviously restrict, will itself be a genuine sortal.

Although this argument seems thoroughly confused, I think we can see what Wiggins was getting at. While g_1 and h_1 could not fail to be so related that (A) holds, they could fail to be so related that something can be, at one and the same time, both a g_1 and an h_1. Or as we might put it, they could fail to be "cosatisfiable." But in that case they could not both be restricted by f'' if the latter is a legitimate sortal—indeed, they could not both be restricted by it if it is a satisfiable concept. What must be shown is that since, by hypothesis, the g_1 and h_1 in the example are both restricted by the genuine sortal f'', and so are cosatisfiable, there must be a common sortal which both restrict. This is precisely the thesis I earlier referred to as (II). And while Wiggins barely hints at it, there does seem to me to be a plausible argument for (II). Where two sortals f and g are such that an f and a g can exactly coincide at a given time, that is, can occupy exactly the same place at the same time, what will show them not to be cosatisfiable will be the fact that a particular f and a particular g can coincide at one time without coinciding throughout their histories. For example, if a person can have different bodies at different times, and so can first coincide with a given body and then cease to coincide with it, this shows that the sortals *person* and *human body* are not cosatisfiable. But this implies that if sortals g_1 and h_1 are cosatisfiable, they must be such that it is necessarily the case that a g_1 and an h_1 cannot coincide at one time without coinciding throughout their histories. And this can be so only if g_1 and h_1 share the same criterion of identity, the same principle for tracing their instances through space and time. They will share the same criterion of identity if they restrict a common sortal [as was noted in the argument for (I)], and it is difficult to see how else they could do so.

It should be noted that the argument just given presupposes the principle that it is impossible for two things of the same kind (two instances of the same sortal) to coincide at one time and not at other times. This is a principle Wiggins would accept (since he thinks that it is impossible for two things of the same kind to occupy the same place at the same time), but it is perhaps not self-evident. If it were false, then, because every sortal is cosatisfiable with itself, it would not be the case that, if sortals f and f' are cosatisfiable, then an f and an f' must coincide throughout their histories if they coincide at any time at all. But I think that even if this principle were false, the following principle would still be true: if f and f' are cosatisfiable, then if an f and an f' coincide at t, and neither coincides with more than one f or more than one f' at t, then the f and the f' must be identical and so must coincide throughout their histories. And this is sufficient to yield the result that if two sortals are cosatisfiable they must share the same criterion of identity.

Wiggins' main target in Part IV is the view that there are two or more independent and potentially conflicting criteria of personal identity, two of these being the criterion of bodily continuity and the criterion of memory. Wiggins' own position is conveniently summarized in the following passage:

The spatio-temporal criterion and memory criterion [of personal identity], when it is founded in the notion of cause, inform and regulate one another reciprocally—indeed they are really aspects of a single criterion. For the requirement of spatio-temporal continuity is quite empty until we say continuity *under what concept* (see Part Two). And . . . we cannot specify the right concept without mention of the behavior, characteristic functioning, and capacities of a person, including the capacity to remember some sufficient amount of his past. It is this characteristic functioning which gives the relevant kind of spatio-temporal continuity for the kinds of parcel of matter we individuate when we individuate persons. (pp. 45–46)

What is essential to personal identity, on this view, is not bodily continuity as such, but rather the continuity of a person's "life and vital functions." These "define an individual in the category of substance. They define a person." As a matter of scientific fact, the characterization in functional terms of such individuals confers on the human brain the rôle of being the "individuating nucleus" of a person, and for this reason it is conceivable that owing to brain transplantation the same person should have different bodies at different times. It is not logically necessary that the brain should be the "individuating nucleus" of a person but it is apparently Wiggins' view that it is logically necessary that *some* "parcel of matter" should have this rôle—for he holds that the notion a person should be analyzed in such a way that

coincidence under the concept *person* logically required *the continuance in one organized parcel of all that was causally sufficient and causally necessary to the continuance of essential and characteristic functioning, no autonomously sufficient part achieving autonomous and functionally separate existence.* (p. 55)

I am not absolutely sure how this last passage is to be understood, but I take Wiggins to be saying that if person X at t_2 is identical with person Y at t_1 then X, while he need not be housed in the same "bodily shell" which earlier housed Y, must have as the "seat" of his memory and other mental capacities the very same bodily part—whether it be the brain, the heart, or the liver—which had earlier been the seat of Y's memory and other mental capacities. It is not at all clear to me that this is so. For it seems to me conceivable that the following should be (or should have been) the case. The two hemispheres of the brain, we can imagine, alternate in controlling bodily functions and in being the seat of memory and other mental capacities. At regular intervals, say every twenty-four hours, whichever hemisphere has been playing this rôle "induces" its current state in the other hemisphere, and then goes into a neutral and dormant state. While in a dormant state a brain hemisphere is indistinguishable from any other dormant brain hemisphere. If all this were so, it seems that we could have a case of "change of body" in which no bodily part, no matter at all, would be retained by the person in his change of bodily ownership. What we do is to remove the dormant hemisphere of A's brain and replace it temporarily with the dormant hemisphere of B's brain. Then, after A's active brain hemisphere has induced its state in B's dormant brain hemisphere, making it active, we restore the latter to its original place in B's skull. Now B's body, or what had been B's body, will include all of the same matter as before, including the same brain, yet (so we will suppose) the memory claims that issue from its mouth will correspond to A's past, the personality traits manifested in its behavior will be A's rather than B's, and so on. If in the brain-transfer example Wiggins discusses we can say that Brownson (the brain recipient) is identical with Brown (the brain donor), it seems to me that we can say here that the postoperative inhabitant of what had been B's body, call him C, is the same person as A. For we are imagining that C's memories, abilities, personality traits, and so on, are causally related to A's past experiences and actions, and, what is even more important, that the causal relations between them are of the same kind as those that hold in normal cases (in this imaginary world) between different temporal phases of a single person's mental life. Given that this is so, one would think that a memory criterion of personal identity which is "founded in the notion of cause" should yield the verdict that C is the same person as A.

Wiggins' reason for holding that personal identity involves the "continuance in one organized parcel . . . etc." is that he thinks that only by including this requirement in a memory criterion can we make it such as to exclude, logically, the possibility of what he calls "splitting," that is, of there being two persons existing at one time who both satisfy the criterion for being identical with a single person existing at an earlier time. A putative case of splitting that he considers is one in which the two hemispheres of someone's (Brown's) brain are separated and "housed" in different bodies, and in which, the two hemispheres being "equipollent," the resulting persons (Brown I and Brown II) both claim to remember the same things and are equally intelligent. Wiggins holds, rightly I think, that as long as we "operate person . . . in the category of substance" our criterion of personal identity should be such as to give the verdict that Brown I and Brown II are not the same person and that neither is the same as Brown. (He does envisage another use of "same person" that might come into play here, in which a person would be a "clone," a "concrete universal" or "quasi-universal," and in which Brown, Brown I, and Brown II could be said to be the same

person in the sense of belonging to the same "clone person.") My guess
is that, if Wiggins were presented with my example of the preceding
paragraph, he would say that any criterion that gave the verdict that C
is the same person as A would be unsatisfactory in that it would fail to
exclude, logically, the possibility of splitting—for surely it is possible,
logically, that after inducing its state in one of B's brain hemispheres
A's brain hemisphere should have retained its state, and remained active so that subsequently memory claims corresponding to A's past
would issue both from the mouth of body A and the mouth of body B.
But it seems to me possible to allow that C (the postoperative owner
of body B) would not be the same person as A in the case just described
and still to maintain that in the example as originally described C *would*
be the same person as A. Letting R be the causal relationship between
C's memories, abilities, and so on, and A's past life, which inclines us
to say that C is A, we can offer the following as a logically sufficient
condition of personal identity: If X's memories, and the like at t stand
in R to Y's past life, *and* if there is no one other than X who at t or at
some time prior to t has memories, and so on which stand in R to Y's
past life, then X is the same person as Y. (This presupposes that we
already have a necessary condition of personal identity that can be
used to establish that someone is "other than X"; but clearly we do
have this, for clearly Z is other than X if X and Z occupy different
places at the same time.)

The criterion just suggested excludes splitting by making X's
having a certain relationship to Y sufficient for X's being identical with
Y *unless* X has a "competitor" (Wiggins' term) for being identical with
Y—that is, unless there is some Z ($\neq$ X) which also stands in that relationship to Y. Wiggins twice objects to this way of excluding splitting,
but one of his objections rests on a mistake and the other is inapplicable
to the present case. He twice invokes the principle that if "p" is grounds
for "q", then "p and r" (for any r) is grounds for "q," and argues that,
if a certain fact is grounds for the truth of an identity statement, then it
must be grounds for it even in the case where there is known to be a
"competitor" (see footnotes 38 and 47, p. 69 and pp. 72–73). But the
principle invoked is false, unless "grounds" means "entailing grounds,"
and in any case the objection is inapplicable if the statement of the
grounds includes an assertion of the nonexistence of any competitors.
Wiggins does make the point, which is due originally to B. A. O.
Williams, that in an important class of cases the claim that there is no
competitor would involve "a proposition of unlimited generality about
the whole universe, viz. that there was no competitor *anywhere* to be
found," and remarks that "I do not believe that 'a = a'' has such a
close resemblance to a general proposition" (p. 73). This does, I think,

constitute a strong objection to the view that exact similarity (together with the absence of competitors) can provide a sufficient criterion of identity, and also of some formulations of the memory criterion, and it provides a strong if not conclusive reason for denying that there can be substantial spatiotemporal discontinuities in the history of an object or person. But it has no bearing on the memory criterion suggested above; the causal chain connecting C's memories and the like with A's past life is a spatiotemporally continuous one, and it can be established without a survey of the entire universe whether some other person's memories are connected with A's past by the same sort of causal chain.

It seems to me, then, that a memory criterion of personal identity can logically exclude splitting without including Wiggins' requirement of "the continuance in one organized parcel . . . etc." But this requires, what Wiggins rightly insists on, a causal theory of memory, and I think that it also requires the assumption that causal chains, or at any rate those that link memories with remembered actions and experiences, be spatiotemporally continuous. Thus I entirely agree with Wiggins' view that a satisfactory memory criterion and a satisfactory spatiotemporal continuity criterion will necessarily coincide.

Identity and Substitutivity

RICHARD CARTWRIGHT

Massachusetts Institute of Technology

Since the publication of Frege's "Über Sinn und Bedeutung,"[1] there has been a good deal of discussion of something variously referred to as Leibniz' Law, Leibniz' Principle, Leibniz' Rule, or — in what one is led to suppose is a reference to the same thing — the Principle of Substitutivity. Much of the discussion has, I think, been interesting and valuable, but I think also that some of it has been marred by a failure to be perfectly clear what the law or principle in question is. Evidently it is something in connection with which it is somehow relevant to talk about 9 and the number of the planets, the Evening Star and the Morning Star, and Giorgione and Barbarelli. But it is not always sufficiently appreciated that whether and how these are relevant to Leibniz' Law depends upon which of several distinct propositions that Law is taken to be.

Let us begin at the beginning, namely, with the passage from Leibniz' writings to which the name 'Leibniz' Law' presumably alludes. In C. I. Lewis' translation this reads as follows:

Two terms are the *same* if one can be substituted for the other without altering the truth of any statement. If we have A and B and A enters into some true proposition, and the substitution of B for A wherever it appears, results in a new proposition which is likewise true, and if this can be done for every such proposition,

[1] *Zeitschrift für Philosophie und philosophische Kritik*, vol. 100 (1892), pp. 25–50.

then A and B are said to be the *same;* and conversely, if A and B are the same, they can be substituted for one another as I have said.[2]

It is doubtful that Leibniz here succeeded in saying what he wanted to say. For one thing, the passage contains an unfortunate confusion of use and mention: words, or expressions, are substituted for one another and not, as Leibniz suggests, the things to which the words refer. For another, his use of the word 'proposition' appears to me to obscure an important distinction. Substitution is an operation performed upon sentences and yielding sentences as values; but, as Leibniz himself urged in other places,[3] it is what is expressed, or formulated, in sentences that is properly said to be true. Allowing, then, for these deficiencies of exposition, we may take Leibniz to have been enunciating the following:

(A)   for all expressions α and β, $\ulcorner \alpha = \beta \urcorner$ expresses a true proposition if and only if, for all sentences S and S', if S' is like S save for containing an occurrence of β where S contains an occurrence of α, then S expresses a true proposition only if S' does also.

Even this does not have all the accuracy and precision one might hope for, but I think it will do for present purposes.

Let us agree to use the words 'substitution of β for α is truth preserving' to express the condition which, according to (A), is both necessary and sufficient for $\ulcorner \alpha = \beta \urcorner$ to express a true proposition. Then we may say that (A) is the conjunction of

(B)   for all expressions α and β, $\ulcorner \alpha = \beta \urcorner$ expresses a true proposition if substitution of β for α is truth preserving

with

(C)   for all expressions α and β, $\ulcorner \alpha = \beta \urcorner$ expresses a true proposition only if substitution of β for α is truth preserving.

Now it should be remarked at once that recent references to "the Principle of Substitutivity" are references to (C) rather than (A). Thus

[2] *A Survey of Symbolic Logic* (New York: Dover, 1960), p. 291.
[3] *E.g., New Essays concerning Human Understanding,* translated by A. G. Langley (LaSalle, Ill.: Open Court, 1949), pp. 450–451.

Quine formulates what he calls "the principle of substitutivity" in these words: "given a true statement of identity, one of its two terms may be substituted for the other in any true statement and the result will be true."[4] And, making allowances for what I should regard as an equivocal use of the word 'statement', this amounts to (C) rather than (A). Though historical purists will perhaps regret that (C) is sometimes referred to as "Leibniz' Law," it could hardly be claimed that departing in this way from Leibniz' formulation is of any great consequence: the logical relationships among (A), (B), and (C) are simply too transparent.

There is, however, another departure from Leibniz that is apt to seem a good deal more radical. Frequently what is put forward as "Leibniz' Law" is

(D) if $x = y$, then every property of x is a property of y.

Here, notice, there is no talk of substitution, indeed no talk of expressions at all. We are given instead a necessary condition for an *object x* to be identical with an *object y*. And there would thus appear to be all the difference between (C) and (D) that there is between the world and discourse about it. Yet I think it is often supposed that (D) somehow comes to the same thing as (C), that (D) is only a "material mode" version of (C). So at any rate we might infer, given that either is apt to be called "Leibniz' Law." But is this view correct? Only if (D) implies (C). But *does* (D) imply (C)?

Let us agree to call (C) *the Principle of Substitutivity* and (D) *the Principle of Identity*. My question is, Does the Principle of Identity imply the Principle of Substitutivity? The question can be sharpened with the help of some further terminological conventions. Let S and S' be any sentences. I shall say that the pair (S, S') *is a counterexample to the Principle of Substitutivity* if and only if there are expressions α and β such that (1) $\ulcorner \alpha = \beta \urcorner$ expresses a true proposition, (2) S' is like S save for containing an occurrence of β where S contains an occurrence of α, (3) S expresses a true proposition, and (4) S' expresses a false proposition; and if, in addition, $\ulcorner S \cdot \sim S' \cdot \alpha = \beta \urcorner$ expresses a proposition from which the negation of the Principle of Identity follows, then (and only then) I shall say that the pair (S, S') *falsifies the Principle of Identity*. Now, the Principle of Substitutivity is false if and only if there is a counterexample to it, and the Principle of Identity implies the Principle of Substitutivity if and only if the falsity of the

[4] *From a Logical Point of View,* Second edition (New York and Evanston: Harper and Row, 1963), p. 139.

Principle of Substitutivity implies the falsity of the Principle of Identity. So to ask whether the Principle of Identity implies the Principle of Substitutivity is to ask whether from the proposition that there is a counterexample to the Principle of Substitutivity one can legitimately infer the falsity of the Principle of Identity. But surely such an inference would be legitimate only if any counterexample to the Principle of Substitutivity itself falsified the Principle of Identity. Thus we may appropriately ask, Does every counterexample to the Principle of Substitutivity falsify the Principle of Identity?

In discussing this question it is important to recognize once and for all that there *are* counterexamples to the Principle of Substitutivity. The Principle is simply false. Let S_1 and S_2 be, respectively, 'Giorgione was so-called because of his size' and 'Barbarelli was so-called because of his size'. These are alike, save that S_2 contains the name 'Barbarelli' where S_1 contains the name 'Giorgione', the sentence 'Giorgione = Barbarelli' expresses a true proposition; and S_1 expresses a true proposition and S_2 a false proposition. It follows that the pair (S_1, S_2) is a counterexample to the Principle of Substitutivity and hence that the Principle is false.[5]

Some respond to this by pointing out that the proposition expressed by S_1 is also expressed by the different sentence, "Giorgione was called 'Giorgione' because of his size," and that here substitution of 'Barbarelli' for the first occurrence of 'Giorgione' yields a sentence which, in contrast with S_2, expresses a true proposition. But the proper response to this is: true but irrelevant. For, however it may be with other pairs of sentences, the fact remains that the pair (S_1, S_2) is a counterexample. Again, it is sometimes said that the occurrence of 'Giorgione' in S_1 is not purely referential (not purely designative, oblique). But far from saving the Principle of Substitutivity, this only acknowledges that the pair (S_1, S_2) is indeed a counterexample to it. For we are also told that an occurrence of a name in a sentence counts as purely referential only if substitution for that occurrence of any and every co-designative expression preserves truth value. And, even if accompanied by an independent criterion of purely referential occurrence, this second response is really no more relevant than the first. For the Principle of Substitutivity, as formulated above, contains no qualifications; it purports to cover *all* occurrences of *all* expressions.

The question remains, however, whether the pair (S_1, S_2) falsifies the Principle of Identity. If it does, then from the propositions expressed by S_1 and S_2 it must follow that Giorgione has some property that Barbarelli lacks. What could that property be? Evidently it is not

[5] *Cf.* Quine, *loc. cit.*

the property of being called 'Giorgione' because of one's size, since Giorgione and Barbarelli share that property. Nor will it do to say that it is the property of being so-called because of one's size, for this only invites the question, Being called *what* because of one's size? A more likely suggestion is that the property in question is that which a given object has if and only if the proposition that the object in question is so-called because of its size is a true proposition. Thus it might be suggested that if we let P be the property which a thing x has just in case the proposition that x is so-called because of its size is true, then, since the proposition that Giorgione was so-called because of his size is true, Giorgione has P, and, since the proposition that Barbarelli was so-called because of his size is false, Barbarelli lacks P; and from this, together with the identity of Giorgione with Barbarelli, it might be concluded that the pair (S_1, S_2) falsifies the Principle of Identity.

But the contention that there is such a property as P, possessed by Giorgione though not by Barbarelli, can be seen to be incoherent. The defender of P affirms

(1) Giorgione has P

and can scarcely deny

(2) Giorgione is called 'Barbarelli'.

From (1) and (2) it follows by existential generalization that

(3) there is someone called 'Barbarelli' and he has P;

and, by the proposed definition of P, this is equivalent to

(4) there is someone called 'Barbarelli' and the proposition that he is so-called because of his size is true.

But if we can make sense of (4) at all, we shall have to count it false: no one called 'Barbarelli' is so-called because of his size.

What is the advocate of P to say? He cannot object to the inference from (1) and (2) to (3). Existential generalization on (2) is surely permissible. And to contend that it is not permissible in the case of (1) is in effect to concede that there is no such property as P, for it is absurd to suggest that it is possible that Giorgione should have a certain property and yet that there should not be something that has that property. And, in any case, existential generalization on (1) is essential to the project of deducing the negation of the Principle of

Identity. For that was to be accomplished by arguing that from the propositions that Giorgione has P, that Barbarelli does not, and that Giorgione is identical with Barbarelli, it follows that *there is* something x and something y such that x has P, y does not, and yet x is identical with y.

Perhaps, then, the advocate of P will contend that the English sentence just now used to express (4) is simply not an accurate formulation of the proposition obtained by properly expanding (3) in accordance with the definition of P. He will point out that the expression 'so-called', as it occurs in that sentence, inevitably picks up 'Barbarelli' as antecedent and that accordingly the sentence is naturally read as expressing a proposition from which it follows that someone is called 'Barbarelli' because of his size. Of course, it is unlikely that there is an appropriate English sentence without this defect. So perhaps it will be suggested that we retain the sentence already used but assiduously avert our eyes from the reference back to 'Barbarelli'. Otherwise put, we shall perhaps be told that the proposition obtained by proper definitional expansion of (3) is one from which it follows that

(5)   there is someone such that the proposition that he is so-called because of his size is true,

where now 'so-called' stands on its own, free from the misleading suggestions of a surrounding linguistic environment.

But obviously the expression 'so-called' is just the kind of expression that *cannot* thus stand on its own. To make sense of sentences in which it occurs, to determine what propositions they express, it is necessary to look to the environment — linguistic or otherwise — of the expression 'so-called'. And if this fails to reveal a referent, no proposition has as yet been formulated. It was, in part, the failure to recognize this that led to the proposed definition of P. According to that definition, a given object has P just in case the proposition that it is so-called because of its size is true. But how is this to be understood? If we take the expression 'so-called' to have a *fixed* referent — the name 'Giorgione', say — then P will not serve to falsify the Principle of Identity; and if we are to understand that the referent of 'so-called' changes with each difference in choice of name for the given object, then the definition presupposes what is false, namely, that there is such a thing as *the* proposition that the object in question is so-called because of its size.

I suspect I have in a way been attacking a strawman. Perhaps no one would suppose that there is such a property as the alleged P or that the pair (S_1, S_2) falsifies the Principle of Identity. Nevertheless the attack is not without point. It shows that not every counterexample to the Principle of Substitutivity is a counterexample to the Principle of Identity and therefore that the Principle of Identity does not imply the Principle of Substitutivity. And this, it seems to me, is something that ought to be recognized once and for all.

But of course, for all that has been said so far, it remains possible that *some* counterexamples to the Principle of Substitutivity *do* falsify the Principle of Identity and hence that the Principle of Identity is, like the Principle of Substitutivity, simply false. This view has had its proponents. One of them, the late E. J. Lemmon, wrote as follows:

> ... '$x = y$' may be true, even though x has an attribute (for example, that of necessarily being x) which y has not got. Thus the morning star, though it *is* the evening star, has the attribute of being necessarily the morning star, which the evening star does not have. This ... will be unpalatable to many, but I believe it to be a paradox of intensionality that should be accepted on a par with the paradoxes of infinity that we have now come to accept (for example, that a totality may be equinumerous with a proper part of itself). ... The paradoxes of the infinite are paradoxical only because we normally think in terms of finite classes; this paradox of intensionality is paradoxical only because we normally think, with Leibniz, in extensional terms.[6]

Lemmon's alleged exception to the Principle of Identity at once suggests hosts of others. We can agree that whereas it is a necessary truth that 9 is greater than 7, it is only contingently true that the number of planets is greater than 7; and from this I suppose Lemmon and others of his persuasion would say it follows that 9 has a property the number of the planets lacks; and this in spite of the astronomical fact that 9 *is* the number of the planets. Again, though 9 is identical with 3^2, we may suppose Herbert knows that 9 is greater than 7 but is ignorant of the fact that 3^2 is greater than 7. And from this it will perhaps be concluded that although 9 has the property of being known by Herbert to be greater than 7, 3^2 does not.

Lemmon anticipated—correctly, I think—that many would find his position unpalatable. If y lacks a property x has, then to most people it will seem evident and undeniable that y cannot be the very same object as x. But what is one to say to those few who see the matter differently? I think it wise to concede at once that demonstration is out of the question. To *prove* there are no counterexamples to the Prin-

---

[6] "A Theory of Attributes Based on Modal Logic," *Acta Philosophica Fennica* (1963), p. 98.

ciple of Identity would require appeal to some more fundamental principle, and it is doubtful that any such is available. Still, there are strategies open to the Leibnizian. He may try to exhibit disturbing consequences of the negation of the Principle of Identity, hoping thereby to present considerations that will at least influence the intellect of the non-Leibnizian. He may try to show that one or another alleged counterexample is not really such. And he may seek to show that the non-Leibnizian is led to his position through bad arguments and intellectual confusions.

Demonstration of the nonequivalence of the Principle of Identity and the Principle of Substitutivity is itself an effort in this direction, for I suspect some have rejected the Principle of Identity only because they have confused it with the Principle of Substitutivity. In what follows I shall attempt further efforts, though of a quite limited nature. What I have to say concerns a single example; and although my discussion of it is somewhat detailed, I doubt that it is exhaustive.

Consider, then, the pair (S_3, S_4), where S_3 is the sentence '9 is necessarily greater than 7' and S_4 the sentence 'the number of planets is necessarily greater than 7'. Now of course my main concern is to determine whether this pair falsifies the Principle of Identity. But I think it will be of some value to attend first to the question whether it really is, as it is usually thought to be, a counterexample to the Principle of Substitutivity. There is a straightforward enough argument: from the premises

(6) S_3 expresses a true proposition if and only if '9 is greater than 7' expresses a necessary proposition,

(7) S_4 expresses a true proposition if and only if 'the number of planets is greater than 7' expresses a necessary proposition,

(8) '9 is greater than 7' expresses a necessary proposition,

and

(9) 'the number of planets is greater than 7' does not express a necessary proposition

it is inferred that

(10) S_3 expresses a true proposition, while S_4 expresses a false proposition;

and this coupled with

(11)   '9 = the number of planets' expresses a true proposition

yields the desired conclusion.

The argument is clearly valid, and I shall suppose there is no doubt that (6), (8), (9), and (11) are true. Hence, if (7) is true, the conclusion will have to be granted. But is (7) true?

Those who think it is would perhaps invoke the following general principle:

(E)   if α is any singular term and ϕ any predicate expression, $\ulcorner\alpha$ is necessarily $\phi\urcorner$ expresses a true proposition if and only if $\ulcorner\alpha$ is $\phi\urcorner$ expresses a necessary proposition.

And certainly *if* (E) is unexceptionable, (7) has to be counted true. But is (E) unexceptionable? Consider in this connection the sentence, S_5, 'the proposition at the top of page 210 of *Word and Object* is necessarily true'. Does this express a true proposition or not? Notice that, given (E), we can answer without knowing *what* proposition *is* at the top of page 210 of *Word and Object* — indeed, without knowing whether there is any proposition at all at the top of that page. For according to (E), S_5 expresses a true proposition if and only if the sentence, 'the proposition at the top of page 210 of *Word and Object* is true' expresses a necessary proposition. And clearly this last sentence does not express a necessary proposition; that is, the proposition

(12)   the proposition at the top of page 210 of *Word and Object* is true

is not a necessary truth. But this shows that something is wrong with (E). Asked whether S_5 expresses a true proposition, we surely have some inclination to suppose that we cannot answer unless we *do* know what proposition appears at the top of page 210 of *Word and Object*. That is, it is altogether natural to take S_5 to express a proposition which is true if and only if

(13)   there is exactly one proposition at the top of page 210 of *Word and Object*, which proposition is necessarily true.

And so understood, S_5 expresses a true proposition, for the proposition at the top of page 210 of *Word and Object* is the proposition that for every positive integer x, the class of positive integers less than or equal to x has x members, and this is necessarily true.

There is no need to insist that S_5 *has* to be read in such a way that it expresses a true proposition if and only if (13) is true. No doubt it can also be read in such a way that it expresses a true proposition if and only if (12) is necessary. But then S_5 will have to be counted ambiguous, and it is precisely this ambiguity that is not taken account of in (E).

Now, I think the same sort of ambiguity is present in S_4. No doubt that sentence can be so understood that it expresses a true proposition if and only if the sentence, 'the number of planets is greater than 7' expresses a necessary proposition. And, so understood, it does not express a true proposition since

(14)   the number of planets is greater than 7

is not a necessary truth. But I should suppose that S_4 can just as easily be understood in such a way that it expresses a proposition which is true if and only if it is true that

(15)   there is a unique number of planets, which number is necessarily greater than 7.

This is the way it would be understood by someone who supposed — what it is perfectly natural to suppose — that one cannot say whether S_4 expresses a true proposition unless one knows *which* number *is* the number of the planets. And understood in this way S_4 expresses a true proposition: There is a unique number of planets and it is necessarily greater than 7.

So, read in one way S_4 expresses a false proposition, and read in another, equally natural way it expresses a true proposition. Is there a similar ambiguity in S_3? I think there is, though I think it occasions no disparity in truth-value. S_3 can be understood *de dicto*, that is, as expressing the proposition that

(16)   9 is greater than 7

is a necessary truth. But it can also be understood *de re*, that is, as asserting of the number 9 that it is necessarily greater than 7. Under either interpretation it seems to me to express a true proposition.

What, then, is to be said of the pair (S_3, S_4)? Is it or is it not a counterexample to the Principle of Substitutivity? The fact is that in the formulation of that principle cases of sentential ambiguity were simply not anticipated. The principle was formulated under the useful fiction that a sentence expresses at most one proposition. The fiction *is* a useful one. Let us preserve it by leaving the Principle of Substitutivity undisturbed and ruling that S_3 and S_4 are to be understood *de re*, while the new sentences S_6 'necessarily, 9 is greater than 7', and S_7, 'necessarily, the number of the planets is greater than 7' are to be understood *de dicto*. I suspect there is some sanction in English usage for these rulings, but whether there is or not is of little importance once the propositions in question have been distinguished. And thus we may say that whereas the pair (S_6, S_7) is a counterexample to the Principle of Substitutivity, the pair (S_3, S_4) is not.

But the question remains whether the pair (S_6, S_7) falsifies the Principle of Identity. If it does, then from

(17) necessarily, 9 is greater than 7,

(18) 9 = the number of planets,

and

(19) not (necessarily the number of planets is greater than 7)

it must follow that 9 has a property that the number of planets lacks. What might this property be? The quick answer is: the property of being necessarily greater than 7. But exactly what property is this? The question is urgent, for we might have supposed that the property of being necessarily greater than 7 is the property which, in S_3 and S_4 is *correctly* attributed to *both* 9 and the number of the planets; and what is presently needed is a property which in S_6 is correctly attributed to 9 but which in S_7 is *in*correctly attributed to the number of the planets. Perhaps we should ask how, in the light of (17) and (19), 9 is supposed to differ from the number of the planets. What is supposed to be true of 9 that is not true of the number of the planets? It might be suggested that in view of (17) it is true of 9 that necessarily it is greater than 7, while in view of (19) it is not true of the number of the planets that necessarily it is greater than 7. Given our conventions concerning the word 'necessarily', the suggestion comes to this: It is true of 9 that the proposition that it is greater than 7 is necessary, but it is not true of the number of planets that the proposition that *it* is greater than 7 is necessary. And so it will perhaps be suggested that if we define Q as the property which a thing x has if and only if the proposition that x is greater than 7 is necessary, then from (17) it will follow that 9 has Q and from (19) it will follow that the number of planets does not have Q.

The suggestion is worth some exploration. The advocate of Q

will of course agree that there is a unique number of planets. This is an immediate consequence of

(20) $(m)(m$ is a number of the planets iff $m = 9)$,

which is simply a fact of astronomy. Something, then, and one thing only, is a number of the planets. Does it have Q or not? This question, which I suppose certainly ought to have an answer, is bound to embarrass the advocate of Q. From (20) and

(21)   9 has Q

it follows that

(22) $(\exists n)((m)(m$ is a number of the planets iff $m = n)$ and n has $Q)$.

But equally, from the undeniable

(23) $(m)(m$ is a number of the planets iff $m =$ the number of planets)

and the non-Leibnizian's

(24)   the number of planets lacks Q

it follows that

(25) $(\exists n)((m)(m$ is a number of the planets iff $m = n)$ and n lacks $Q)$.

The advocate of Q is thus committed to both (22) and (25): to the proposition that there is a unique number of planets and it has Q, and to the proposition that there is a unique number of planets and it lacks Q. But anyone who affirms both these is surely ill-equipped to answer the question whether, given that there is a unique number of planets, it has Q or not.

The point is not that (22) and (25) are incompatible. I think they are, but to invoke this would beg the question; for a contradiction follows from the conjunction of (22) and (25) only on the assumption of the Principle of Identity. Nor is the point that on Russell's theory of descriptions (22) is the expansion of

(26)   the number of the planets has Q

and thus that the advocate of Q is committed to the very thing he wishes to deny. I suppose it is open to someone simply to reject Russell's theory. The point is rather this: If I am told that exactly one thing numbers the planets, I expect to be able to ask whether it – that number – has Q; and I expect my question to have a determinate answer. But no answer can be given by one who affirms both (22) and (25).

I suspect it will be suggested that my words, 'There is a unique number of planets. Does it have Q?' amount to 'Does the number of planets have Q?' and that this is a question the advocate of Q is quite prepared to answer. After all, one of his claims is that the number of planets lacks Q. Now, I myself do not object to this rephrasing of my question. But I should like it noted that it is just the possibility of this sort of paraphrase that lends credence to Russell's theory – a theory that we have seen the advocate of Q must reject. And in any case, it seems to me that the question needs no paraphrase and that a friend of Q ought himself to find its original formulation perfectly intelligible. Recall that Q is supposed to be the property that an object has just in case the proposition that it is greater than 7 is a necessary truth. Well, there is an object – and one only – that numbers the planets. Can we not consider, then, the proposition that *it* is greater than 7? And should not reflection reveal whether this proposition is a necessary truth? I submit that reflection can reveal nothing better than *both* (22) and (25).

The difficulty originates in what seems to me to be an illegitimate form of definition. We are invited to speak of the property which an object x has if and only if the proposition that x is greater than 7 is a necessary truth. But it ought to be clear by now that it is simply a mistake to suppose that in the case of any given object there is such a thing as *the* proposition that it is greater than 7. Ever so many propositions will qualify as propositions that it, the object in question, is greater than 7. The point is obvious but often overlooked. There is an unfortunate temptation to suppose that it is possible to specify a function, in the mathematical sense, by stipulating that its domain is a particular well-defined class of objects and by stipulating further that, for any element x of that class, the value of the function for the argument x is the proposition that x is such-and-such – greater than 7, or whatever. But the fact is that these stipulations simply do not succeed in specifying a function. Suppose, for example, the domain of the alleged function is to be the class having 9 as sole member and suppose the value for x as argument is to be the proposition that *x* is greater than 7. What is the value for 9 as argument? If the proposition that 9 is greater than 7 qualifies, so too does the different proposition that the number of the planets is greater than 7; for the number of the planets is the only member of the class whose sole member is 9. Thus the alleged function is not single-valued and hence not properly a function at all.

Let me put the point another way. Consider the propositions

(27)   9 is greater than 7

and

(28)   8 is greater than 7.

In (27) it is said of 9 that it is greater than 7, and in (28) it is said of 8 that *it* is greater than 7. Thus (27) and (28) are alike in that in each it is said of something that it is greater than 7. But that of which this is said in (27) is not the same as that of which this is said in (28). This is how the propositions differ. It is what makes them *two*. In the light of this it is tempting to go on to suppose that (27) can be fully identified by saying that it is the proposition in which it is said of 9 that it is greater than 7: We specify the object concerning which something is said and specify further what is said of it. But the supposition that this succeeds in distinguishing (27) from all other propositions is not true. That of which in (27) something is said is the number 9, that is, the number of the planets; hence (27) has not yet been distinguished from the proposition that the number of the planets is greater than 7.

What strikes me as especially odd in the case of the definition of *Q* is that those who would use it to show the falsity of the Principle of Identity must implicitly recognize its illegitimacy. They speak, on the one hand, of *the* proposition that *x* is greater than 7, for arbitrary but unspecified choice of *x*; yet, on the other hand, it is crucial to their argument that for one and the same object *x* there be distinct propositions to the effect that *x* is greater than 7: After all, one such proposition is to be necessarily true, another only contingently so. Were there not such distinct propositions, it could hardly emerge that 9 has *Q* while something identical with it does not.

Of course, a really determined proponent of *Q* will not waver in the face of what I have been saying. He will insist that, given any object *x*, there *is* such a thing as *the* proposition that *x* is greater than 7. He will insist, in particular, that the necessary truth that 9 is greater than 7 really is identical with the contingent truth that the number of the planets is greater than 7. And he will see in this only another exception to the Principle of Identity. Now frankly this strikes me as a desperation move. But how is one to reply? To show that two things — propositions or any other things — really *are* two, nothing will suffice short of mentioning something true of one of them that is not true of the other. Perhaps in the end all that can be said is that the Principle of Identity is a self-evident truth.

Identity and Necessity

SAUL KRIPKE

The Rockefeller University

A problem which has arisen frequently in contemporary philosophy is: "How are *contingent* identity statements possible?" This question is phrased by analogy with the way Kant phrased his question "How are synthetic a priori judgments possible?" In both cases, it has usually been taken for granted in the one case by Kant that synthetic a priori judgments were possible, and in the other case in contemporary philosophical literature that contingent statements of identity are possible. I do not intend to deal with the Kantian question except to mention this analogy: After a rather thick book was written trying to answer the question how synthetic a priori judgments were possible, others came along later who claimed that the solution to the problem was that synthetic a priori judgments were, of course, impossible and that a book trying to show otherwise was written in vain. I will not discuss who was right on the possibility of synthetic a priori judgments. But in the case of contingent statements of identity, most philosophers have felt that the notion of a contingent identity statement ran into something like the following paradox. An argument like the following can be given against the possibility of contingent identity statements: [1]

---

[1] This paper was presented orally, without a written text, to the New York University lecture series on identity which makes up this volume. The lecture was taped, and the present paper represents a transcription of these tapes, edited only slightly with no attempt to change the style of the original. If the reader imagines the sentences of this paper as being delivered, extemporaneously, with proper pauses and emphases, this may facilitate his comprehension. Nevertheless, there may still be passages which are hard to follow, and the time allotted necessitated a condensed presentation of the argu-

First, the law of the substitutivity of identity says that, for any objects x and y, if x is identical to y, then if x has a certain property F, so does y:

(1) $(x)(y) [(x = y) \supset (Fx \supset Fy)]$

On the other hand, every object surely is necessarily self-identical:

(2) $(x) \,\square\, (x = x)$

But

(3) $(x)(y) (x = y) \supset [\square\, (x = x) \supset \square\, (x = y)]$

is a substitution instance of (1), the substitutivity law. From (2) and (3), we can conclude that, for every x and y, if x equals y, then, it is necessary that x equals y:

(4) $(x)(y) ((x = y) \supset \square\, (x = y))$

This is because the clause $\square\, (x = x)$ of the conditional drops out because it is known to be true.

This is an argument which has been stated many times in recent philosophy. Its conclusion, however, has often been regarded as highly paradoxical. For example, David Wiggins, in his paper, "Identity-Statements," says,

> Now there undoubtedly exist contingent identity-statements. Let $a = b$ be one of them. From its simple truth and (5) [= (4) above] we can derive '$\square(a = b)$'. But how then can there be any contingent identity statements?[2]

He then says that five various reactions to this argument are possible, and rejects all of these reactions, and reacts himself. I do not want to discuss all the possible reactions to this statement, except to mention the second of those Wiggins rejects. This says,

> We might accept the result and plead that provided 'a' and 'b' are proper names nothing is amiss. The consequence of this is that no

ment. (A longer version of some of these views, still rather compressed and still representing a transcript of oral remarks, will appear elsewhere.) Occasionally, reservations, amplifications, and gratifications of my remarks had to be repressed, especially in the discussion of theoretical identification and the mind-body problem. The footnotes, which were added to the original, would have become even more unwieldy if this had not been done.

[2] R. J. Butler, ed., *Analytical Philosophy, Second Series*, Basil Blackwell, Oxford, 1965, p. 41.

contingent identity-statements can be made by means of proper names.

And then he says that he is discontented with this solution and many other philosophers have been discontented with this solution, too, while still others have advocated it.

What makes the statement (4) seem surprising? It says, for any objects x and y, if x is y, then it is necessary that x is y. I have already mentioned that someone might object to this argument on the grounds that premise (2) is already false, that it is not the case that everything is necessarily self-identical. Well, for example, am I myself necessarily self-identical? Someone might argue that in some situations which we can imagine I would not even have existed and therefore the statement "Saul Kripke is Saul Kripke" would have been false or it would not be the case that I was self-identical. Perhaps, it would have been neither true nor false, in such a world, to say that Saul Kripke is self-identical. Well, that may be so, but really it depends on one's philosophical view of a topic that I will not discuss, that is, what is to be said about truth values of statements mentioning objects that do not exist in the actual world or any given possible world or counterfactual situation. Let us interpret necessity here weakly. We can count statements as necessary if whenever the objects mentioned therein exist, the statement would be true. If we wished to be very careful about this, we would have to go into the question of existence as a predicate and ask if the statement can be reformulated in the form: For every x it is necessary that, if x exists, then x is self-identical. I will not go into this particular form of subtlety here because it is not going to be relevant to my main theme. Nor am I really going to consider formula (4). Anyone who believes formula (2) is, in my opinion, committed to formula (4). If x and y are the same things and we can talk about modal properties of an object at all, that is, in the usual parlance, we can speak of modality *de re* and an object *necessarily* having certain properties as such, then formula (1), I think, has to hold. Where x is any property at all, including a property involving modal operators, and if x and y are the same object and x had a certain property F, then y has to have the same property F. And this is so even if the property F is itself of the form of necessarily having some other property G, in particular that of necessarily being identical to a certain object. Well, I will not discuss the formula (4) itself because by itself it does not assert, of any particular true statement of identity, that it is necessary. It does not say anything about *statements* at all. It says for every *object x* and *object y*, if x and y are the same object, then it is necessary that x and y are the same object. And this, I think, if we think about it (anyway, if someone does not think so, I will not argue for it here), really amounts to something very little different from the statement (2). Since x, by definition of identity, is the only object identical with x, "$(y)(y = x \supset Fy)$" seems to me to be little more than a garrulous way of saying 'Fx', and thus (x) $(y)(y = x \supset Fx)$ says the same as $(x)Fx$ no matter what 'F' is—in particular, even if 'F' stands for the property of necessary identity with x. So if x has this property (of necessary identity with x), trivially everything identical with x has it, as (4) asserts. But, from statement (4) one may apparently be able to deduce various particular statements of identity must be necessary and this is then supposed to be a very paradoxical consequence.

Wiggins says, "Now there undoubtedly exist contingent identity statements." One example of a contingent identity statement is the statement that the first Postmaster General of the United States is identical with the inventor of bifocals, or that both of these are identical with the man claimed by the *Saturday Evening Post* as its founder (*falsely* claimed, I gather, by the way). Now some such statements are plainly contingent. It plainly is a contingent fact that one and the same man both invented bifocals and took on the job of Postmaster General of the United States. How can we reconcile this with the truth of statement (4)? Well, that, too, is an issue I do not want to go into in detail except to be very dogmatic about it. It was I think settled quite well by Bertrand Russell in his notion of the scope of a description. According to Russell, one can, for example, say with propriety that the author of Hamlet might not have written "Hamlet," or even that the author of Hamlet might not have been the author of "Hamlet." Now here, of course, we do not deny the necessity of the identity of an object with itself; but we say it is true concerning a certain man that he in fact was the unique person to have written "Hamlet" and secondly that the man, who in fact was the man who wrote "Hamlet," might not have written "Hamlet." In other words, if Shakespeare had decided not to write tragedies, he might not have written "Hamlet." Under these circumstances, the man who in fact wrote "Hamlet" would not have written "Hamlet." Russell brings this out by saying that in such a statement, the first occurrence of the description "the author of 'Hamlet' " has large scope.[3] That is, we say "The author of 'Hamlet' has the following property: that he might not have written 'Hamlet.' " We *do not* assert that the following statement might have been the case, namely that the author of "Hamlet" did not write "Hamlet," for that is not true. That would be to say that it might have been the case that someone wrote "Hamlet" and yet did not write "Hamlet," which would be a contradiction. Now, aside from the details of Russell's particular for-

---

[3] The second occurrence of the description has small scope.

mulation of it, which depends on his theory of descriptions, this seems to be the distinction that any theory of descriptions has to make. For example, if someone were to meet the President of Harvard and take him to be a Teaching Fellow, he might say: "I took the President of Harvard for a Teaching Fellow." By this he does not mean that he took the proposition "The President of Harvard is a Teaching Fellow" to be true. He could have meant this, for example, had he believed that some sort of democratic system had gone so far at Harvard that the President of it decided to take on the task of being a Teaching Fellow. But that probably is not what he means. What he means instead, as Russell points out, is "Someone is President of Harvard and I took him to be a Teaching Fellow." In one of Russell's examples someone says, "I thought your yacht is much larger than it is." And the other man replies, "No, my yacht is not much larger than it is."

Provided that the notion of modality *de re*, and thus of quantifying into modal contexts, makes any sense at all, we have quite an adequate solution to the p.oblem of avoiding paradoxes if we substitute descriptions for the universal quantifiers in (4) because the only consequence we will draw,[4] for example, in the bifocals case, is that there is a man who both happened to have invented bifocals and happened to have been the first Postmaster General of the United States, and is necessarily self-identical. There is an object x such that x invented bifocals, and as a matter of contingent fact an object y, such that y is the first Postmaster General of the United States, and finally, it is necessary, that x is y. What are x and y here? Here, x and y are both Benjamin Franklin, and it can certainly be necessary that Benjamin Franklin is identical with himself. So, there is no problem in the case of descriptions if we accept Russell's notion of scope.[5] And I just dogmatically

---

[4] In Russell's theory, $F(\imath x G x)$ follows from $(x)Fx$ and $(\exists!x)Gx$, provided that the description in $F(\imath x G x)$ has the entire context for its scope (in Russell's 1905 terminology, has a 'primary occurrence'). Only then is $F(\imath x G x)$ 'about' the denotation of '$\imath x G x$'. Applying this rule to (14), we get the results indicated in the text. Notice that, in the ambiguous form $\Box(\imath x G x = \imath x H x)$, if one or both of the descriptions have 'primary occurrences' the formula does not assert the necessity of $\imath x G x = \imath x H x$; if both have secondary occurrences, it does. Thus in a language without explicit scope indicators, descriptions must be construed with the smallest possible scope — only then will $\sim A$ be the negation of A, $\Box A$ the necessitation of A, and the like.

[5] An earlier distinction with the same purpose was, of course, the medieval one of *de dicto–de re*. That Russell's distinction of scope eliminates modal paradoxes has been pointed out by many logicians, especially by Smullyan.

So as to avoid misunderstanding, let me emphasize that I am of course not asserting that Russell's notion of scope solves Quine's problem of 'essentialism'; what it does show, especially in conjunction with modern model-theoretic approaches to modal logic, is that quantified modal logic need not deny the truth of all instances of $(x)(y)(x = y \cdot \supset \cdot Fx \supset Fy)$, nor of all instances of '$(x)(Gx \supset Ga)$' (where 'a' is to be replaced by a nonvacuous definite description whose scope is all of 'Ga'), in order to avoid

want to drop that question here and go on to the question about names which Wiggins raises. And Wiggins says he might accept the result and plead that, provided a and b are proper names, nothing is amiss. And then he rejects this.

Now what is the special problem about proper names? At least if one is not familiar with the philosophical literature about this matter, one naively feels something like the following about proper names. First, if someone says "Cicero was an orator," then he uses the name 'Cicero' in that statement simply to pick out a certain object and then to ascribe a certain property to the object, namely, in this case, he ascribes to a certain man the property of having been an orator. If someone else uses another name, such as say 'Tully', he is still speaking about the same man. One ascribes the same property, if one says "Tully is an orator," to the same man. So to speak, the fact, or state of affairs, represented by the statement is the same whether one says "Cicero is an orator" or one says "Tully is an orator." It would, therefore, seem that the function of names is *simply* to refer, and not to describe the objects so named by such properties as "being the inventor of bifocals" or "being the first Postmaster General." It would seem that Leibniz' law and the law (1) should not only hold in the universally quantified form, but also in the form "if $a = b$ and Fa, then Fb," wherever 'a' and 'b' stand in place of names and 'F' stands in place of a predicate expressing a genuine property of the object:

$$(a = b \cdot Fa) \supset Fb$$

We can run the same argument through again to obtain the conclusion where 'a' and 'b' replace any names, "if $a = b$, then necessarily $a = b$." And so, we could venture this conclusion: that whenever 'a' and 'b' are proper names, if a is b, that it is necessary that a is b. Identity statements between proper names have to be necessary if they are going to be true at all. This view in fact has been advocated, for ex-

making it a necessary truth that one and the same man invented bifocals and headed the original Postal Department. Russell's contextual definition of descriptions need not be adopted in order to ensure these results; but other logical theories, Fregean or other, which take descriptions as primitive must somehow express the same logical facts. Frege showed that a simple, non-iterated context containing a definite description with small scope, which cannot be interpreted as being 'about' the denotation of the description, can be interpreted as about its 'sense'. Some logicians have been interested in the question of the conditions under which, in an intensional context, a description with small scope is equivalent to the same one with large scope. One of the virtues of a Russellian treatment of descriptions in modal logic is that the answer (roughly that the description be a 'rigid designator' in the sense of this lecture) then often follows from the other postulates for quantified modal logic; no special postulates are needed, as in Hintikka's treatment. Even if descriptions are taken as primitive, special postulation of when scope is irrelevant can often be deduced from more basic axioms.

ample, by Ruth Barcan Marcus in a paper of hers on the philosophical interpretation of modal logic.[6] According to this view, whenever, for example, someone makes a correct statement of identity between two names, such as, for example, that Cicero is Tully, his statement has to be necessary if it is true. But such a conclusion *seems* plainly to be false. (I, like other philosophers, have a habit of understatement in which "it seems plainly false" means "it is plainly false." Actually, I think the view is true, though not quite in the form defended by Mrs. Marcus.) At any rate, it seems plainly false. One example was given by Professor Quine in his reply to Professor Marcus at the symposium: "I think I see trouble anyway in the contrast between proper names and descriptions as Professor Marcus draws it. The paradigm of the assigning of proper names is tagging. We may tag the planet Venus some fine evening with the proper name 'Hesperus'. We may tag the same planet again someday before sun rise with the proper name 'Phosphorus'." (Quine thinks that something like that actually was done once.) "When, at last, we discover that we have tagged the same planet twice, our discovery is empirical, and not because the proper names were descriptions." According to what we are told, the planet Venus seen in the morning was originally thought to be a star and was called "the Morning Star," or (to get rid of any question of using a description) was called 'Phosphorus'. One and the same planet, when seen in the evening, was thought to be another star, the Evening Star, and was called "Hesperus." Later on, astronomers discovered that Phosphorus and Hesperus were one and the same. Surely no amount of a priori ratiocination on their part could conceivably have made it possible for them to deduce that Phosphorus is Hesperus. In fact, given the information they had, it might have turned out the other way. Therefore, it is argued, the statement 'Hesperus is Phosphorus' has to be an ordinary contingent, empirical truth, one which might have come out otherwise, and so the view that true identity statements between names are necessary has to be false. Another example which Quine gives in *Word and Object* is taken from Professor Schrödinger, the famous pioneer of quantum mechanics: A certain mountain can be seen from both Tibet and Nepal. When seen from one direction it was called 'Gaurisanker'; when seen from another direction, it was called 'Everest'; and then, later on, the empirical discovery was made that Gaurisanker *is* Everest. (Quine further says that he gathers the example is actually geographically incorrect. I guess one should not rely on physicists for geographical information.)

6 "Modalities and Intensional Languages," *Boston Studies in the Philosophy of Science*, Vol. 1, Humanities Press, New York, 1963, pp. 71 ff. See also the "Comments" by Quine and the ensuing discussion.

Of course, one possible reaction to this argument is to deny that names like 'Cicero', 'Tully', 'Gaurisanker', and 'Everest' really are proper names. "Look," someone might say (someone has said it: his name was 'Bertrand Russell'), "just because statements like "Hesperus is Phosphorus" and "Gaurisanker is Everest" are contingent, we can see that the names in question are not really purely referential. You are not, in Mrs. Marcus' phrase, just 'tagging' an object; you are actually describing it. What does the contingent fact that Hesperus is Phosphorus amount to? Well, it amounts to the fact that *the* star in a certain portion of the sky in the evening is *the* star in a certain portion of the sky in the morning. Similarly, the contingent fact that Gaurisanker is Everest amounts to the fact that the mountain viewed from such and such an angle in Nepal is the mountain viewed from such and such another angle in Tibet. Therefore, such names as 'Hesperus' and 'Phosphorus' can only be abbreviations for descriptions. The term 'Phosphorus' *has* to mean "the star seen . . . ," or (let us be cautious because it actually turned out not to be a star), "the *heavenly body* seen from such and such a position at such and such a time in the morning," and the name 'Hesperus' has to mean "the heavenly body seen in such and such a position at such and such a time in the evening." So, Russell concludes, if we want to reserve the term "name" for things which really just name an object without describing it, the only real proper names we can have are names of our own immediate sense data, objects of our own 'immediate acquaintance'. The only such names which occur in language are demonstratives like "this" and "that." And it is easy to see that this requirement of necessity of identity, understood as exempting identities between names from all imaginable doubt, can indeed be guaranteed only for demonstrative names of immediate sense data; for only in such cases can an identity statement between two different names have a general immunity from Cartesian doubt. There are some other things Russell has sometimes allowed as objects of acquaintance, such as one's self; we need not go into details here. Other philosophers (for example, Mrs. Marcus in her reply, at least in the verbal discussion as I remember it—I do not know if this got into print, so perhaps this should not be 'tagged' on her [7]) have said, "If names are really just tags, genuine tags, then a good dictionary should be able to tell us that they are names of the same object." You have an object *a* and an object *b* with names 'John' and 'Joe'. Then, according to Mrs. Marcus, a dictionary should be able to tell you whether or not 'John' and 'Joe' are names of the same object. Of course, I do not know what ideal dictionaries should do, but ordinary

[7] It should. See her remark on p. 115, *op. cit.,* in the discussion following the papers.

proper names do not seem to satisfy this requirement. You certainly *can*, in the case of ordinary proper names, make quite empirical discoveries that, let's say, Hesperus is Phosphorus, though we thought otherwise. We can be in doubt as to whether Gaurisanker is Everest or Cicero is in fact Tully. Even now, we could conceivably discover that we were wrong in supposing that Hesperus was Phosphorus. Maybe the astronomers made an error. So it seems that this view is wrong and that if by a name we do not mean some artificial notion of names such as Russell's, but a proper name in the ordinary sense, then there can be contingent identity statements using proper names, and the view to the contrary seems plainly wrong.

In recent philosophy a large number of other identity statements have been emphasized as examples of contingent identity statements, different, perhaps, from either of the types I have mentioned before. One of them is, for example, the statement "Heat is the motion of molecules." First, science is supposed to have discovered this. Empirical scientists in their investigations have been supposed to discover (and, I suppose, they did) that the external phenomenon which we call "heat" is, in fact, molecular agitation. Another example of such a discovery is that water is H_2O, and yet other examples are that gold is the element with such and such an atomic number, that light is a stream of photons, and so on. These are all in some sense of "identity statement" identity statements. Second, it is thought, they are plainly contingent identity statements, just because they were scientific discoveries. After all, heat might have turned out not to have been the motion of molecules. There were other alternative theories of heat proposed, for example, the caloric theory of heat. If these theories of heat had been correct, then heat would not have been the motion of molecules, but instead, some substance suffusing the hot object, called "caloric." And it was a matter of course of science and not of any logical necessity that the one theory turned out to be correct and the other theory turned out to be incorrect.

So, here again, we have, apparently, another plain example of a contingent identity statement. This has been supposed to be a very important example because of its connection with the mind-body problem. There have been many philosophers who have wanted to be materialists, and to be materialists in a particular form, which is known today as "the identity theory." According to this theory, a certain mental state, such as a person's being in pain, is identical with a certain state of his brain (or, perhaps, of his entire body, according to some theorists), at any rate, a certain material or neural state of his brain or body. And so, according to this theory, my being in pain at this instant, if I were, would be identical with my body's being or my brain's being in a certain state. Others have objected that this cannot be because, after all, we can imagine my pain existing even if the state of the body did not. We can perhaps imagine my not being embodied at all and still being in pain, or, conversely, we could imagine my body existing and being in the very same state even if there were no pain. In fact, conceivably, it could be in this state even though there were no mind 'back of it', so to speak, at all. The usual reply has been to concede that all of these things might have been the case, but to argue that these are irrelevant to the question of the identity of the mental state and the physical state. This identity, it is said, is just another contingent scientific identification, similar to the identification of heat with molecular motion, or water with H_2O. Just as we can imagine heat without any molecular motion, so we can imagine a mental state without any corresponding brain state. But, just as the first fact is not damaging to the identification of heat and the motion of molecules, so the second fact is not at all damaging to the identification of a mental state with the corresponding brain state. And so, many recent philosophers have held it to be very important for our theoretical understanding of the mind-body problem that there can be contingent identity statements of this form.

To state finally what *I* think, as opposed to what seems to be the case, or what others think, I think that in both cases, the case of names and the case of the theoretical identifications, the identity statements are necessary and not contingent. That is to say, they are necessary if *true;* of course, false identity statements are not necessary. How can one possibly defend such a view? Perhaps I lack a complete answer to this question, even though I am convinced that the view is true. But to begin an answer, let me make some distinctions that I want to use. The first is between a *rigid* and a *nonrigid designator*. What do these terms mean? As an example of a nonrigid designator, I can give an expression such as 'the inventor of bifocals'. Let us suppose it was Benjamin Franklin who invented bifocals, and so the expression, 'the inventor of bifocals', designates or refers to a certain man, namely, Benjamin Franklin. However, we can easily imagine that the world could have been different, that under different circumstances someone else would have come upon this invention before Benjamin Franklin did, and in that case, *he* would have been the inventor of bifocals. So, in this sense, the expression 'the inventor of bifocals' is nonrigid: Under certain circumstances one man would have been the inventor of bifocals; under other circumstances, another man would have. In contrast, consider the expression 'the square root of 25'. Independently of the empirical facts, we can give an arithmetical proof that the square root

of 25 is in fact the number 5, and because we have proved this mathe-
matically, what we have proved is necessary. If we think of numbers as
entities at all, and let us suppose, at least for the purpose of this lecture,
that we do, then the expression 'the square root of 25' necessarily
designates a certain number, namely 5. Such an expression I call 'a
rigid designator'. Some philosophers think that anyone who even uses
the notions of rigid or nonrigid designator has already shown that he
has fallen into a certain confusion or has not paid attention to certain
facts. What do I mean by 'rigid designator'? I mean a term that designates the same object in all possible worlds. To get rid of one confusion which certainly is not mine, I do not use "might have designated
a different object" to refer to the fact that language might have been
used differently. For example, the expression 'the inventor of bifocals'
might have been used by inhabitants of this planet always to refer to
the man who corrupted Hadleyburg. This would have been the case,
if, first, the people on this planet had not spoken English, but some
other language, which phonetically overlapped with English; and if,
second, in that language the expression 'the inventor of bifocals' meant
the 'man who corrupted Hadleyburg'. Then it would refer, of course,
in their language, to whoever in fact corrupted Hadleyburg in this
counterfactual situation. That is not what I mean. What I mean by saying that a description might have referred to something different, I
mean that in *our* language as *we* use it in describing a counterfactual
situation, there might have been a different object satisfying the descriptive conditions *we* give for reference. So, for example, we use the
phrase 'the inventor of bifocals', when we are talking about another
possible world or a counterfactual situation, to refer to whoever in that
counterfactual situation would have invented bifocals, not to the person whom people *in* that counterfactual situation would have called
the inventor of bifocals'. *They* might have spoken a different language
which phonetically overlapped with English in which 'the inventor of
bifocals' is used in some other way. I am *not* concerned with that question here. For that matter, they might have been deaf and dumb, or
there might have been no people at all. (There still could have been an
inventor of bifocals even if there were no people—God, or Satan, will
do.)

   Second, in talking about the notion of a rigid designator, I do not
mean to imply that the object referred to has to exist in all possible
worlds, that is, that it has to necessarily exist. Some things, perhaps
mathematical entities such as the positive integers, if they exist at all,
necessarily exist. Some people have held that God both exists and
necessarily exists; others, that He contingently exists; others, that He

contingently fails to exist; and others, that He necessarily fails to exist: [8] all four options have been tried. But at any rate, when I use the notion of rigid designator, I do not imply that the object referred to necessarily exists. All I mean is that in any possible world where the object in question *does* exist, in any situation where the object *would* exist, we use the designator in question to designate that object. In a situation where the object does not exist, then we should say that the designator has no referent and that the object in question so designated does not exist.

As I said, many philosophers would find the very notion of rigid designator objectionable per se. And the objection that people make may be stated as follows: Look, you're talking about situations which are counterfactual, that is to say, you're talking about other possible worlds. Now these worlds are completely disjoint, after all, from the actual world which is not just another possible world; it is the actual world. So, before you talk about, let us say, such an object as Richard Nixon in another possible world at all, you have to say which object in this other possible world would *be* Richard Nixon. Let us talk about a situation in which, as *you* would say, Richard Nixon would have been a member of SDS. Certainly the member of SDS you are talking about is someone very different in many of his properties from Nixon. Before we even can say whether this man would have been Richard Nixon or not, we have to set up criteria of identity across possible worlds. Here are these other possible worlds. There are all kinds of objects in them with different properties from those of any actual object. Some of them resemble Nixon in some ways, some of them resemble Nixon in other ways. Well, which of these objects is Nixon? One has to give a criterion of identity. And this shows how the very notion of rigid designator runs in a circle. Suppose we designate a certain number as the number of planets. Then, if that is our favorite way, so to speak, of designating this number, then in any other possible worlds we will have to identify whatever number is the number of planets with the number 9, which in the actual world is the number of planets. So, it is argued by various philosophers, for example, implicitly by Quine, and explicitly by many others in his wake, we cannot really ask whether a designator is rigid or nonrigid because we first need a criterion of identity across possible worlds. An extreme view has even been held that, since possible worlds are so disjoint from our own, we cannot really say that any object in them is the *same* as an object existing now but only that there

[8] If there is no deity, and especially if the nonexistence of a deity is *necessary*, it is dubious that we can use "He" to refer to a deity. The use in the text must be taken to be non-literal.

are some objects which resemble things in the actual world, more or less. We, therefore, should not really speak of what would have been true of Nixon in another possible world but, only of what 'counterparts' (the term which David Lewis uses [9]) of Nixon there would have been. Some people in other possible worlds have dogs whom they call 'Checkers'. Others favor the ABM but do not have any dog called Checkers. There are various people who resemble Nixon more or less, but none of them can really be said to be Nixon; they are only *counterparts* of Nixon, and you choose which one is the best counterpart by noting which resembles Nixon the most closely, according to your favorite criteria. Such views are widespread, both among the defenders of quantified modal logic and among its detractors.

All of this talk seems to me to have taken the metaphor of possible worlds much too seriously in some way. It is as if a 'possible world' were like a foreign country, or distant planet way out there. It is as if we see dimly through a telescope various actors on this distant planet. Actually David Lewis' view seems the most reasonable if one takes this picture literally. No one far away on another planet can be strictly identical with someone here. But, even if we have some marvelous methods of transportation to take one and the same person from planet to planet, we really need some epistemological criteria of identity to be able to say whether someone on this distant planet is the same person as someone here.

All of this seems to me to be a totally misguided way of looking at things. What it amounts to is the view that counterfactual situations have to be described purely qualitatively. So, we cannot say, for example, "If Nixon had only given a sufficient bribe to Senator X, he would have gotten Carswell through" because that refers to certain people, Nixon and Carswell, and talks about what things would be true of them in a counterfactual situation. We must say instead "If a man who has a hairline like such and such, and holds such and such political opinions had given a bribe to a man who was a senator and had such and such other qualities, then a man who was a judge in the South and had many other qualities resembling Carswell would have been confirmed." In other words, we must describe counterfactual situations purely qualitatively and then ask the question, "Given that the situation contains people or things with such and such qualities, which of these people is (or is a counterpart of) Nixon, which is Carswell, and so on?" This seems to me to be wrong. Who is to prevent us from saying

[9] David K. Lewis, "Counterpart Theory and Quantified Modal Logic," *Journal of Philosophy* 65 (1968), pp. 113 ff.

"Nixon might have gotten Carswell through had he done certain things"? We are speaking of *Nixon* and asking what, in certain counterfactual situations, would have been true of *him*. We can say that if Nixon had done such and such, he would have lost the election to Humphrey. Those I am opposing would argue, "Yes, but how do you find out if the man you are talking about is in fact Nixon?" It would indeed be very hard to find out, if you were looking at the whole situation through a telescope, but that is not what we are doing here. Possible worlds are not something to which an epistemological question like this applies. And if the phrase 'possible worlds' is what makes anyone think some such question applies, he should just *drop* this phrase and use some other expression, say "counterfactual situation," which might be less misleading. If we say "If Nixon had bribed such and such a Senator, Nixon would have gotten Carswell through," what is *given* in the very description of that situation is that it is a situation in which we are speaking of Nixon, and of Carswell, and of such and such a Senator. And there seems to be no less objection to *stipulating* that we are speaking of certain *people* than there can be objection to stipulating that we are speaking of certain *qualities*. Advocates of the other view take speaking of certain qualities as unobjectionable. They do not say, "How do we know that this quality (in another possible world) is that of redness?" But they do find speaking of certain *people* objectionable. But I see no more reason to object in the one case than in the other. I think it really comes from the idea of possible worlds as existing out there, but very far off, viewable only through a special telescope. Even more objectionable is the view of David Lewis. According to Lewis, when we say "Under certain circumstances Nixon would have gotten Carswell through," we really mean "Some man, other than Nixon but closely resembling him, would have gotten some judge, other than Carswell but closely resembling him, through." Maybe that is so, that some man closely resembling Nixon could have gotten some man closely resembling Carswell through. But *that* would not comfort either Nixon or Carswell, nor would it make Nixon kick himself and say "*I* should have done such and such to get Carswell through." The question is whether under certain circumstances Nixon *himself* could have gotten *Carswell* through. And I think the objection is simply based on a misguided picture.

Instead, we can perfectly well talk about rigid and nonrigid designators. Moreover, we have a simple, intuitive test for them. We can say, for example, that the number of planets might have been a different number from the number it in fact is. For example, there might have been only seven planets. We can say that the inventor of bifocals might have been someone other than the man who *in fact* invented bifocals.[10] We cannot say, though, that the square root of 81 might have been a different number from the number it in fact is, for that number just has to be 9. If we apply this intuitive test to proper names, such as for example 'Richard Nixon', they would seem intuitively to come out to be rigid designators. First, when we talk even about the counter-factual situation in which we suppose Nixon to have done different things, we assume we are still talking about Nixon himself. We say, "If Nixon had bribed a certain Senator, he would have gotten Carswell through," and we assume that by 'Nixon' and 'Carswell' we are still referring to the very same people as in the actual world. And it seems that we cannot say "Nixon might have been a different man from the man he in fact was," unless, of course, we mean it metaphorically: He might have been a different *sort* of person (if you believe in free will and that people are not inherently corrupt). You might think the state-ment true in that sense, but Nixon could not have been in the other literal sense a different person from the person he, in fact, is, even though the thirty-seventh President of the United States might have been Humphrey. So the phrase "the thirty-seventh President" is non-rigid, but 'Nixon', it would seem, is rigid.

Let me make another distinction before I go back to the question of identity statements. This distinction is very fundamental and also hard to see through. In recent discussion, many philosophers who have debated the meaningfulness of various categories of truths, have re-garded them as identical. Some of those who identify them are vocif-erous defenders of them, and others, such as Quine, say they are all identically meaningless. But usually they're not distinguished. These are categories such as 'analytic', 'necessary', 'a priori', and sometimes

---

[10] Some philosophers think that definite descriptions, in English, are ambiguous, that sometimes 'the inventor of bifocals' rigidly designates the man who in fact invented bifocals. I am tentatively inclined to reject this view, construed as a thesis about Eng-glish (as opposed to a possible hypothetical language), but I will not argue the question here.

What I do wish to note is that, contrary to some opinions, this alleged ambiguity cannot replace the Russellian notion of the scope of a description. Consider the sen-tence, "The number of planets might have been necessarily even." This sentence plainly can be read so as to express a truth; had there been eight planets, the number of planets would have been necessarily even. Yet without scope distinctions, both a 'ref-erential' (rigid) and a non-rigid reading of the description will make the statement false. (Since the number of planets is nine, the rigid reading amounts to the falsity that nine might have been necessarily even.)

The 'rigid' reading is equivalent to the Russellian primary occurrence; the non-rigid, to innermost scope—some, following Donnellan, perhaps loosely, have called this reading the 'attributive' use. The possibility of intermediate scopes is then ignored. In the present instance, the intended reading of $\Diamond\Box$ (the number of planets is even) makes the scope of the description $\Box$ (the number of planets is even), neither the largest nor the smallest possible.

even 'certain'. I will not talk about all of these but only about the notions of a prioricity and necessity. Very often these are held to be synonyms. (Many philosophers probably should not be described as holding them to be synonyms; they simply *use* them interchangeably.) I wish to distinguish them. What do we mean by calling a statement *necessary?* We simply mean that the statement in question, first, is true, and, second, that it could not have been otherwise. When we say that something is *contingently* true, we mean that, though it is in fact the case, it could have been the case that things would have been otherwise. If we wish to assign this distinction to a branch of philosophy, we should assign it to metaphysics. To the contrary, there is the notion of an *a priori truth*. An a priori truth is supposed to be one which can be *known* to be true independently of all experience. Notice that this does not in and of itself say anything about all possible worlds, unless this is put into the definition. All that it says is that it can be known to be true of the actual world, independently of all experience. It may, by some philosophical argument, follow from our knowing, independently of experience, that something is true of the actual world, that it has to be known to be true also of all possible worlds. But if this is to be established, it requires some philosophical argument to establish it. Now, *this* notion, if we were to assign it to a branch of philosophy, belongs, not to metaphysics, but to epistemology. It has to do with the way we can know certain things to be in fact true. Now, it may be the case, of course, that anything which is necessary is something which *can* be known a priori. (Notice, by the way, the notion a priori truth as thus defined has in it *another* modality: it *can* be known independently of all experience. It is a little complicated because there is a double modality here.) I will not have time to explore these notions in full detail here, but one thing we can see from the outset is that these two notions are by no means trivially the same. If they are coextensive, it takes some philosophical argument to establish it. As stated, they belong to different domains of philosophy. One of them has something to do with *knowledge,* of what can be known in certain ways about the *actual* world. The other one has to do with *metaphysics,* how the world *could* have been; given that it is the way it is, could it have been otherwise, in certain ways? Now I hold, as a matter of fact, that neither class of statements is contained in the other. But, all we need to talk about here is this: Is everything that is necessary knowable a priori or known a priori? Consider the following example: the Goldbach conjecture. This says that every even number is the sum of two primes. It is a mathematical statement and if it is true at all, it has to be necessary. Certainly, one could not say that though in fact every even number is the sum of two primes, there could have been some extra number which was even and not the sum of two primes. What would that mean? On the other hand, the answer to the question whether every even number *is* in fact the sum of two primes is unknown, and we have no method at present for deciding. So we certainly do not know, a priori or even a posteriori, that every even number is the sum of two primes. (Well, perhaps we have some evidence in that no counterexample has been found.) But we certainly do not know a priori anyway, that every even number is, in fact, the sum of two primes. But, of course, the definition just says "*can* be known independently of experience," and someone might say that if it is true, we *could* know it independently of experience. It is hard to see exactly what this claim means. It might be so. One thing it might mean is that if it were true we could *prove* it. This claim is certainly wrong if it is generally applied to mathematical statements and we have to work within some fixed system. This is what Godel proved. And even if we mean an 'intuitive proof in general' it might just be the case (at least, this view is as clear and as probable as the contrary) that though the statement is true, there is just no way the human mind could ever prove it. Of course, one way an *infinite* mind might be able to prove it is by looking through each natural number one by one and checking. In this sense, of course, it can, perhaps, be known a priori, but only by an infinite mind, and then this gets into other complicated questions. I do not want to discuss questions about the conceivability of performing an infinite number of acts like looking through each number one by one. A vast philosophical literature has been written on this: Some have declared it is logically impossible; others that it is logically possible; and some do not know. The main point is that it is not trivial that just because such a statement is necessary it can be known a priori. Some considerable clarification is required before we decide that it can be so known. And so this shows that even if everything necessary is a priori in some sense, it should not be taken as a trivial matter of definition. It is a substantive philosophical thesis which requires some work.

Another example that one might give relates to the problem of essentialism. Here is a lectern. A question which has often been raised in philosophy is: What are its essential properties? What properties, aside from trivial ones like self-identity, are such that this object has to have them if it exists at all,[11] are such that if an object did not have it,

---

[11] This definition is the usual formulation of the notion of essential property, but an exception must be made for existence itself; on the definition given, existence would be trivially essential. We should regard existence as essential to an object only if the object necessarily exists. Perhaps there are other recherché properties, involving existence, for which the definition is similarly objectionable. (I thank Michael Slote for this observation.)

it would not be this object? [12] For example, being made of wood, and not of ice, might be an essential property of this lectern. Let us just take the weaker statement that it is not made of ice. That will establish it as strongly as we need it, perhaps as dramatically. Supposing this lectern is in fact made of wood, could this very lectern have been made from the very beginning of its existence from ice, say frozen from water in the Thames? One has a considerable feeling that it could *not*, though in fact one certainly could have made a lectern of water from the Thames, frozen it into ice by some process, and put it right there in place of this thing. If one had done so, one would have made, of course, a *different* object. It would not have been *this very lectern*, and so one would not have a case in which this very lectern here was made of ice, or was made from water from the Thames. The question of whether it could afterward, say in a minute from now, turn into ice is something else. So, it would seem, if an example like this is correct — and this is what advocates of essentialism have held — that this lectern could not have been made of ice, that is in any counterfactual situation of which we would say that this lectern existed at all, we would have to say also that it was not made from water from the Thames frozen into ice. Some have rejected, of course, any such notion of essential property as meaningless. Usually, it is because (and I think this is what Quine, for example, would say) they have held that it depends on the notion of identity across possible worlds, and that this is itself meaningless. Since I have rejected this view already, I will not deal with it again. We can talk about *this very object*, and whether it could have had certain properties which it does not in fact have. For example, it could have been in another room from the room it in fact is in, even at this very time, but it could not have been made from the very beginning from water frozen into ice.

If the essentialist view is correct, it can only be correct if we sharply distinguish between the notions of a posteriori and a priori truth on the one hand, and contingent and necessary truth on the

---

[12] The two clauses of the sentence footnoted give equivalent definitions of the notion of essential property, since $\Box((\exists x)\,(x = a) \supset Fa)$ is equivalent to $\Box(x)\,({\sim}\,Fx \supset x \neq a)$. The second formulation, however, has served as a powerful seducer in favor of theories of 'identification across possible worlds'. For it suggests that we consider 'an object *b* in another possible world' and test whether it is identifiable with *a* by asking whether it lacks any of the essential properties of *a*. Let me therefore emphasize that, although an essential property is (trivially) a property without which an object cannot be *a*, it by no means follows that the essential, purely qualitative properties of *a* jointly form a sufficient condition for being *a*, nor that *any* purely qualitative conditions are sufficient for an object to be *a*. Further, even if necessary and sufficient qualitative conditions for an object to be Nixon may exist, there would still be little justification for the demand for a purely qualitative description of all counterfactual situations. We can ask whether Nixon might have been a Democrat without engaging in these subtleties.

other hand, for although the statement that this table, if it exists at all, was not made of ice, is necessary, it certainly is not something that we know a priori. What we know is that first, lecterns usually are not made of ice, they are usually made of wood. This looks like wood. It does not feel cold and it probably would if it were made of ice. Therefore, I conclude, probably this is not made of ice. Here my entire judgment is a posteriori. I could find out that an ingenious trick has been played upon me and that, in fact, this lectern is made of ice; but what I am saying is, given that it is in fact not made of ice, in fact is made of wood, one cannot imagine that under certain circumstances it could have been made of ice. So we have to say that though we cannot know a priori whether this table was made of ice or not, given that it is not made of ice, it is *necessarily* not made of ice. In other words, if P is the statement that the lectern is not made of ice, one knows by a priori philosophical analysis, some conditional of the form "if P, then necessarily P." If the table is not made of ice, it is necessarily not made of ice. On the other hand, then, we know by empirical investigation that P, the antecedent of the conditional, is true — that this table is not made of ice. We can conclude by *modus ponens:*

$$P \supset \Box P$$
$$\frac{P}{\Box P}$$

The conclusion — '$\Box P$' — is that it is necessary that the table not be made of ice, and this conclusion is known a posteriori, since one of the premises on which it is based is a posteriori. So, the notion of essential properties can be maintained only by distinguishing between the notions of a priori and necessary truth, and I do maintain it.

Let us return to the question of identities. Concerning the statement 'Hesperus is Phosphorus' or the statement 'Cicero is Tully', one can find all of these out by empirical investigation, and we might turn out to be wrong in our empirical beliefs. So, it is usually argued, such statements must therefore be contingent. Some have embraced the other side of the coin and have held "Because of this argument about necessity, identity statements between names have to be knowable a priori, so, only a very special category of names, possibly, really works as names; the other things are bogus names, disguised descriptions, or something of the sort. However, a certain very narrow class of statements of identity are known a priori, and these are the ones which contain the genuine names." If one accepts the distinctions that I have made, one need not jump to either conclusion. One can hold that certain statements of identity between names, though often known a posteriori, and maybe not knowable a priori, are in fact necessary, if true. So, we have some room to hold this. But, of course, to have some room to hold it does not mean that we should hold it. So let us see what the evidence is. First, recall the remark that I made that proper names seem to be rigid designators, as when we use the name 'Nixon' to talk about a certain man, even in counterfactual situations. If we say, "If Nixon had not written the letter to Saxbe, maybe he would have gotten Carswell through," we are in this statement talking about Nixon, Saxbe, and Carswell, the very same men as in the actual world, and what would have happened to them under certain counterfactual circumstances. If names are rigid designators, then there can be no question about identities being necessary, because 'a' and 'b' will be rigid designators of a certain man or thing x. Then even in every possible world, a and b will both refer to this same object x, and to no other, and so there will be no situation in which a might not have been b. That would have to be a situation in which the object which we are also now calling 'x' would not have been identical with itself. Then one could not possibly have a situation in which Cicero would not have been Tully or Hesperus would not have been Phosphorus.[13]

Aside from the identification of necessity with a priority, what has made people feel the other way? There are two things which have made people feel the other way.[14] Some people tend to regard identity statements as metalinguistic statements, to identify the statement "Hesperus is Phosphorus" with the metalinguistic statement, " 'Hesperus' and 'Phosphorus' are names of the same heavenly body." And that, of course, might have been false. We might have used the terms 'Hesperus' and 'Phosphorus' as names of *two* different heavenly bodies. But, of course, this has nothing to do with the necessity of identity. In the same sense "2 + 2 = 4" might have been false. The phrases

[13] I thus agree with Quine, that "Hesperus is Phosphorus" is (or can be) an empirical discovery; with Marcus, that it is necessary. Both Quine and Marcus, according to the present standpoint, err in identifying the epistemological and the metaphysical issues.

[14] The two confusions alleged, especially the second, are both related to the confusion of the metaphysical question of the necessity of "Hesperus is Phosphorus" with the epistemological question of its a prioricity. For if Hesperus is identified by its position in the sky in the evening, and Phosphorus by its position in the morning, an investigator may well know, in advance of empirical research, that Hesperus is Phosphorus if and only if one and the same body occupies position x in the evening and position y in the morning. The a priori material equivalence of the two statements, however, does not imply their strict (necessary) equivalence. (The same remarks apply to the case of heat and molecular motion below.) Similar remarks apply to some extent to the relationship between "Hesperus is Phosphorus" and " 'Hesperus' and 'Phosphorus' name the same thing." A confusion that also operates is, of course, the confusion between what *we* would say of a counterfactual situation and how people *in* that situation would have described it; this confusion, too, is probably related to the confusion between a prioricity and necessity.

"2 + 2" and "4" might have been used to refer to two different numbers. One can imagine a language, for example, in which "+", "2", and "=" were used in the standard way, but "4" was used as the name of, say, the square root of minus 1, as we should call it, "*i*." Then "2 + 2 = 4" would be false, for 2 plus 2 is not equal to the square root of minus 1. But this is not what we want. We do not want just to say that a certain statement which we in fact use to express something true could have expressed something false. We want to use the statement in *our* way and see if it could have been false. Let us do this. What is the idea people have? They say, "Look, Hesperus might not have been Phosphorus. Here a certain planet was seen in the morning, and it was seen in the evening; and it just turned out later on as a matter of empirical fact that they were one and the same planet. If things had turned out otherwise, they would have been two different planets, or two different heavenly bodies, so how can you say that such a statement is necessary?"

Now there are two things that such people can mean. First, they can mean that we do not know a priori whether Hesperus is Phosphorus. This I have already conceded. Second, they may mean that they can actually imagine circumstances that they would call circumstances in which Hesperus would not have been Phosphorus. Let us think what would be such a circumstance, using these terms here as *names* of a planet. For example, it could have been the case that Venus did indeed rise in the morning in exactly the position in which we saw it, but that on the other hand, in the position which is in fact occupied by Venus in the evening, Venus was not there, and Mars took its place. This is all counterfactual because in fact Venus is there. Now one can also imagine that in this counterfactual other possible world, the earth would have been inhabited by people and that they should have used the names 'Phosphorus' for Venus in the morning and 'Hesperus' for Mars in the evening. Now, this is all very good, but would it be a situation in which Hesperus was not Phosphorus? Of course, it is a situation in which people would have been able to *say,* truly, "Hesperus is not Phosphorus"; but we are supposed to describe things in our language, not in theirs. So let us describe it in our language. Well, how could it actually happen that Venus would not be in that position in the evening? For example, let us say that there is some comet that comes around every evening and yanks things over a little bit. (That would be a very simple scientific way of imagining it: not really too simple — that is very hard to imagine actually.) It just happens to come around every evening, and things get yanked over a little bit. Mars gets yanked over to the very position where Venus is, then the comet yanks things back to their normal position in the morning. Thinking of this planet which we now call 'Phosphorus', what should we say? Well, we can say that the comet passes it and yanks Phosphorus over so that it is not in the position normally occupied by Phosphorus in the evening. If we do say this, and really use 'Phosphorus' as the name of a planet, then we have to say that, under such circumstances, Phosphorus in the evening would not be in the position where we, in fact, saw it; or alternatively, Hesperus in the evening would not be in the position in which we, in fact, saw it. We might say that under such circumstances, we would not have called Hesperus 'Hesperus' because Hesperus would have been in a different position. But that still would not make Phosphorus different from Hesperus; but what would then be the case instead is that Hesperus would have been in a different position from the position it in fact is and, perhaps, not in such a position that people would have called it 'Hesperus'. But that would not be a situation in which Phosphorus would not have been Hesperus.

Let us take another example which may be clearer. Suppose someone uses 'Tully' to refer to the Roman orator who denounced Cataline and uses the name 'Cicero' to refer to the man whose works he had to study in third-year Latin in high school. Of course, he may not know in advance that the very same man who denounced Cataline wrote these works, and that is a contingent statement. But the fact that this statement is contingent should not make us think that the statement that Cicero is Tully, if it is true, and it is in fact true, is contingent. Suppose, for example, that Cicero actually did denounce Cataline, but thought that this political achievement was so great that he should not bother writing any literary works. Would we say that these would be circumstances under which he would not have been Cicero? It seems to me that the answer is no, that instead we would say that, under such circumstances, Cicero would not have written any literary works. It is not a necessary property of Cicero — the way the shadow follows the man — that he should have written certain works; we can easily imagine a situation in which Shakespeare would not have written the works of Shakespeare, or one in which Cicero would not have written the works of Cicero. What may be the case is that we *fix the reference* of the term 'Cicero' by use of some descriptive phrase, such as 'the author of these works'. But once we have this reference fixed, we then use the name 'Cicero' *rigidly* to designate the man who in fact we have identified by his authorship of these works. We do not use it to designate whoever would have written these works in place of Cicero, if someone else wrote them. It might have been the case that the man who wrote these works was not the man who denounced Cataline. Cassius might have written these works. But we would not then say that Cicero would have been Cassius, unless we were speaking in a very loose and metaphorical way. We would say that Cicero, whom we may have identified and come to know by his works, would not have written them, and that someone else, say Cassius, would have written them in his place.

Such examples are not grounds for thinking that identity statements are contingent. To take them as such grounds is to misconstrue the relation between a *name* and a *description used to fix its reference,* to take them to be *synonyms.* Even if we fix the reference of such a name as 'Cicero' as the man who wrote such and such works, in speaking of counterfactual situations, when we speak of Cicero, we do not then speak of whoever in such counterfactual situations *would* have written such and such works, but rather of Cicero, whom we have identified by the contingent property that he is the man who in fact, that is, in the actual world, wrote certain works.[15]

I hope this is reasonably clear in a brief compass. Now, actually I have been presupposing something I do not really believe to be, in general, true. Let us suppose that we do fix the reference of a name by a description. Even if we do so, we do not then make the name *synonymous* with the description, but instead we use the name *rigidly* to refer to the object so named, even in talking about counterfactual situations where the thing named would not satisfy the description in question. Now, this is what I think in fact is true for those cases of naming where the reference is fixed by description. But, in fact, I also think, contrary to most recent theorists, that the reference of names is rarely or almost never fixed by means of description. And by this I do not just mean what Searle says: "It's not a single description, but rather a cluster, a family of properties which fixes the reference." I mean that properties in this sense are not used *at all.* But I do not have the time to go into this here. So, let us suppose that at least one half of prevailing views about naming is true, that the reference is fixed by descriptions. Even were that true, the name would not be synonymous with the descrip-

---

[15] If someone protests, regarding the lectern, that it *could* after all have *turned out* to have been made of ice, and therefore could have been made of ice, I would reply that what he really means is that *a lectern* could have looked just like this one, and have been placed in the same position as this one, and yet have been made of ice. In short, I could have been in the *same epistemological situation* in relation to *a lectern made of ice* as I actually am in relation to *this* lectern. In the main text, I have argued that the same reply should be given to protests that Hesperus could have turned out to be other than Phosphorus, or Cicero other than Tully. Here, then, the notion of 'counterpart' comes into its own. For it is not this table, but an epistemic 'counterpart', which was hewn from ice; not Hesperus-Phosphorus-Venus, but two distinct counterparts thereof, in two of the roles Venus actually plays (that of Evening Star and Morning Star), which are different. Precisely because of this fact, it is not *this table* which could have been made of ice. Statements about the modal properties of *this table* never refer to counterparts. However, if someone confuses the epistemological and the metaphysical problems, he will be well on the way to the counterpart theory Lewis and others have advocated.

tion, but would be used to *name* an object which we pick out by the contingent fact that it satisfies a certain description. And so, even though we can imagine a case where the man who wrote these works would not have been the man who denounced Cataline, we should not say that that would be a case in which Cicero would not have been Tully. We should say that it is a case in which Cicero did not write these works, but rather that Cassius did. And the identity of Cicero and Tully still holds.

Let me turn to the case of heat and the motion of molecules. Here surely is a case that is contingent identity! Recent philosophy has emphasized this again and again. So, if it is a case of contingent identity, then let us imagine under what circumstances it would be false. Now, concerning this statement I hold that the circumstances philosophers apparently have in mind as circumstances under which it would have been false are not in fact such circumstances. First, of course, it is argued that "Heat is the motion of molecules" is an a posteriori judgment; scientific investigation might have turned out otherwise. As I said before, this shows nothing against the view that it is necessary – at least if I am right. But here, surely, people had very specific circumstances in mind under which, so they thought, the judgment that heat is the motion of molecules would have been false. What were these circumstances? One can distill them out of the fact that we found out empirically that heat is the motion of molecules. How was this? What did we find out first when we found out that heat is the motion of molecules? There is a certain external phenomenon which we can sense by the sense of touch, and it produces a sensation which we call "the sensation of heat." We then discover that the external phenomenon which produces this sensation, which we sense, by means of our sense of touch, is in fact that of molecular agitation in the thing that we touch, a very high degree of molecular agitation. So, it might be thought, to imagine a situation in which heat would not have been the motion of molecules, we need only imagine a situation in which we would have had the very same sensation and it would have been produced by something other than the motion of molecules. Similarly, if we wanted to imagine a situation in which light was not a stream of photons, we could imagine a situation in which we were sensitive to something else in exactly the same way, producing what we call visual experiences, though not through a stream of photons. To make the case stronger, or to look at another side of the coin, we could also consider a situation in which we *are* concerned with the motion of molecules but in which such motion does not give us the sensation of heat. And it might also have happened that we, or, at least, the creatures inhabiting this planet, might have been so constituted that, let us say, an increase in the motion of molecules did not give us this sensation but that, on the contrary, a slowing down of the molecules did give us the very same sensation. This would be a situation, so it might be thought, in which heat would not be the motion of molecules, or, more precisely, in which temperature would not be mean molecular kinetic energy.

But I think it would not be so. Let us think about the situation again. First, let us think about it in the actual world. Imagine right now the world invaded by a number of Martians, who do indeed get the very sensation that we call "the sensation of heat" when they feel some ice which has slow molecular motion, and who do not get a sensation of heat — in fact, maybe just the reverse — when they put their hand near a fire which causes a lot of molecular agitation. Would we say, "Ah, this casts some doubt on heat being the motion of molecules, because there are these other people who don't get the same sensation"? Obviously not, and no one would think so. We would say instead that the Martians somehow feel the very sensation we get when we feel heat when they feel cold and that they do not get a sensation of heat when they feel heat. But now let us think of a counterfactual situation.[16] Suppose the earth had from the very beginning been inhabited by such creatures. First, imagine it inhabited by no creatures at all: then there is no one to feel any sensations of heat. But we would not say that under such circumstances it would necessarily be the case that heat did not exist; we would say that heat might have existed, for example, if there were fires that heated up the air.

Let us suppose the laws of physics were not very different: Fires do heat up the air. Then there would have been heat even though there were no creatures around to feel it. Now let us suppose evolution takes place, and life is created, and there are some creatures around. But they are not like us, they are more like the Martians. Now would we say that heat has suddenly turned to cold, because of the way the creatures of this planet sense it? No, I think we should describe this situation as a situation in which, though the creatures on this planet got our sensation of heat, they did not get it when they were exposed to heat. They got it when they were exposed to cold. And that is something we can surely well imagine. We can imagine it just as we can imagine our planet being invaded by creatures of this sort. Think of it in two steps. First

---

[16] Isn't the situation I just described also counterfactual? At least it may well be, if such Martians never in fact invade. Strictly speaking, the distinction I wish to draw compares how we *would* speak *in* a (possibly counterfactual) situation, *if* it obtained, and how we *do* speak *of* a counterfactual situation, knowing that it does not obtain — i.e., the distinction between the language we would have used in a situation and the language we *do* use to describe it. (Consider the description: "Suppose we all spoke German." This description is in English.) The former case can be made vivid by imagining the counterfactual situation to be actual.

there is a stage where there are no creatures at all, and one can certainly imagine the planet still having both heat and cold, though no one is around to sense it. Then the planet comes through an evolutionary process to be peopled with beings of different neural structure from ourselves. Then these creatures could be such that they were insensitive to heat; they did not feel it in the way we do; but on the other hand, they felt cold in much the same way that we feel heat. But still, heat would be heat, and cold would be cold. And particularly, then, this goes in no way against saying that in this counterfactual situation heat would still *be* the molecular motion, *be* that which is produced by fires, and so on, just as it would have been if there had been no creatures on the planet at all. Similarly, we could imagine that the planet was inhabited by creatures who got visual sensations when there were sound waves in the air. We should not therefore say, "Under such circumstances, sound would have been light." Instead we should say, "The planet was inhabited by creatures who were in some sense visually sensitive to sound, and maybe even visually sensitive to light." If this is correct, it can still be and will still be a necessary truth that heat is the motion of molecules and that light is a stream of photons.

To state the view succinctly: we use both the terms 'heat' and 'the motion of molecules' as rigid designators for a certain external phenomenon. Since heat is in fact the motion of molecules, and the designators are rigid, by the argument I have given here, it is going to be *necessary* that heat is the motion of molecules. What gives us the illusion of contingency is the fact we have identified the heat by the contingent fact that there happen to be creatures on this planet — (namely, ourselves) who are sensitive to it in a certain way, that is, who are sensitive to the motion of molecules or to heat — these are one and the same thing. And this is contingent. So we use the description, 'that which causes such and such sensations, or that which we sense in such and such a way', to identify heat. But in using this fact we use a contingent property of heat, just as we use the contingent property of Cicero as having written such and such works to identify him. We then use the terms 'heat' in the one case and 'Cicero' in the other *rigidly* to designate the objects for which they stand. And of course the term 'the motion of molecules' is rigid; it always stands for the motion of molecules, never for any other phenomenon. So, as Bishop Butler said, "everything is what it is and not another thing." Therefore, "Heat is the motion of molecules" will be necessary, not contingent, and one only has the *illusion* of contingency in the way one could have the illusion of contingency in thinking that this table might have been made of ice. We might think one could imagine it, but if we try, we can see on reflection that what we are really imagining is just there being another lectern in this very position here which was in fact made of ice. The fact that we may identify this lectern by being the object we see and touch in such and such a position is something else.

Now how does this relate to the problem of mind and body? It is usually held that this is a contingent identity statement just like "Heat is the motion of molecules." That cannot be. It cannot be a contingent identity statement just like "Heat is the motion of molecules" because, if I am right, "Heat is the motion of molecules" is not a contingent identity statement. Let us look at this statement. For example, "My being in pain at such and such a time is my being in such and such a brain state at such and such a time," or, "Pain in general is such and such a neural (brain) state."

This is held to be contingent on the following grounds. First, we can imagine the brain state existing though there is no pain at all. It is only a scientific fact that whenever we are in a certain brain state we have a pain. Second, one might imagine a creature being in pain, but not being in any specified brain state at all, maybe not having a brain at all. People even think, at least prima facie, though they may be wrong, that they can imagine totally disembodied creatures, at any rate certainly not creatures with bodies anything like our own. So it seems that we can imagine definite circumstances under which this relationship would have been false. Now, if these circumstances are circumstances, notice that we cannot deal with them simply by saying that this is just an illusion, something we can apparently imagine, but in fact cannot in the way we thought erroneously that we could imagine a situation in which heat was not the motion of molecules. Because although we can say that we pick out heat contingently by the contingent property that it affects us in such and such a way, we cannot similarly say that we pick out pain contingently by the fact that it affects us in such and such a way. On such a picture there would be the brain state, and we pick it out by the contingent fact that it affects us as pain. Now that might be true of the brain state, but it cannot be true of the pain. The experience itself has to be *this experience*, and I cannot say that it is contingent property of the pain I now have that it is a pain.[17] In fact, it would seem

---

[17] The most popular identity theories advocated today explicitly fail to satisfy this simple requirement. For these theories usually hold that a mental state is a brain state, and that what makes the brain state into a mental state is its 'causal role', the fact that it tends to produce certain behavior (as intentions produce actions, or pain, pain behavior) and to be produced by certain stimuli (e.g. pain, by pinpricks). If the relations between the brain state and its causes and effects are regarded as contingent, then *being such-and-such-a-mental state* is a contingent property of the brain state. Let X be a pain. The causal-role identity theorist holds (1) that X is a brain state, (2) that the fact that X is a pain is to be analyzed (roughly) as the fact that X is produced by certain stimuli and produces certain behavior. The fact mentioned in (2) is, of course, regarded

that both the terms, 'my pain' and 'my being in such and such a brain state' are, first of all, both rigid designators. That is, whenever anything is such and such a pain, it is essentially that very object, namely, such and such a pain, and wherever anything is such and such a brain state, it is essentially that very object, namely, such and such a brain state. So both of these are rigid designators. One cannot say this pain might have been something else, some other state. These are both rigid designators.

Second, the way we would think of picking them out – namely, the pain by its being an experience of a certain sort, and the brain state by its being the state of a certain material object, being of such and such molecular configuration – both of these pick out their objects essentially and not accidentally, that is, they pick them out by essential properties. Whenever the molecules *are* in this configuration, we *do* have such and such a brain state. Whenever you feel *this*, you do have a pain. So it seems that the identity theorist is in some trouble, for, since we have two rigid designators, the identity statement in question is necessary. Because they pick out their objects essentially, we cannot say the case where you seem to imagine the identity statement false is really an illusion like the illusion one gets in the case of heat and molecular motion, because that illusion depended on the fact that we pick out heat by a certain contingent property. So there is very little room to maneuver; perhaps none.[18] The identity theorist, who holds that pain

as contingent; the brain state X might well exist and not tend to produce the appropriate behavior in the absence of other conditions. Thus (1) and (2) assert that a certain pain X might have existed, yet not have been a pain. This seems to me self-evidently absurd. Imagine any pain: is it possible that *it itself* could have existed, yet not have been a pain?

If $X = Y$, then X and Y share all properties, including modal properties. If X is a pain and Y the corresponding brain state, then *being a pain* is an essential property of X, and *being a brain state* is an essential property of Y. If the correspondence relation is, in fact, identity, then it must be *necessary* of Y that it corresponds to a pain, and *necessary* of X that it correspond to a brain state, indeed to this particular brain state, Y. Both assertions seem false; it *seems* clearly possible that X should have existed without the corresponding brain state; or that the brain state should have existed without being felt as pain. Identity theorists cannot, contrary to their almost universal present practice, accept these intuitions; they must deny them, and explain them away. This is none too easy a thing to do.

[18] A brief restatement of the argument may be helpful here. If "pain" and "C-fiber stimulation" are rigid designators of phenomena, one who identifies them must regard the identity as necessary. How can this necessity be reconciled with the apparent fact that C-fiber stimulation might have turned out not to be correlated with pain at all? We might try to reply by analogy to the case of heat and molecular motion; the latter identity, too, is necessary, yet someone may believe that, before scientific investigation showed otherwise, molecular motion might have turned out not to be heat. The reply is, of course, that what really is possible is that people (or some rational sentient beings) could have been in the *same epistemic situation* as we actually are, and identify

is the brain state, also has to hold that it necessarily is the brain state. He therefore cannot concede, but has to deny, that there would have been situations under which one would have had pain but not the corresponding brain state. Now usually in arguments on the identity theory, this is very far from being denied. In fact, it is conceded from the outset by the materialist as well as by his opponent. He says, "Of course, it *could* have been the case that we had pains without the brain states. It is a contingent identity." But that cannot be. He has to hold that we are under some illusion in thinking that we can imagine that there could have been pains without brain states. And the only model I can think of for what the illusion might be, or at least the model given by the analogy the materialists themselves suggest, namely, heat and molecular motion, simply does not work in this case. So the materialist is up against a very stiff challenge. He has to show that these things we think we can see to be possible are in fact not possible. He has to show that these things which we can imagine are not in fact things we can imagine. And that requires some very different philosophical argument from the sort which has been given in the case of heat and molecular motion. And it would have to be a deeper and subtler argument than I can fathom and subtler than has ever appeared in any materialist literature that I have read. So the conclusion of this investigation would be that the analytical tools we are using go against the identity thesis and so go against the general thesis that mental states are just physical states.[19]

a phenomenon in the same way we identify heat, namely, by feeling it by the sensation we call "the sensation of heat," without the phenomenon being molecular motion. Further, the beings might not have been sensitive to molecular motion (i.e., to heat) by any neural mechanism whatsoever. It is impossible to explain the apparent possibility of C-fiber stimulations not having been pain in the same way. Here, too, we would have to suppose that we could have been in the same epistemological situation, and identify something in the same way we identify pain, without its corresponding to C-fiber stimulation. But the way we identify pain is by feeling it, and if a C-fiber stimulation could have occurred without our feeling any pain, then the C-fiber stimulation would have occurred without there *being* any pain, contrary to the necessity of the identity. The trouble is that although 'heat' is a rigid designator, heat is picked out by the contingent property of its being felt in a certain way; pain, on the other hand, is picked out by an essential (indeed necessary and sufficient) property. For a sensation to be *felt* as pain is for it to *be* pain.

[19] All arguments against the identity theory which rely on the necessity of identity, or on the notion of essential property, are, of course, inspired by Descartes' argument for his dualism. The earlier arguments which superficially were rebutted by the analogies of heat and molecular motion, and the bifocals inventor who was also Postmaster General, had such an inspiration; and so does my argument here. R. Albritton and M. Slote have informed me that they independently have attempted to give essentialist arguments against the identity theory, and probably others have done so as well.

The simplest Cartesian argument can perhaps be restated as follows: Let 'A' be a *name* (rigid designator) of Descartes' body. Then Descartes argues that since he could exist even if A did not, $\lozenge$ (Descartes $\neq A$), hence Descartes $\neq A$. Those who have ac-

The next topic would be my own solution to the mind-body problem, but that I do not have.

cused him of a modal fallacy have forgotten that '*A*' is rigid. His argument is valid, and his conclusion is correct, provided its (perhaps dubitable) premise is accepted. On the other hand, provided that Descartes is regarded as having ceased to exist upon his death, "Descartes ≠ *A*" can be established without the use of a modal argument; for if so, no doubt *A* survived Descartes when *A* was a corpse. Thus *A* had a property (existing at a certain time) which Descartes did not. The same argument can establish that a statue is not the hunk of stone, or the congery of molecules, of which it is composed. Mere non-identity, then, may be a weak conclusion. (See D. Wiggins, *Philosophical Review*, Vol. 77 (1968), pp. 90 ff.) The Cartesian modal argument, however, surely can be deployed to maintain relevant stronger conclusions as well.

Essentialism, Self-Identity, and Quantifying In

JOHN WOODS

Department of Philosophy
Centre for Linguistic Studies
University of Toronto

1. Our contempt for metaphysical doctrines of essentialism tends to vary inversely with how well we manage to understand them. In fact, essentialism, as it is currently and fashionably conceived, is enough of a bogey man to afford a very strong-seeming attack upon quantified modal logic ($q \cdot m \cdot l \cdot$).[1] Everyone who has thought about such matters seems to agree that there is something or other wrong with $q \cdot m \cdot l \cdot$. One of the more common complaints is that $q \cdot m \cdot l \cdot$ commits one to essentialism, and that essentialism is incoherent. There is reason to think that the objection is meant to go in the other direction as well: $q \cdot m \cdot l \cdot$ is needed for the formulation of essentialism, but $q \cdot m \cdot l \cdot$ is seriously suspect especially as regards axioms for the mix (of quantifiers and modal operators); so much the worse for essentialism. Now, although there can be no gainsaying the trouble prompted by quantification into modal contexts, it is far from obvious, and quite probably untrue, that what prove to be embarrassments for quantified modal logic are of any real importance for at least one historically prominent breed of essentialism. In particular, even if $q \cdot m \cdot l \cdot$ does

---

[1] By '$q \cdot m \cdot l \cdot$' I mean any quantificational system Γ admitting theorems of the form $\lceil \mathcal{Q} \mathcal{M} \phi \rceil$, where $\mathcal{Q}$ is a quantifier $\mathcal{M}$ a modal operator and ϕ any wff of Γ. In particular, it is to be understood that ϕ may be an *open* sentence of Γ.

commit us to essentialism as characterized, say, by Quine [30, page 199], and even if, thus characterized, essentialism is incredible (as surely it is), there is no very good reason to think that what Quine calls essentialism is essentialism in fact. It is not, in any event, what I shall mean by essentialism, which I think lies closer than Quine's creation to what some philosophers have actually intended by the word. The species of the doctrine I have in mind I am tempted to attribute to Arnauld — subject, of course, to contradiction, such being the penalty for attributions to *Messieurs du Port Royal:*

> ... This is why, Monsieur, it seems to me, that I ought to regard as involved in my individual concept only what is of such a nature that I would no longer be myself if it were not in me, while, on the other hand, everything which is of such a nature that it might either happen to me or not happen to me without my ceasing to be myself, should not be considered as involved in my individual concept; ... This is my thought, which, I believe, conforms wholly to what has always been held by all the philosophers in the world (Included in [31, page 95]).

It is a thesis of this essay that certain essentialistic sentences can be formulated without the resources of $q \cdot m \cdot l \cdot$. If so, it hardly matters for the essentialist what the status of $q \cdot m \cdot l \cdot$ might be, however dubious. I mean to make an eponym out of poor Arnauld, and so shall mean by Arnauldic essentialism, *with respect to individuals,*[2] any thesis meeting the following two conditions:

Where **a** is an individual (it is named by '*a*'), $\mathscr{P}$ the set of properties possessed by **a**, $\mathscr{E} = \{g_0, g_1, g_2, \ldots\}$ a subset[3] of $\mathscr{P}$ (the g_i designated by '$G_i x$'),[4] and setting "$\mathscr{E}$ is satisfied by x" to mean that x has each of the properties $g_i \in \mathscr{E}$, then it shall be true to say that **a** satisfies $\mathscr{E}$ essentially, if and only if, *sub specie logicae*

> (I) **a** has the g_i, and for any x, if x satisfies or were to satisfy $\mathscr{E}$ then x is or would be the very individual **a**; and for all x, if x lacked some g_i, then x would not and could not be the individual **a**.

---

[2] The quite different matter of *general* essence (that is, of what properties a thing must have to be of such and such a *kind*) is not here at issue.

[3] 'Subset' rather than 'proper subset' in order to accommodate, if that should prove necessary or desirable, a version of essentialism, sometimes associated with Leibniz, by which an individual has every one of its properties essentially.

[4] More generally, where f_i is any property of an individual, it will be designated by the predicate '$F_i x$'.

(II) There are possible worlds in which nothing whatever satisfies $\mathscr{E}$.

Thus, if $\mathscr{E}$ constitutes **a**'s essence, then either **a** satisfies $\mathscr{E}$ or nothing does or could. We remark that $\mathscr{E}$, in effect, gives a conjunction of properties, jointly but not necessarily separately, essential to **a**. It will simplify the exposition if we imagine the conjunction to be the limiting case in which there is one conjunct only, say g_0. And since no particular purpose any longer is served by subscripts we shall omit them. In consequence, $\mathscr{E} = \{ g \}$. We also now understand any $\mathscr{E}$ to be such that any individual satisfying it at all satisfies it essentially. Even though, for convenience, we put $\mathscr{E} = \{ g \}$, we should not lose sight of an important distinction.

(1) A property f will be said to be *essential* to **a** if it is a member of $\mathscr{E}$ and **a** satisfies $\mathscr{E}$.

(2) A property f is *fully essential* to **a** if having it is both necessary and sufficient unto **a**, that is, if its being $\mathscr{E}$'s sole member would not preclude **a**'s satisfying $\mathscr{E}$.

Condition (I) provides that any possible world in which $\mathscr{E}$ is satisfied is a world in which it is satisfied by the selfsame individual **a** and by **a** alone; and so yields a condition on identity through different possible worlds. From this, any possible world in which **a** does not satisfy $\mathscr{E}$ is a possible world in which there is no such thing as **a**. And, although this conveys the idea that if $\mathscr{E}$ is the set of **a**'s essential properties (namely, $\{g\}$) then **a** has g *necessarily*, condition (II) establishes nonetheless that, when we say that **a** has g necessarily, we are not committed to the statement *de dicto* "$\Box G(a)$." [5] For by the provenance of condition (II) it is evident that truths of the form "**a** has g necessarily" do not preserve the familiar model-theoretic criterion of necessity *de dicto*, by which a statement is necessary if and only if it is true in all possible worlds. Condition (II) explicitly allows for worlds not containing [6] **a** and thus for the circumstance that "$G(a)$" not be true. What

---

[5] The locutions "*de dicto*" and "*de re*" are sometimes construed as expressing syntactic concepts: thus, in a system Γ a wff can be thought of as *de dicto* if it is of the form $\ulcorner \mathscr{M} \mathscr{Q} \phi \urcorner$, for the modal operator $\mathscr{M}$ is regarded as affecting the entire sentence — or *dictum* — $\ulcorner \mathscr{Q} \phi \urcorner$. A sentence of the form $\ulcorner \mathscr{Q} \mathscr{M} \phi \urcorner$ is reckoned to be *de re* because the modal operator affects the variables in ϕ bound by $\mathscr{Q}$ so as to convey the idea that it is the values of those variables — *res* — to which a predicate pertains necessarily (contingently, etc.).

[6] In David Kaplan's memorable idiom, we allow a passage, from a given possible world to another world possible to it, via TWH (Trans-World Heir Lines) to result in the disappearance of a passenger.

(I) and (II) jointly convey is the weaker proposition that in all and only those possible worlds containing **a** will "$G(a)$" be true.[7] In fact, it is proposed (until section 5) that "$G(a)$"'s truth in all and only those possible worlds containing **a** just is what it is for **a** to have g necessarily. If so, we have in this a partial reconstruction of the concept of necessity *de re:* the sentence "$G(a)$" will be necessary *de re* if it is true in all possible worlds in which 'a' names the selfsame individual **a**, provided that in at least one possible world **a** enjoys no tenancy.

The idea that an individual inhabitant of this or some given possible world might not exist in other possible worlds finds *formal semantical expression,* for example, in Kripke [1, page 85]. We may consider the ordered triple (**G**, **K**, **R**)[8] as a *quantified modal structure,* with **H** ∈ **K**, and ψ a function which assigns to **H** a set $\psi(\mathbf{H})$, called its domain. Then (where **H** is understood to be the formal analogue of a possible world) our point is that $\psi(\mathbf{H})$ need not be one and the same set for different arguments **H**.

Hintikka [2, page 73], on the other hand, is prompted to say that "a singular term (say a) really specifies a well-defined individual . . . if and only if it refers to one and the same individual not only in the actual world (or, more generally, in whatever possible world we are considering) but also in all the alternative worlds which could have been realized instead of it. . . ." As Hintikka goes on to remark, this is tantamount to saying that the name's referring to that very individual is a matter of necessity; and so it will be a matter of necessity, as well, that there should be such a thing as that individual. However, it should be emphasized that Hintikka holds this view not so much because he thinks it captures an intuitive and plausible thesis concerning what exists in all alternative possible worlds (namely, at least all that exists in *this* one), but rather, Hintikka's interest in it is to marshall sentences of the form $\ulcorner(Ev)N(v = v)\urcorner$ with which to repatriate certain patterns of inference that appear to break down in quantified modal contexts.[9] As

---

[7] Thus (I) and (II) sound such essentialistic themes as: "If g is essential to **a**, then the Creator could not create **a** without endowing it with g"; "If g is essential to **a**, then g came into being precisely with **a**'s coming into being."

[8] Intuitively, **G** is the actual world, **K** the set of all possible worlds, and **R** a reflexive relation on **K**. R is an alternativeness relation fixing the possibility of a world relative to a given world.

As an explanation of the modal operator '□', the idea of truth in all possible worlds is overpicturesque; and the idea of holding in some set bearing some reflexive relation to some set is too uninterpreted. On the question what are the *intended realizations* of such things as Kripke structures, see van Fraassen [37].

[9] It is known that no consistent interpreted system of $q \cdot m \cdot l \cdot$ with identity, which admits formulas of the form $\ulcorner\Box_1 \Box_2 \ldots \Box_m \Sigma v \Box_1 \Box_2 \ldots \Box_n \phi v\urcorner$, is semantically complete unless it contains as an axiom or a theorem the formula $\ulcorner\Box_1 \Box_2 \ldots \Box_m \Pi_{v_0} \Sigma_{v_1}$ $(\Box_1 \Box_2 \ldots \Box_n (v_0 = v_1))\urcorner$, m and n being any natural numbers. This is, in effect, to say

I have already mentioned, what proves problematic for the modal logician need not for the essentialist, since his is a thesis the formal expression of which need not involve those aspects of quantified modal logic which understandably have come under fire.[10] That being so, it is not at all clear that essentialism can tolerate, to say nothing of needing, the proposal that if 'a' refers to **a** in a given possible world, then it refers to a in every world possible relative to it. Accordingly, I shall adopt Kripke's conditions on possible worldhood. Intuitively, this is as it should be, since for the essentialist of current persuasion,

that it is a condition on alternativeness with respect to the world containing a given individual **a** that any alternative possible world also contain it. So, in the case of individuals, if it is actual, it must be necessary. Problematic though it may be, this is a view of world alternativeness that need not here exercise us. For, though the view is part and parcel of a powerful and intuitive interpretation of $q \cdot m \cdot l \cdot$, the essentialist need not espouse any such formulas, hence he can, if so inclined, declare himself a total skeptic regarding the very possibility of an intelligibly interpreted $q \cdot m \cdot l \cdot$.

[10] The seemingly most serious difficulty with $q \cdot m \cdot l \cdot$ is the question of how to understand quantification into modal environments. Quine has argued that it cannot be understood. In [6, pages 156 ff.], Quine makes this argument: for any theory, an open sentence whose free variables are 'x' and 'y' is an expression of identity only in case it meets the condition

(1) $\forall x \forall y (x = y \cdot \supset \cdot Fx \equiv Fy)$.

But if we introduce the predicate '$\Box(x = \text{①})$' for the predicate '$F\text{①}$' in '$x = y \cdot \supset \cdot Fx \equiv Fy$' in (1), then by closure and simplification we get the consequence

(2) $\forall x \forall y (x = y) \cdot \supset \Box(x = y)$.

But this means that in the class of identity statements there can be no distinction between necessary truths and contingent truths. This may not be a deep objection, but the following one is (Quine [30, pages 197–198]).

Suppose we find it intuitively plausible to suppose that the following is a condition on identity:

(3) $\forall y (Fy \equiv \cdot y = x) \& \forall y (Gy \equiv \cdot y = x) \cdot \supset \Box(\forall y(Fy \equiv Gy))$.

Then, put 'p' for any true sentence, and let **x** be an item in our universe of discourse. Assume as well that $z = x$ is true. Then, we have

(4) $\forall y (p \& y = z \cdot \equiv \cdot y = x)$.

(5) $\forall y (y = z \cdot \equiv \cdot y = x)$.

Now introduce '$p \& \text{①} = z$' for '$F\text{①}$' and '$\text{①} = z$' for '$G\text{①}$' in (3). This yields

(6) $\forall y (p \& y = z \cdot \equiv \cdot y = x) \& \forall y(y = z \cdot \equiv y = x) \cdot \supset \Box(\forall y(p \& y = z \cdot \equiv \cdot y = z)$.

But (6) implies

(7) $p \& z = z \cdot \equiv \cdot z = z$

and (7) implies

(8) p.

Yet since a necessary truth implies only necessary truths, we are forced to conclude

(9) $\Box p$.

By these lights, for the entire class of statements, it is impossible to differentiate truths from necessary truths; modal distinctions collapse into ordinary alethic ones.

that is, of what looks very like a third-grade modal involvement,[11] necessity *de dicto* seems a matter of relations of linguistic meaning, or conceptual connection, or *something* like that,[12] whereas necessity *de re* is a matter of the properties a thing must have in order to be the very thing it is, a matter of what must be what by whatever name or none. And it seems to be no part of this latter notion that essential to a thing's being the very thing it is is that it should be found in all worlds possible relative to the world that actually contains it.

In representing the essentialist as favouring expression of his views in an idiom delivering necessities *de re,* it is not meant to be suggested that for necessities *de re* there are no logically equivalent truths whose whole modal content can be represented *de dicto.* That there is *some* such equivalence is in fact a view that I wish to espouse; [13] and it may even be urged that the equivalence in question is reductive in the sense that from essentialist truths *de re* there is an effective map on truths *de dicto* (in a certain canonical form) for which latter alone modal language enjoys any claim to intelligibility. Still, it will be important to recognize that if it is a truth *de re* that every man is necessarily rational and a truth *de dicto* that necessarily every man is rational, it is for the essentialist distinctively and irreducibly a *third* truth that necessarily every man is necessarily rational.[14]

On the face of it, the essentialist's arithmetic is accurate, and talk of there being a difference, of the kind mentioned, between modalities *de re* and *de dicto* makes reasonable sense and may even be true. Of course, the opinion most widely received is that essentialism, at least in so far as it involves necessities *de re,* simply cannot bear scrutiny; in particular, that although some, possibly supportable, interpretations are available for *de dicto* modalities none is forthcoming, or likely, for modalities *de re.* Modalities *de dicto,* it is cautiously ventured, *can* be represented by properties of Kripke models on modal structures [1] [3], or of Hintikka-model systems of model sets [2][4], but, it is supposed, no corresponding achievement is even remotely near to hand for modalities *de re.* Such skepticism appears to result both from a failure to understand the *de re* idiom in any deep way, to be able to provide for it a satisfactory semantics, and from a related bewildered unconfidence that such understanding is possible.[15] However, the modal

---

[11] Quine [6, pages 156 ff.].

[12] See, for example, van Fraassen [37, pages 155–159].

[13] In section 3.

[14] For a slightly more stable example put 'even integer' for 'man' and 'divisible by 2' for 'rational'.

[15] The full story of the skeptic's confusion is a familiar one and will not be detailed here. See Quine [5], [6], William and Martha Kneale [7]. For recent attempts at accomplishments thought to be so remote, see Thomason and Stalnaker [32], and Parsons [33].

skeptic does not usually take the mere statement of his bewilderment as a proper proof of his skepticism, does not take a boggle for a demonstration, and some of the time it is possible to read him as offering the *de re*ist a sort of challenge: "Translate the *de re* into the *de dicto* and then there shall be some chance of my understanding you." [16]

I propose here to respond to the skeptic's challenge by presenting considerations in support of two main theses: first, that there are acceptable means of meeting it, that is, of translating essentialist claims *de re* into reductively equivalent sentences all of whose modal symbols are in positions *de dicto;* but, second, that one particular way of meeting the challenge does not meet it in fact. Very roughly, the procedure that I think does not work is one that represents all essentialist truths *de re* as rehabilitatable cases of Sleigh's Fallacy. The Fallacy, in its most general form, is the mistake of placing a modal symbol into the interior of a context over *all* of which alone it correctly operates. (The Fallacy owes its name to Robert Sleigh, who in a colleague's words ". . . is expert at detecting and extirpating it" (Plantinga [8]).) [17] In the case of singular sentences involving a single occurrence of a modal, treatment is administered by removal, to the extreme left of the offending sentence, of the modal word originally occurring in its interior, with the result that the modal symbol now adjoins a sentence, not a predicate, and modifies a statement, not an attribute.[18] If the resulting sentence is true, it is taken as clarifying what was confusedly displayed *de re* in the original; and if the resulting sentence is false, that will not only show that the original was false (not just confused) but will provide some explanation of why this is so. Two examples will illustrate the point. If, informally, "2 is necessarily prime" seems in order and "Sally is necessarily nice" not, the method of rehabilitation will confirm the appearances and offer an explanation of them: "2 is necessarily prime" is mapped onto the *de dicto* truth "□2 is prime" and "Sally is necessarily nice" onto the *de dicto* falsehood "□ Sally is

---

[16] See, for example, von Wright [10, pages 26–28], William Kneale [34, pages 629 ff.]. Quine [5, pages 148 ff], and Plantinga [9, pages 241 ff.].

It is worth remarking that our skeptic is skeptical of the chances of making sense of the very basic idea of a thing's having certain properties necessarily and independently of the means by which the thing is denoted and the property expressed. It is another matter that modal logic, in general, should be prey to sundry quirks and abnormalities. This latter might serve in reinforcement of the basic doubts, but not as their source.

[17] An example of Sleigh's Fallacy would be the fallacy of concluding that Harry is necessarily myopic from the facts that Harry is a Chelmsford and all Chelmsfords are myopic.

[18] There are some very subtle variations of rehabilitation, for example, Plantinga's [9]. However even by Plantinga's scheme it remains a central idea that a truth in the form "$G(a)$ necessarily" is logically equivalent to a truth in which the modal operates on the proposition expressed by "$G(a)$", given that 'a' merely names a and 'G' merely designates g ([9, pages 248–252]). A further refinement is noted in footnote 29.

nice." And, as this latter is untrue because "Sally is nice" is not a *necessary* truth even if true, neither is it acceptable in its original formulation *de re*.[19]

I will suggest that this is a remedy which has yet to effect a cure. The *Treat-it-as-a-Sleigh-Fallacy-and-see-whether-it-rehabilitates* Method purports to establish an equivalence which is reductive in the sense of preserving truth while providing for the elimination of modalities *de re*. But there is reason to think of the correspondence in question that it is not properly reductive, not only because it does not convey the philosophic content of essentialism, but also because it is not even an equivalence—mapping as it does truths onto falsehoods.

2. I assume a close-to-standard, first-order logic with identity and individual constants. In place of the usual '∃' and '∀' I adopt the "existence-neutral" quantifiers 'Σ' and 'Π' by the intended interpretation of which the consistency of "Σx (x does not exist)" is undetermined.[20] Two quantifier rules are employed: a Σ-introduction Rule, *from* ϕ *to infer* $\ulcorner\Sigma v\phi\urcorner$; and a Σ-elimination Rule, from $\ulcorner\Sigma_v\phi_v\urcorner$ *to infer* ϕ_α, provided 'α' is free for 'v'.

Definite descriptions are, for now, treated as names. To motivate this decision, we need see that definite descriptions cause trouble of two kinds.

First, they seem to afford unavoidable means of proliferating essentialistic-looking sentences well beyond what, Leibniz aside, even the most enthusiastic essentialist would be happy with. For, let G be any predicate or assortment of predicates uniquely true of an individual **a**. Then we may form the definite description '$(\imath x)Gx$' with which to refer to **a**. But, by Quine's lights [5, pages 155–156], "$\Box G(\imath x)Gx$" is an inconsistent sentence, hence "$\Box G(\imath x)Gx$" is true.[21] Thus if Harry

---

[19] For passages which suggest a not altogether dithyrambic endorsement of this policy see, for example, Kneale [34, page 629] and Quine [5, page 148].

[20] Nothing more is intended than that there might be things that do not exist, such as Santa Claus, Sherlock Holmes, and perhaps the number 2. It is not here proposed that $\ulcorner\Sigma v_0(v_1 = v_0)\urcorner$ ("There is something or other") is or that it is not a theorem, though in section 4 I shall say that it is not. For present purposes it will do no harm to regard 'Σ' simply as a terminological alternative to '∃'. If it is thought a pressing matter, it will do to interpret $\ulcorner\Sigma v\phi\urcorner$ in the manner of Leonard, thus: $\ulcorner\Sigma v\phi\urcorner$ is true iff for some singular term t, $\ulcorner t/v\phi\urcorner$ is true, or $\ulcorner\exists v\phi\urcorner$ is true.

[21] Clearly a counterfeit of Arnauldic essentialism. It seems, by the way, to have been Locke's view that Aristotle was merely a counterfeit essentialist. It is hard to accept Locke's characterization of Aristotelian essentialism, but it is no less hard to accept than Quine's characterization of it. For they come to the same, libelous, thing.

It is interesting, however, that these are not theorems of standard description theories. In Hintikka's system [36] we have $\vdash\ulcorner\phi(\imath v)\phi\urcorner$; but this is hardly a standard theory since in it we do not have $\vdash\ulcorner v = v\urcorner$. It might also be observed that to accept $\ulcorner\phi(\imath v)\phi\urcorner$ as a theorem seems tantamount to accepting Meinong's Principle regarding the round square which, in turn, seems open to Russell's crushing refutation, and which in [18] prompted the introduction of the special inference-inhibiting predicate '$\mathscr{F}x$'.

is the only man in the room with a stuffy nose, then "The man with the stuffy nose has a stuffy nose" will be necessary, and Harry will have clogged sinuses essentially.[22]

The other difficulty is that even for *essential* properties, h, of a thing a, reference to a by means of a definite description containing a designator, H, of that property should not depend upon a view of definite description which makes "$H(\imath x)Hx$" a necessary truth *de dicto*. For how, without necessary existence, can a truth of the form $\ulcorner\phi(\imath v)\phi\urcorner$ be true in all possible worlds? Even in all possible worlds containing the ϕ-er, if ϕ is not an essential property of it? One, I think reasonable, way of escaping this consequence is to abandon the view that $\ulcorner\neg\phi(\imath v)\phi\urcorner$ is logically inconsistent, by taking the option that definite descriptions in singular referential positions have, to borrow Strawson's metaphor, "grown capital letters" [23, page 186]. "The Holy Roman Empire was neither Holy nor Roman."

The solution just proposed automatically takes care of our first difficulty. Semantically speaking, definite descriptions, having grown their capital letters, are indistinguishable from individual constants.

Of course there are other remedies; for example, we might treat all descriptions in the manner of Russell. Or we might try to resist saying that $\ulcorner\neg\phi(\imath v)\phi\urcorner$ is inconsistent in any sense strong enough to excite a pullulation of essential properties. Such an approach is essayed in section 5. For now, enough said of descriptions.

A "Σ closure" of an open sentence ϕ is understood to be the well-formed sentence (that is, a sentence with no free variables) that would result if we placed the quantifier in exactly one grammatically available region of ϕ. By a "constant closure" of an open sentence we mean the well-formed sentence that results when we uniformly replace some *one* variable in each of its free occurrences with a constant.

Consider now the open sentence "$\Box Fx$" and its constant closure

(1) $\Box Fa$

It is open to inquire whether "$\Box Fx$" admits of just one Σ closure, that is, whether there is one and only one syntactically approved method of converting "$\Box Fx$" into a wff by adding 'Σx'. It would seem not, since, on the face of it
both

(2) $\Sigma x\Box Fx$

---

[22] Actually, even further surfeit is unavoidable, for let "H" be any predicate merely true of **a**; then we may form the description 'the *H*-er I'm presently thinking of', which, by Quine's claim, takes us to a full Leibnizian essentialism.

and

(3) $\Box\Sigma xFx$

are well-formed sentences. The point is quite general: it does not quite ring true that, what is to all intents and purposes the very same syntactic maneuver, namely, closure on terms, should force '$\Box$' into that particular pattern of versatility, always giving, for constant closure on $\ulcorner\Box\phi v\urcorner$, a result *de dicto*, yet for Σ closure, a result *de re*. And this, it might be conceded, argues for the grammatical admissibility of both (2) and (3).

Such liberality is, of course, not matched, not even attempted, by the Rule of Σ introduction, by the authority of which the inference from (1) results in a sentence in which the quantifier occurs only in left-most position, as in (2). But might there not be (as there is in some systems of $q \cdot m \cdot l \cdot$)[23] a *second* Rule of Σ introduction which would sanction the inference from (1) to (3)? (By analogy with

(4) $\vdash\phi$ only if $\vdash\Sigma v\phi$

in whose consequent '$\vdash$', and not the quantifier, is retained in the left-most position.) It is natural to think that the answer must be yes, if only for the reason that if it is necessary that **a** have f it surely is necessary that *something* have it.[24]

---

[23] For example, Fitch [24].

[24] That $\ulcorner\Box\phi\urcorner$ should admit of two distinct Σ-introduction Rules is not a characteristic of necessity alone, nor indeed of alethic modalities alone. A parallel logical structure is exhibited by the epistemic modality, knowledge. Putting 'K' for "It is known that" and replacing '$\Box$' with 'K' in $\ulcorner\Box\phi\urcorner$ we obtain

(1) $K(\phi)$.

But it is well known that (1) admits of two "existential" inferences, one *de re* and the other *de dicto*, thus:

(2) $\Sigma v((v = \alpha) \ \& \ K(\phi v))$,

and

(3) $K(\Sigma v((v = \alpha) \ \& \ \phi v))$.

From "It is known that Tommy Tweed is bearded" it follows *either* that the man who Tommy Tweed is is known to be bearded, *or* that it is known that Tommy Tweed, whoever he might be, is bearded. We have a kind of ambiguity, *de re/de dicto*, attaching to (1), depending on whether in the Existential Generalization of (1) the modal K does or does not cross over variables bound by quantification.

Some philosophers, such as von Wright [10] and Hintikka [4], have remarked the impressive generality of basic modal logics and have held that the verbs of propositional attitude share a rudimentary modal behavior.

So regarded these too admit of modal ambiguity. For, from

I need claim no more for these conjectures than that they attach momentary respectability to the inference from (1) to (3); but if an actual precedent were desired one could always cite, with a caution appropriate to its notoriety, the Barcan formula,[25]

(5) $\Sigma v \Box \phi \Rightarrow \Box \Sigma v \phi$

by which to proceed from (1) to (3), via (2).

It is an evident, and important, fact about (3) that it violates customary prohibitions of necessary existence.[26] Even if we were to accommodate the hypothesis of the unique case of God's necessary existence the inference would still be unsound. God is not presumed to have all attributes [27] and the inference from (1) to (3) will therefore fail for certain interpretations of 'Fx'. Thus it is false that

(4) John hopes Sally will be there.

The conclusion *de dicto* is

(5) John hopes that $\Sigma x((x = \text{Sally}) \& x$ will be there,

whereas the conclusion *de re* is

(6) $\Sigma x((x = \text{Sally}) \& $ John hopes that x will be there).

And if we accept the extreme-seeming contention (Hintikka [11]) that the verbs of perception are naturally construed as modals, then from

(7) Tommy Tweed sees Sally

we obtain either the *de dicto*

(8) Tommy Tweed knows that $\Sigma x((x = \text{Sally} \& $ he sees $x)$

or the *de re*

(9) $\Sigma x((x = \text{Sally} \& $ Tommy Tweed (knows that he) sees $x)$.

[25] For one, of several, critical discussions of the Barcan formulae, see Myhill [12]. Speaking of the Barcan formulae, it is arguable that $(1)^\ulcorner \Box_1 \Box_2 \ldots \Box_m (\forall x \forall_y (x = y \cdot \supset \Box_1 \Box_2 \ldots \Box_n (x = y)^1$ is not provable in any syntactically consistent modal theory Γ meeting the conditions: (1) Γ is an extension of S8 or any weaker theory, by addition of a standard quantificational and identity profile, that is, of axioms and rules of quantification theory and identity theory, or second-order predicate logic. (2) In Γ the added axioms are modalized by prefixing a '$\Box$'. (3) Γ contains the Barcan axiom $\ulcorner \Diamond \Sigma v \phi \dashv \Sigma v \Diamond \phi^1$. But any such theory as Γ in which (1) is not provable is semantically incomplete. See Føllesdall [36]

[26] There is no happy nominalization of 'there is' (why should there be, 'there is' being a quantifier?). One ubiquitous candidate, 'being', has been romanticized and revisionistically ontologized out of all recognizable shape; and another, 'subsistence', on grammatical grounds alone, is disqualified, for it nominalizes the very different verb 'to subsist'. The nominalizationlessness of 'to be' is probably further explained by the fact that the copula is not easily made out to be a verb in the first place. Compare with 'to exist' which effortlessly gives 'existence'. However, I here accept the fiction that 'existence' *is* an allowable nominalization of 'to be' and occasionally will so employ it.

[27] Our ecumenism, it should be confessed, extends to deities neither neoplatonistic nor pantheistic.

(6)   God is (arithmetically) prime,

yet true, by hypothesis, that

(7) $\Box(2$ is prime),

and true, again by hypothesis, that God *alone* has necessary existence. So (7) would be untrue.

There is good, even compelling, reason to forsake the inference from (1) to (3), and so doing to renounce the Barcan formula,[28] and to turn our attention to (2). By moving the modal symbol past all quantifiers binding occurrences of x, we show ourselves to be espousing, it would seem, no more than necessary *attribution*, restoring, for now, to its proper parliamentary shelf all questions of necessary existence. Even so, by the original Σ-introduction Rule on (1), and by the necessity of (1) in conjunction with the dogma that from necessity necessity alone follows, we are back to necessary existence at

(8) $\Box\Sigma x\Box Fx$

Yet if (2), but not (8), were to follow from (1), we would have a contingent truth, following from a necessary one, in violation of still another philosophical stricture; as (in reverse), by Σ elimination on (2), we commit the related indiscretion, if that is what it is, of inferring a necessary truth from a contingent one (Belnap [13, pages 2 ff.]).

Suppose we grant that this last difficulty can satisfactorily be dealt with; statement (1), nonetheless, should give us pause. For how can it be true that "Socrates is rational" is a necessary truth while evidently contingent that there is such as he? Otherwise put, how can "Socrates is rational" be true in all possible worlds and "There is such as Socrates" true only in those worlds that count Socrates among their number, when it is *not* true that these two sets of possible worlds coincide, that is, that Socrates inhabits all possible worlds or even all possible alternative worlds to the world he does inhabit? So if we are to suppose that the inference from (1) should go only to (2), and if we believe this on the grounds that the modal symbol affects only the predicate, evoking no more than the *de-re*ist idea of necessary attribution, it still happens, as we have seen, that Σ *elimination* on (2) takes us straight back to a statement *de dicto*.[29]

---

[28] Renouncing, as well, the Σ-introduction Rule, for sentences *in the form given.*

[29] Plantinga [9] sidesteps the problem, basically, by rewriting sentences $\ulcorner\Box\phi\alpha\urcorner$ in some such fashion as $\ulcorner\neg\Diamond$ neg $\phi\alpha\urcorner$ ("It is necessarily false that α *lacks* ϕ"). $\ulcorner\neg\phi\alpha\urcorner$ will

I shall speak of the circumstance in which a sentence of the form
(1) is necessary and a sentence of the form (2) contingent as a circumstance of modal ambiguity regarding '□'. It is clearly that, since it is
the disposition of the modal symbol that imposes upon (1) and (2)
such radically different truth conditions. So disposed, (1) is true in
every possible world, but (2) quite conceivably in just one. The
difference in truth conditions can be taken as establishing that in (1) and
(2) '□' plays different semantical roles — that in (1) and (2) '□' "means
different things." [30] Whence the entirely unsurprising result that the
inference from (1) to (2) is suspect.

Now since it happens that modal ambiguity at (1) and (2) accounts
for the collapse of the inference, a return to univocity should instantly

be true in every possible world, both those that do and those that do not contain α.
Thus "2 is not prime" fails in those worlds containing 2, since there 2 will be prime,
and fails too in those worlds not containing 2 (since there 2 cannot either have or lack
primehood); whence "$\neg \Diamond$ neg (2 is prime)." And although "There is such as 2," that is,
"$\Sigma x(x = 2)$," follows from "neg (2 is prime)," it does not follow distinctively, but rather
as one among *all* that follows from an impossible proposition, namely, everything.
This is an interesting maneuver and prompts all kinds of queries. It would be enough
to say that I do not adopt Plantinga's solution, mainly because I think that there are
other measures, equally effective, which allow us to see essentialism in a little clearer
light. But there is also the point that Plantinga's essentialism cannot be expressed in
any *given* language (because of countably many names and uncountable many nominata [for example, the reals]). My own proposal is not liable to such a restriction.

[30] The ambiguity is reflected by the fact that only modalities *de dicto* seem clearly to
iterate. For the nonalethic modalities, such as 'K' ('It is known that' or 'Knowly'),
'H' ('It is hoped that' or 'Hopedly') and (if we agree with Hintikka — see footnote 24)
'P' ('It is perceived that' or 'Perceivedly'), similar modal behavior again is evident.
Take the inference from (1) to (2), replacing in turn '□' with 'K', 'H' and 'P'. One example will make the point. From

(10) $H(Fa)$

we obtain by Σ-introduction

(11) $\Sigma x H(Fx)$;

and back again to (10), by Σ elimination.

Intuitively (and roughly) it seems correct to say that in every *optative alternative*
[possible world] to the world for which (10) is true, that is, in every world *compatible*
with the world in which it is hoped (say) that Tommy Tweed is bearded, there is someone x hoped to be bearded.

In this Hintikka-like optative logic the italicized expressions in the paragraph preceding serve to place qualifications on the interpretation of the inference of (11) from
(10), without which it would be invalid. What is important to notice is that a similar
device could be used to salvage the inference of (2) from (1). Define an *alethic alternative* to a world regarding which (1) is true as a possible world containing the individual
a. Then in every possible world compatible with the world for which (1) is true (2) also
is true. So amended, the inference would require (2) to be true in every alethic alternative to (1) in case (1) is true.

The present comparison serves to support the claim that the misinference, (1) to
(2), is characteristic of a considerable variety of different modalities and is no isolated
quirk of necessity.

restore it. One means of eliminating ambiguity would be to construe Σ elimination on (2) as giving not (1), but something rather more like

(9) $a \square F$

where the modal symbol has been driven into the sentence and there affects only the predicate.[31] Notationally this is nonstandard, perhaps disastrous; and, because our purposes can equally well be served by it, I shall adopt the following procedure for "modalizing" predicates, a procedure by which a predicate, once modalized, remains so under Σ elimination. The method in question provides for attaching to a predicate, 'Fx' say, a modal superscript, thus: '$F_x^{\square}$'. The result is itself a predicate, an open sentence (to be read 'x is necessarily F'), for which the constant closure and Σ closure are, respectively,

(10) $F_a^{\square}$

and

(11) $\Sigma x F_x^{\square}$

It is now proposed that (10) and (11) replace (1) and (2). Questions of interpretation momentarily aside, we remark that the new notation extends to modalized predicates the same uniform syntactic regimentability that first-order logic already visits upon ordinary unmodalized predicates.

Although it may be conceded that old and familiar inference patterns have been reinstated, it may not be clear that their repair is due to anything other than notational sleight of hand. In particular, it will have to be ascertained whether this new idiom *de re* can so be explicated as to do justice to the philosophic content of essentialism, yet still to admit of a reduction *de dicto*.

3. (a) Could $\ulcorner \phi_\alpha^{\square} \urcorner$ ever be true? (b) What is meant by $\ulcorner \phi_\alpha^{\square} \urcorner$? (c) What is meant by $\ulcorner \phi\alpha$ essentially$\urcorner$? (d) Do $\ulcorner \phi_\alpha^{\square} \urcorner$ and $\ulcorner \phi\alpha$ *essentially*$\urcorner$ mean the same? Beginning with (c) I will deal with these in reverse order. Along the way (d) will take care of itself.

It is a requirement on what follows (α) that essentialism receive a characterization which avoids the consequence that such things as have essential properties exist necessarily and which avoids equally the circumstance that singular truths ascribing essential properties are necessities *de dicto;* (β) that at least one essential property actually

---

[31] By analogy with "$\Sigma x \square Fx$."

be displayed; (γ) that some idea be given of the scope of essentialism; that is to say, of the kinds of individuals plausibly supposed to admit of essential attribution; and (δ) some idea be given as to scope, in another sense, regarding namely the kinds of properties plausibly supposed to be essential.

What is meant by ⌜φα essentially⌝? In the light of the remarks of section 1, I propose self-identity as the paradigmatic *fully essential* property. On the face of it, the choice is apt, for, if self-identity is not a property such that for anything having it its failure to have it would constitute its very nonexistence, then no property would. What is more, self-identity is, in one clear sense, an utterly general property, true of everything there is (in confirmation of the basic essentialist thesis that essentialism is universal[32] in the sense that every individual has an essence).

Philosophic opinion on self-identity forms a spectrum, defined at one end by Bishop Butler's homily—brought into modern, and extravagant, prominence by Moore—to the effect that everything is what it is and not another thing; and, at the other pole, by Wittgenstein's tractarian skepticism to the effect that statements of self-identity ascribe nothing. My own inclinations place me in the Butlerian region of the spectrum, although it should be admitted that there is something so primeval about identity as to occasion periodic perplexity about the structure of that relation. It is a very easy thing to agree with those, such as Scott [14], for whom identity is so basic a concept that its properties are not properly a part of logic. It cannot be denied that self-identity is a funny kind of property. Certainly it is not a *universal* since it is not instantiable by more than one individual. It is not, that is to say, a property such that every individual has it, even though it is true that every individual is self-identical. The proof that self-identity is not a universal is quite straightforward:

(1) it is such that anything having it is the very thing it is, and none other.
(2) there is more than one individual.

Evidently self-identity behaves very like a Bergmannian, *character* [29, pages 244–245], which "depends₁" upon the entities having it. That is, the cardinality of the set of being-self-identicals is exactly that of the set of individuals and varies exactly as this latter set varies. Every individual has *its* self-identity, and every case of self-identity

[32] Not of course universal in the Leibnizian sense that a thing's every property is essential to it.

is unique to just one individual. Of course, such a view is by no means original with Bergmann. The basic model, or prototype, of dependency$_1$ is (appropriately enough) that of a Scholastic *essence*. (See Aquinas [25, Chapter 3], and Suarez [26, Section II, paragraph 8.)

The difference between ordinary properties and self-identity is that ordinary properties are universals and are, as we once were able to say, 'One not Many', whereas self-identity is Many and not One. This leaves us with two related chores:

1. of providing an interpretation of the claim that everything is self-identical without having to say or imply that more than one individual has an identity other than its own,
2. of providing an intelligible characterization of self-identity.

The first task is easily enough accomplished: $\ulcorner \Pi v(v = v) \urcorner$ is a theorem; and no formula $\ulcorner (\Pi v_0)(\Pi v_1)(v_0 = v_1) \urcorner$ is a theorem, save in a world of just one thing.

We distinguish the sense in which self-identity is general from generality of another kind. For suppose that *being susceptible of reference* (= being assignable to variables accessible to quantification) is a property. Then that selfsame property is a property of everything there is. If it is a property of **a**, then it, that very property, is a property of everything.

As for the second task, that too is fairly straightforwardly accomplished. As a first pass, we make the following contextual definition.

Def   (d_0)   **a** is self-identical iff $\Sigma x((a = x) \ \& \ \Pi y((y = x) \equiv (y = a)))$.

But this will not quite suffice, for the property conveyed by the definition just is the property,

$$(\lambda a)((\Sigma x)(x = a)),^{33}$$

of being identical with *something or other*. But that is a property of everything and cannot serve as our paradigmatic essential property, which is a property of at most one thing. Instead of the idea of being identical with something or other, we need to convey the notion of being identical with **a**, if it is the essence of **a** we happen to be considering; of being identical with **b**, if it is **b** we are considering; and so on. One way of putting this requirement is to say that we need to hit

---

[33] Where '*t*' is any singular term, then "*t* = *x*" $\Rightarrow$ "$\Pi y(y = x \cdot \equiv \cdot y = t)$." So the definiens of the contextual definition simplifies to: "$(\Sigma x)(x = a)$." On the standard reading of the quantifier, the condition defines *existence,* on the present reading '*being*', both of which are reasonably thought to be universals.

upon a way of associating a property not with the open sentence "$x = x$," true of everything there is, but of finding the properties that go with "$x = a$," "$x = b$," "$x = c$," and so on. This is what our second pass seeks to capture:

Def   (d_i) **a** is self-identical iff $\Sigma x \Pi y \ (y = x \cdot \equiv \cdot y = a)$.

What our second pass intends is that we associate with the *definiens* not the property of *being (identical with) something or other*, but rather the property of *being* **a**, a property possessed, if at all, by **a** alone.

If our explication proves satisfactory, it should be remarked that whatever might be the felt ontological peculiarities attaching to self-identity, we can express that idea by means of the customary and relatively uncomplicated resources of quantification theory and a standard theory of identity.

Essential propertyhood, with respect to an arbitrary individual **a** is now inductively defined as follows.

Def.   (d1) Self-identity is a fully essential, hence an essential, property of **a**.

(d2) For some essential property g_i of **a** and for any g_k, g_k is an essential property of **a** iff $G_k a \ \& \ (\neg G_k a \dashv 3 \ \neg G_i a)$.

That is, a property of **a** is essential if **a**'s not having it would mean, to speak very loosely, that **a** lacked a second of its essential properties; but that would mean that it would lack a third, and so on as it were, until it lost self-identity.[34]

Still there are problems. For surely it is a condition, that any account of essentialism must meet, that

(L*) If "$a = b$" is true and **a** necessarily (*de re*) has f then **b** necessarily (*de re*) has f.

(L*) is an instance of what is equivalent to that incontrovertible part (L) of Leibniz' Law, sometimes known as the principle of the indiscernibility of identicals. But suppose our property f is the property associated with the predicate '$x = a$'. Then we have or seem to have the fol-

---

[34] It is not of course supposed that the circumstance in which self-identity were to fail an individual is the absurdity in which that individual finds itself exhibiting that ontological gaucherie of quite literally not being itself. Rather, the failure in question would result in there being none such as it.

lowing consistent triad, contrary to (L*):

$$F \overset{\square}{a}$$
$$a = b$$
$$\neg F \overset{\square}{b}$$

This poses something of a dilemma, for either we must abandon (L*), which I am not prepared to do, or we must make it a reasonable thing to say of our triad that it is *not* in fact consistent. This latter can, I think, be managed. For let **a** be Cicero and **b** Tully and *f* some arbitrary property of each. Now since Tully and Cicero are one, then, by (L*), they have all their properties in common. *A fortiori* they have all their essential properties in common. Self-identity (or being necessarily *de re* Cicero) is an essential property of Cicero, hence of Tully — the same man by another name. So the triad is not consistent after all.

It must be admitted, however, that it has the *look* of consistency. But the look is deceiving. We tend to see the first member of the triad, '$a = \square a$' not just as true but as necessary *de dicto,* as a theorem and valid wff of any theory of identity extended by our method of predicate modalization; and certainly we can see that neither of the remaining members of the triad, '$a = b$' and '$b = \square a$', is a theorem; so it must be possible for us to have '$a = \square a$' and "$b = \square a$." The fallacy begins to glare: from $\ulcorner \vdash \phi \urcorner$ and $\ulcorner$ not $\vdash \psi \urcorner$ it is inferred that $\ulcorner \phi$ is true$\urcorner$ and $\ulcorner \psi$ is false$\urcorner$ are jointly possible. But, quite apart from the fact that in our treatment "$a = \square a$" is *not* a theorem and not a necessary truth *de dicto,* the reasoning is fallacious, for it conflates truth with theoremhood and, unwittingly I assume, affects the quite general collapse of modal distinctions.

Now, our definition comfortably complies with all but one of requirements (α) to (δ). It exhibits a particular essential property and enforces the universality of essentialism. The definition also serves as a rough kind of test for what is to count as an essential property. Regrettably, however, self-identity does not seem to oblige the first requirement not to commit to necessary existence those things having essential properties, and not to force essentialist attributions into forms *de dicto.* For if a property, being essential, is such as to guarantee, for anything having it, its non-self-identity in case it should not have it, then, because $\ulcorner \Pi v(v = v) \urcorner$ is a theorem, that an individual **a** has a given property *g* essentially must be necessary *de dicto.* And if, being *de dicto,* it is a truth in every possible world, it is equally a truth in every possible world that there is such as **a**, hence "$\square \Sigma x(a = x)$" will be true. It is usual in first-order logics with identity that $\ulcorner \Sigma v_0(v_1 = v_0) \urcorner$ is a theorem; [35] and by the convention that only those names (individual constants) are admitted that do in fact name, it is in such logics inescapable that "$\Sigma x(a = x)$" is necessary *de dicto* and that attributions of essential properties are necessarily true when true at all.

Evidently, since ordinary first-order logic neither yields nor permits the desired account, and since what proves intransigent is a theorem of questionable logical credentials, it is perfectly in order to seek for some amendment of standard logic. Details of the amendment are reserved for section 4, but it is here conceded that the proposed changes should not be *ad hoc* in the precise sense of having nothing to recommend them other than allowing a characterization of essentialism in compliance with the four requirements (α) to (δ). For the present both "$\Sigma x(a = x)$" and "$\Sigma x(y = x)$" will be understood as holding, not in every possible world, but merely in every possible world containing **a** (respectively something or other).

What is meant by $\ulcorner \phi_\alpha^\square \urcorner$? By the remarks of the paragraph above and late in section 2, it may be evident that $\ulcorner \phi_\alpha^\square \urcorner$ is to be regarded as not less than logically equivalent to $\ulcorner \phi\alpha$ *essentially*.$\urcorner$ Thus:

Def.   (d3) $\phi_\alpha^\square$ iff $\phi\alpha$ & $\neg\phi \ \alpha \dashv 3 \ \neg\Sigma v(\alpha = v))$.[36]

That is to say, **a** has *g* necessarily if and only if it has *g* and its not having *g* *strictly implies* that there is none such as it.

We here remark that if the account of self-identity and essential "propertyhood" is correct, then it should, in some very obvious way, be redundant to say of an individual **a** that it has self-identity *essentially* or *necessarily*. And it is. For, observe, by (d3)

a has self-identity necessarily iff $\Sigma x\Pi y(y = x \cdot \equiv \cdot y = a)$ & $(\neg\Sigma x\Pi y(y = x \cdot \equiv \cdot y = a)\dashv 3 \ \neg\Sigma x(x = a)$.

The formula is plainly redundant.

There does not seem to be much doubt that (d3) provides, for necessary attribution, as do (d1) and (d2), for essential attribution,

---

[35] A theorem sometimes criticized on the grounds that it is not properly a truth of logic, and that it is a theorem mainly by assumption.

[36] In any system Γ of modal logic in which the sentential formula $S, \ulcorner \square p \dashv 3 \ (p \ \& \ (\neg p \dashv 3 \ q)\urcorner$ is preserved for arbitrary q, (d3) will distinguish the *de re* $\ulcorner \phi_\alpha^\square \urcorner$ from the *de dicto* $\ulcorner \square \phi\alpha \urcorner$ by virtue of its 'if' part alone. For (d3) is just a special case of S with $\ulcorner \neg\Sigma v$ $(\alpha = v)\urcorner$ for q. In Γ it is possible to retain a definition, having 'only if' force, if one replaces (d3) with

(d3*) $\phi_\alpha^\square$ iff $\phi\alpha$ & $(\neg\phi\alpha \dashv 3 \ \neg\Sigma v(\alpha = v))$ & $\neg(\neg\phi\alpha \dashv 3 \ \Sigma v(\alpha = v))$.

That is, not *every* formula is true in case a *de re* necessity were to fail to hold.

the two desiderata of fidelity to the philosophic intent of essentialism and of selection of an idiom that admits of reduction *de dicto*. In the biconditional (d3) '$\dashv$', the symbol for strict implication, is the only modal, and of course, it reduces in the usual way to a *de dicto* modalization of '$\supset$', the symbol for truth-functional or material implication. What is necessary *de dicto*, however, is not the whole explicans of (d3). Rather it is only one conjunct of it; the remaining one is contingent. In explicit *de dicto* form (d3) just is

$$(d3') \quad \phi_\alpha^\square \text{ iff } \phi\alpha \ \& \ \square(\neg\phi\alpha \supset \neg\Sigma v(\alpha = v))$$

wherein $\ulcorner\neg\phi\alpha \supset \neg\Sigma v(\alpha = v)\urcorner$ is necessary and $\ulcorner\phi\alpha\urcorner$ not. Thus it happens that if **a** has g necessarily, it is contingent that it has it at all, but not contingent that it has it necessarily *if* it has it has it all. It also emerges that our essentialistic sentences are formulable entirely without the resources of $q \cdot m \cdot l \cdot$. For although in (d3') both a quantifier and a modal operator occur, the operator does not occur *within the scope of the quantifier*. So (d3') is not a formula of $q \cdot m \cdot l \cdot$.

(We remark, parenthetically, that a Leibniz essentialism is derivable simply by "extensionalizing" (d3), by there replacing '$\dashv$' by '$\supset$'. Then for any property f that an individual **a** may happen to have, "Fa" is true and the antecedent of the conditional false, in verification of the entire conditional. It then follows that **a**'s every property is essential to it and that **a** has necessarily every property it has. It is interesting that extensional essentialism is *total* essentialism and that the extensionalist can be an essentialist about some properties only by being one about all — which may well be why usually he is an essentialist about none.)[37]

Could $\ulcorner\phi_\alpha^\square\urcorner$ ever be true? It is necessary to distinguish two questions: (1) what properties *are* essential properties and (2) what

---

[37] Notice that (d3) suggests a counterpart for the related construction *de re*,$\ulcorner\phi\alpha$-contingently$\urcorner$ or $\ulcorner\phi_\alpha^c\urcorner$:

    (d4) ϕ_α^c iff $\phi\alpha$ & $(\neg\phi\alpha \dashv \Sigma v(\alpha = v))$.

That is, **a**'s not having some contingent property it in fact has would visit upon a only an accidental modification.

We can also convey the idea of being a property of something which it would be inconsistent for that something to have, or of being a property which **a** could not have:

    (d5) $\neg\phi\overset{\diamond}{\alpha}$ iff $\neg\phi\alpha$ & $(\phi\alpha \dashv \neg\Sigma v(\alpha = v))$.

Thus, Socrates could not be an inaccessible cardinal, since not only is it the case that he is not, but if he *were* he just could not be who he is — it would not be *Socrates* who is the inaccessible cardinal. Inaccessible cardinalhood being, as St. Thomas was fond of saying, *repugnant* to the likes of Socrates.

things *have* essential properties? As I have àlready averred, self-identity is an essential property [38] and, if the *façon de parler* may be forgiven, everything whatever has it; from which, *to be is to be identical with something*. Thus a cliché receives contemporary (and neoplatonistic) expression in the formula $\ulcorner \Sigma v_0(v_1 = v_0) \urcorner$ which, by capturing the ideas of there being such a thing as so and so *and* of so and so's being *identical* with something, serves to express, what used to be called the co-modality of Being and Unity.[39] But Being and Unity aside, just what things have essential properties and just what are these properties that they have essentially?

A property is essential if and only if, for anything having it, its failure to have it would result in there being no such thing as it. It is a matter of some importance that the clearest and most plausible examples of items having essential properties and of the essential properties that they do in fact have are such abstract and well-defined (we want to say, constructed) things as arithmetic objects; for example, the positive integers. Thus the number 2 is prime; primehood is its essentially. There could not be such as the number 2 without its being prime, and being prime is an essential property in the sense that anything having it has it essentially.[40] However in the case of *non*mathematical flora and fauna it is not at all uncharacteristic that one has

---

[38] An essential property is such that, if it is essential to anything, it is essential to everything having it. It could not happen, for example, that primehood is essential only for the numbers having it, but not for the billygoats having it, since any arithmetically prime billygoat is not a billygoat, but a number.

[39] Hence to be is to *be* the value of a bound variable, and a justly famous soliloquy—"What is there?" "Everything"—goes over into that most unliterary of formal translations: "By what method of closure is $\ulcorner \Sigma v_0(v_1 = v_0) \urcorner$ converted into a truth of greatest generality? "By adjoining 'Πv_1'." It may prove unfortunate that the author of that soliloquy then changed the subject to what *exists*. See Quine [5, pages 1–3].

[40] Depending, of course, upon what is to count as a property. If, for example, we allow arbitrary "disjunctions" of properties to be properties or "material negations" of properties to be properties, then we have counterexamples. For, *being prime or strong* will be had by the number 2 essentially but by Gordie Howe only contingently.

In [19] I tried to discourage what I think might fairly be called the "truth-functional view of property construction": if f is a property and g is a property, so are f-or-g and not-f. And in [20] I have favored the view that the "material negation" of a property can be regarded as a property only in an extended sense, provided that there is some property which is a *contrary* of the property whose "material negation" is under review.

Thomason [21] has attacked [19], chiefly on the grounds that definitions, central to that paper, admit of numerous counterexamples. And since much of [20] also rests upon a thesis of [19], it too seems adversely affected by Thomason's remarks. However, it should be pointed out that Thomason's counterexamples are indeed counterexamples only under an assumption that in [19] I was at pains to deny, namely, that for natural languages the idea of a "semantic primitive" or "atomic predicate" (for example, "x is yellow") makes no more sense than the idea of a natural starting place in California and so makes no sense whatever. This Thomason avers, without argu-

only the unswerving conviction, attended by all appropriate ontological rectitude, that some among these properties must be essential
to them, in virtue of which alone they are individuated. And we need
no reminding of the difficulties occasioned by that conviction when it
comes actually to specifying those properties. It is in that connection,
as we all know, a short and slippery slide to mystical unions of matter
and form, to purely formal (and empty) individuating principles (for
example, "that by which a thing is what it is and none else"), and so on.
In particular, Socrates' rationality seems properly to belong to the
textbook, where so many of what are there offered as examples are
tacitly agreed not to be, having the heuristic virtue of suggestiveness,
not the alethic one of accuracy.

That mathematical objects and their properties serve best to
illustrate essentialism is interesting in two further respects. There is,
first, the difficulty that by the conventional wisdom it is a necessary
truth *de dicto* that 2 is prime. If this should prove to be so then our
best example of an essentialist truth *de re* turns out to be no such
thing, finding formulation in the very idiom that we have been at pains
to deny it. Now it certainly would be a necessary truth *de dicto* that
two is prime if it happened both that every possible world contained
the number 2 and there it were prime. From the conjunction of

(12) $\Box \Sigma x (x = 2)$

and

(13) $2^\Box$ is prime.

ment, in a footnote. It would be interesting to know how the needed argument might
go.

Even so, the decision whether my disparagement of truth functionally compound
properties of arbitrary properties is defensible need not wait upon that argument,
for on the question of truth functionally compound properties our theories coincide.
Not that this settles anything conclusively—concerning properties in particular and
non-individuals in general such hope seems pious.

The related question whether to admit "truth functionally tautological" properties,
for example, *being prime or not being prime,* or "logically nested" properties, for
example, *being an integer, if prime* is not quite as pressing. For, there is no evident
harm in regarding these as conditions which every individual meets in any world he
graces. But for all that, where S is a set, the union of subsets S_i of tautological properties and nested properties, neither S nor any extension of S up to maximal consistency (to expand that concept slightly) can give the essence of any individual. How
could it be otherwise, since all such sets, S_i are satisfied by all individuals? Suppose
we enumerate the sets $S_i - S_1, S_2, \ldots, S_n,$ up to maximal consistency. Then every
S_i differs from every other yet are true of just the same objects. Sets so different but
so radically undiscriminating are perhaps not very usefully thought of as sets of
properties.

It appears that we obtain

(14) $\Box(2^\Box$ is prime);

and from the single truth

(15) $\Box\Sigma x(x = 2)$ & x is prime)

it emerges that

(16) $\Box(2$ is prime),

wherein not a trace of a modalized *predicate* remains.

Apparently the point is a general one: any truth of the form $\ulcorner\Box\Sigma v((\alpha = v)$ & $\phi v)\urcorner$ is logically equivalent to one of the form $\ulcorner\Box\phi\alpha\urcorner$ in which no modal occurs in positions *de re*.

Whether what I have called the "best examples" of truths illustrating the present essentialist thesis are to be allowed to stand, it will have to be ascertained if in fact such items as numbers must be reckoned to have necessary existence. But how are we to decide this question? If numbers were sets, then by the *Axiom of the Empty Set,* there is a set 0 such that nothing is a member of it; and, by the *Axiom of Power Sets,* for every set S there is a family of sets, 2^s, consisting exactly of all subsets of S. In case $S = 0$, $2^s, = \{ 0 \}$. Whether we chose to mimic the integers either by means of Zermelo sets or by means of von Neumann sets, if these axioms could be made out to be necessary in our prevailing *model theoretic* [41] sense and if they could be made out to be sufficiently categorical as to deliver analogues of the integers, then arithmetic essentialism is driven into a rendering *de dicto* of the very sort from which I have been trying to release it.

On both counts there are problems. (1) The empty set, somewhat like the integer 0, is largely a convenience and is postulated not so much because of antecedent firm ontic predilections (does every possible world *have* to contain abstract sets?), but rather to aid in generalizing set theoretic operations. (2) Although Zermelo set theory and von Neumann set theory are not equivalent, are not isomorphic, they simulate the integers with equal intuitive force. This has led

---

[41] I do not intend that there is no good theory of necessary truth in which, for example, the Axiom of the Empty Set finds itself labelled 'necessary'. My point is that it is nonsense to think that *every* good theory of necessity will so classify it. And, as with genuinely alternative theories about any topic, what theory of necessity we adopt is not automatically settled by, for example, the fact that Γ is a good theory, for by hypothesis, its alternative Γ' is a good theory as well.

some philosophers to the opinion that although Zermelo sets and von Neumann sets could not reasonably be expunged from our ontology, the integers very well could be. But in that event we have altogether lost our example, since it will now be false, both *de dicto* and *de re,* that 2 is necessarily prime, there being none such as 2. True, in place of the reduced "fact" that 2 is prime we will have two corresponding theorems, one for Zermelo sets and the other for von Neumann sets, but the question whether *these* are necessary model theoretically speaking is but a variant of the earlier question whether *The Axiom of the Empty Set* is necessary in that sense. I confess that it does not seem to me obvious that it is.

We should bear it in mind, however, that if the existence of the number 2 *is* necessary, that is not a consequence of its having essential properties such as primeness. So we can still avoid the unwelcome conclusion that having any property essentially *makes for* necessary existence.

The second point of interest raised by the mathematical cases is that to the extent that these are constructed entities they will have only such properties as they are defined or proved to have (admitting as well those that follow from those already defined and demonstrated). They are, then, in a way that Socrates could never be, our creatures, items with an initial basic structure imposed by abstraction and postulation. This alone suggests that essentialism with respect to the concrete items of our *quotidian* involvements, Socrates among them, may have to wait upon highly sophisticated abstract theories whose models prove adequate to empirical data (albeit themselves in abstract canonical form) from biology, neurophysics, metallurgy, and the like. Ultimately what properties are essential to an empirical object may only be those conferred upon it by those sentences most deeply embedded in its formal scientific theory.

4. In section 3 the position was taken that, since neither $\ulcorner \Sigma v (\alpha = v) \urcorner$ nor $\ulcorner \Sigma v_0 (v_1 = v_0) \urcorner$ was a theorem, the proffered definitions of essential and necessary attribution could safely specify a condition which, if not met, would involve the negation of sentences of this very profile without, however, forcing the essentialistic sentence into the form of a rehabilitated Sleigh Fallacy. I also remarked that revisions to standard first-order logics resulting in the nontheoremhood of these formulas should not be *ad hoc* in the sense of having nothing to recommend them but an explication of essentialism that met the adequacy conditions (α) to (δ). That revision we now sketch, after, as a preliminary, a brief characterization of a system FQ, due to Meyer and Lambert [15] of universally free logic.

Axioms of FQ (adapted from Church [19]).[42]

101. If A is a truth-functional tautology, A is an axiom.

102. $(x)(A \supset B) \supset (A \supset (x)B)$, where x is not free in A.

103. $(x)(A(x) \supset (E! \, y \supset A(y)))$.

104. $(x)E! \, x$.

105. From A and $A \supset B$, to infer B.

106. From B, to infer $(x)B$.

107. $(x)(A \supset B) \supset ((x)A \supset (x)B)$.

Principal Remarks.

1. The quantifiers receive their standard interpretation. Thus, by Axiom 104, everything (in the range of bound variables) *exists*.
2. $E!$ is a primitive predicate in FQ. However, it can be shown that if the language of FQ is extended by the addition of identity, then "$E! \, x$" is valid if and only if "$\exists y(x = y)$" is valid; and if the language is extended so as to contain individual constants then "$E! \, a$" is valid if and only if "$\exists x(x = a)$" is valid.
3. However neither "$E! \, x$" nor "$E! \, a$" is a theorem of FQ nor a valid wff of FQ.
4. Although identity is reflexive, "$x = x$" is not a valid wff [in our extension] of FQ. Axiom 103 takes us from the reflexivity of identity to the self-identity of Socrates but not "of" the present king of France.

Principal Theorems.

> *Th. I.* Putting '*SQ*' for "standard quantification theory," and where A is an arbitrary wff of FQ, there is some unique distinguished wff A^* of SQ such that, if and only if A is provable in FQ, A^* is provable in SQ.
>
> *Th. II.* FQ is semantically consistent.
>
> *Th. III.* FQ is semantically complete.

[42] The authors' numbering and notation are retained.

Thus, as the authors point out, FQ is not at all a strange or unintuitive logic; in fact SQ is an isolable subsystem of it. It is a fact, by the proof of completeness, that in place of a logic SQ which ignores the empty domain and empty names, we have in FQ a perfectly adequate logic which does not.

An adaptation of FQ.

The notion of necessity *de re* as truth in all possible worlds containing **a** is now easily seen to call for expression in a free logic. Intuitively,

(17) Fa if and only if "Fa" holds in every world containing **a**.

Similarly, in a language quantifying over possible worlds **w**,

(18) Fa if and only if $\Pi w(\alpha \in w \dashv Fa/w)$; that is, for all possible **w**, if **a** $\in$ **w** then Fa is true with respect to **w**.

There is some analogy with a standard inference pattern in free logic:

(19) $\Pi v_0 \phi v_0 \Rightarrow \cdot \Sigma! v_1 \supset \phi v_1$.

That is, it is true of everything in this world that if Fx then if there is (in this world) such a thing as y, it is a truth relative to this world that Fy.

It is a perfectly straightforward matter to extend FQ to FQ^{Σ}.[43]

a. Replace '$\exists$' with the broader 'Σ'. Formally, this interpretation of the quantifier leaves all the results of the system unchanged.
b. Admit individual constants and the identity sign.
c. Contextually define $E!^{\Sigma}$ as follows:

$$E!^{\Sigma} v_0 \quad \text{iff} \quad \Sigma v_1 (v_0 = v_1)$$

That is, "$E!^{\Sigma} a$" reads not "a exists," but rather "there is such a thing as a." The predicate 'exists' is no longer part of the primitive symbolism, now being merely one among many predicates for which the schemata F, G, and so on, serve as dummies.

Principal Remark.

Logically speaking FQ^{Σ} is the same logic as FQ (extended to

43 See Leblanc [27].

admit fixed individuals and the identity relation). FQ^Σ differs only in the translation into a natural language, English, of certain of the symbols of FQ; in effect the '$E!\ v$' and '$\exists v$' of FQ are simply broadened to apply to those particular things that might not exist. If there should be no such things then, '$E!^\Sigma v$' is nothing but a terminological alternative to '$E!\ v$', as is 'Σv' to '$\exists v$'. In FQ^Σ neither $\ulcorner\Sigma v(\alpha = v)\urcorner$ nor $\ulcorner\Sigma v_0(v_1 = v_0)\urcorner$ is a theorem. And, although these are facts of central importance to the essentialism here presented, FQ^Σ evidently does not exist simply to serve the needs of essentialism. To the contrary, free logics exist for the quite general purpose of delivering formal deductive inference from existence assumptions, and in that connexion FQ^Σ *happens* to give what, for us, are two much-needed results. Thus the logic which tolerates expression *de re* of essentialism is not *ad hoc* in the unsupportable sense already mentioned.[44]

Finally, to conclude this section, although my employment of 'Σ' over '$\exists$' is of no particular central importance for the claims here made concerning essentialism, it will not be irrelevant briefly to explain and defend its use.

A "platonist" and "antiplatonist" experience not the slightest difficulty in agreeing, for example, that there exists just one even prime. For his part, moved by such considerations as that there must *be* something about which it is the case that it alone is even and prime, that he and his antiplatonistic protagonist were, after all, referring to something, and that what they referred to is such as to have recognizably provable properties, the platonist finds it impossible to avert the conclusion expressed by the categorical statement of that number's *existence*. The antiplatonist can be understood as one who cannot forbear completing the above chain of reasoning *modus tollens tollendo*. For what disturbs the antiplatonist is the nature of the claim that 2 exists. He is curious to know what the existence of numbers could amount to, what it contrasts with, whether so-called mathematical existence in a species of existence or, as some philosophers have averred,[45] a subterfuge; indeed so extreme is his bewilderment he is even prepared to understand existential claims regarding the integers as locating them in some radically undiscriminating Platonic Heaven. In consequence, he denies the platonists' conclusion; but he since accepts the validity of the argument in behalf of that conclusion, the anti-

---

[44] FQ^Σ gives $\vdash Fa = Fa$ (Axiom 101), but not $\vdash a = a$. (For example, let **a** be Sherlock Holmes, or better, Mrs. Sherlock Holmes.) But, by the full principle of the identity of indiscernibles, we have it from $\vdash Fa = Fa$ that $\vdash a = a$. So FQ^Σ cannot admit the full principle. It does, however, admit what I earlier called its incontrovertible part — the indiscernibility of identicals.

[45] See, for example, R. Routley [16].

platonist is driven to, and takes, the desperate expedient of saying that we do not after all refer to numbers, that they do not after all have properties in any sense which requires us to admit the numbers into the range of variables bound by quantifiers.[46]

It is fairly obvious that the two antagonists are passing each other in the dark, perhaps too that they themselves know it and are at a loss as to how to establish contact. There is a grammatical consideration which helps explain why this should happen. In English "exists" serves two quite different constructions—the copula "to be" and the verb "to exist."[47] It is permissible, in English, to form the following:

(i)   There exists (is) an x such that—
(ii) There exists (is) such a thing as—
(iii) —exists.

The most obvious contrast is between (i) and (iii). In (i) we have what might be called a "purely quantificational situation," a circumstance in which the 'to be' construction, abstractly speaking, performs nothing but a referential role. (i) is admissibly completed only by a predicate, by an open sentence. It is remarked that in (i) 'there exists' behaves like the German '*es gibt*' and not at all like a cognate of 'existence'. In (iii) however, 'exists' occurs not as a cognate of 'to be' but of 'to exist'; it there functions as a predicate and is admissibly completed only by a noun phrase. And unlike (i), in (iii) 'exists' seems to behave similarly to a cognate of '*existieren*' and not, certainly, of '*es gibt*'.[48]

Of course (ii) is like (iii) in the sense that its only admissible sentential completion is by means of a noun phrase; and there is no denying that sometimes (iii) and (ii) are semantically equivalent. But it is perfectly natural and easy to attach to (ii) an interpretation by which it is *not* semantically equivalent to (iii), namely, by analyzing (ii) as follows:

(20) $\Sigma x(x = \ldots)$.

In this way the force of 'there exists' in (ii) is absorbed *by the quantifier* and the predicative nature of the whole construction is reflected *by the adjoined open sentence* '$(x = \ldots)$'. In canonical notation, (i) becomes

(21) $\Sigma x(\ldots x \ldots)$

---

[46] An alternative antiplatonist option, implicit in this paper, is to deny the validity of the platonists' argument and so to affirm that there indeed are some things that do not exist. See Routley [16], [17], and Woods [18].

[47] See footnote 26.

[48] A contrast somewhat similar to '*es gibt*', and '*existieren*' is found, in French, between '*il y a*' and '*exister*'.

and (iii) is rendered

(22)   Exists (x).

The quite palpable differences between (20), (21), and (22) enable us to reproduce, with greater logical clarity, the dialogue between the platonist and the antiplatonist. The platonist observes that 2 is prime, concludes the truth of "$\Sigma x(x$ is prime) " and also "$\Sigma x(x = 2$ & x is prime)," and so the truth of "Exists (2)." The antiplatonist denies "Exists (2) " and thereupon denies "$\Sigma x(x = 2$ & x is prime) " and with it "$\Sigma x(x$ is prime)."

Although the question of the *logical* equivalence of (21) and (22) is not necessarily decided by these remarks, it is clear that they are not semantically equivalent, that they do not mean the same. And this is good enough, for it provides ample room for questioning the validity of that argument accepted by platonist and antiplatonist alike.

We close with the conjecture that (20) and not (21) provides a more natural idiom for the expression of ontological commitment. For on the view that what a theory reckons to fall within its ontology is what are, from the point of view of that theory, the *objects* to which it *refers,* it is evident that (20), unlike (21) captures both ideas. If we allow (21) to function as does 'there are' in ordinary English, and if we hold to the view that what *there are,* are the objectifactory baggage of our language, then we shall have to countenance possibilities, mysteries, chances, hopes, aspirations, attributes, and so on, as being among the objects to which we refer. And this it must be admitted, with Quine and others, is silly. But it is silly not because we cannot refer to the possibility [that James will come], to the mystery [of Sally's behavior], to the chance [of a lifetime], or to the indifference [of the local M.P.]; it is rather than these to which we *do* refer in virtually every stretch of talk are not sensibly made out to be *objects* to which we refer. That something is susceptible of reference is signaled by a construction of the form (21); that it is an *object* of reference, by (20). (20) combines not only the idea that the ontic commitments of a theory are (among) what it refers to ['Σx'] but what, from the standpoint of the theory, are objects ['$(x = \ldots)$']. The explicit presence in (20) of the identity sign serves to remind us that one very prominent and very natural test of *thinghood* is what can sensibly be regarded as entering the identity relation.[49] By this test a referent is a thing if it is identity susceptible, that is, if it satisfies (L) the indiscernibility of identicals. If it satisfies (L), then our referent, now deemed to be a thing, will have all and only

49 See Ruth Marcus [28].

those properties of anything to which it is identical. By the lights of (*L*), correlative with the idea of an object is that of having properties, especially those properties that *individuate* the referent in question. That being so, it is evident that all manner of referents will fail (*L*), for it will not be possible to establish for them the needed condition of having individuating properties in common. Just what are the properties of *the possibility* [that James will come]? Are they sufficiently numerous, or rich, as to make that possibility the very object it is? [50] If not, then that particular referent cannot be made out to be a thing, cannot be an instance of (20).

It is one question whether all referents are objects; it is another whether all objects are such as to exist. Although I am surer about the first than the second, my own answer is, in each case, no.

5. *Appendix (on descriptions).* My conflation, in section 2, of definite singular terms and individual constants, or names, may fairly be called into question thus: that the unique ϕ-er ϕs in all and *only* those worlds containing the ϕ-er is not enough to show that "The unique ϕ-er does not ϕ" is not inconsistent in some pretty serious sense; though not, to be sure, in the sense in which it is the negation of a necessary truth *de dicto;* and it certainly does not show that, semantically speaking, definite descriptions have grown capital letters, for that would be tantamount to claiming that every definite singular term is an idiom.

Let us review the necessity of so treating definite descriptions. Is it in fact true that, owing to the necessary *nonfalsehood* of $\ulcorner\phi(\imath v)\phi\urcorner$, any property ϕ an individual may happen to have all to oneself (such as *being the first wife of Henry VIII*) is a property essential to that individual?

I think enough was said in section 2 to persuade us that

(23) $\phi(\imath v)\phi$

is not a necessary truth *de dicto*. But it seems perfectly reasonable to regard (23) as true in every world containing the unique ϕ-er. That is to say, it seems that

(24) $\phi^{\square}(\imath v)\phi$

is true, though false that

---

[50] And what of properties? Why, if they are not, are they not objects? Because *their* properties are not sufficiently rich or numerous to individuate them. So the trouble is not that one should not quantify over properties, rather that one should scruple at their entering the identity relation.

(25) $\Box\phi(\imath v)\phi$.

By these lights, it cannot any longer be true to say that

(26) $\phi^{\Box}_{\alpha}$

and

(27) $\phi\alpha$ essentially

are, as I averred in section 3, "not less than logically equivalent."
Fortunately, the needed adjustment leaves undisturbed the definitions
both of $\ulcorner\phi^{\Box}_{\alpha}\urcorner$ and of $\ulcorner\phi\alpha$ essentially$\urcorner$, for neither of those definitions
explicitly provided for the rejected coincidence. It emerges, then, that
although $\ulcorner\phi(\imath v)\phi\urcorner$ is a necessary truth *de re*, it need not endow the
ϕ-er with an unwanted essence, ϕ-hood. The inductive definition of
essential propertyhood is such as to make this a perfectly consistent
adjustment, and we are now allowed the view that the set of essentialistic truths is a proper subset of necessities *de re*.

Provided we are very careful about how we *understand* the claim
that $\ulcorner\phi(\imath v)\phi\urcorner$ is necessary *de re*! For let

(28) $(\imath v)\phi = a$

be true, that is, be true in the actual world. Then, on the strength of
(28), are we to say that (23) is true in all and only those worlds containing **a** even though (28) *may not* hold in every world containing **a**.
And are we to say, again on the strength of (28), that (23) will fail in
all worlds not containing **a** even though in those very worlds

(29) $(\imath v)\phi = b$

is true? If

(30) The season's N.H.L. scoring leader is Phil Esposito

is true, then although

(31) The season's scoring leader leads the scoring

will be guaranteed to be true in all worlds containing the scoring leader,
it will be true of Esposito only so long as (30) remains true. But it is

a particularly exciting truth about the National Hockey League that if Keon gets hot, he can falsify (30) but not, he might be glad to know, (31). And what of the deprived world not containing Esposito? Will that be a world in which the N.H.L. cannot have a top scorer?

For (23) to be necessary *de re* it is clearly not enough that it be true only in those worlds containing the individual who happens, in this world, to be the ϕ-er; rather it will be true in every world which contains the ϕ-er, whoever, in those particular worlds, he might be. Thus, we seem to have

$$(32) \quad \Sigma v_0(((\imath v_1)\phi = v_0 \dashv 3 \ \phi v_0) \ \& \ \urcorner((v_0 \neq (\imath v_1)\phi \dashv 3 \ \urcorner\Sigma v_2(v_0 = v_2))).$$

Gloss: Something is the ϕ-er only if it ϕs, but the individual which in fact is the ϕ-er need not so remain; for it could cease to be the ϕ-er without ceasing to *be*.

$$(33) \quad \phi^\square(\imath v_1)\phi$$

is true iff

$$(34) \quad \Sigma v_0(((\imath v_1)\phi = v_0) \ \& \ ((\urcorner\phi v_0 \dashv 3 \ (\urcorner\Sigma v_2(v_0 = v_2)v\Sigma v_2((v_0 = v_2) \ \& \ ((\imath v_1)\phi = v_2)))).$$

Gloss: The ϕ-er necessarily ϕs if and only if there is some individual, v_0 who happens to be the ϕ-er, and v_0's not ϕ-ing would necessarily mean *either* that that individual had ceased to be *or* that some other individual, v_2, had become the ϕ-er, and that this individual is guaranteed to ϕ in all worlds in which that identity is honored.[51]

Bibliography

[1] Kripke, S., "Semantical Considerations on Modal Logic," *Acta Philosophica Fennica*, Fasc. XVI (1963).

[2] Hintikka, J., "The Modes of Modality," *Acta Philosophica Fennica*, Fasc. XVI (1963).

[3] Kripke, S., "Semantical Analysis of Modal Logic," *Zeitschrift für mathematische Logik und Grundlagen der Mathematik* (1963).

[4] Hintikka, J., "Semantics for Propositional Attitudes," in *Studies in Philosophical Logic*, ed. by J. W. Davis *et al.*, Synthese Library, Dordrecht (1969).

[5] Quine, W. V., *From a Logical Point of View*, Harvard (1963).

---

[51] I have learned much of these matters from Alvin Plantinga, Hans Herzberger, Bas van Fraassen, and most especially from Elmar Kremer; to whom all my thanks.

[6] Quine, W. V., *The Ways of Paradox,* New York (1966).

[7] Kneale, W. & M., *The Development of Logic,* Oxford (1962).

[8] Plantinga, A., "It's Actual So It Must Be Possible," *Philosophical Studies* (1961).

[9] Plantinga, A., *"De dicto et de re." Nous* (1969).

[10] Von Wright, G., *An Essay in Modal Logic,* Amsterdam (1951).

[11] Hintikka, J., "The Logic of Perception," in *Perception and Personal Identity,* ed. by N. S. Care and R. H. Grimm, Cleveland (1969).

[12] Myhill, J., "Problems Arising in the Formalization of Intensional Logic," *Logique et Analyse* (1959).

[13] Belnap, N., *A Formal Analysis of Entailment* (1960).

[14] Scott, D., "A Proof of the Independence of the Continuum Hypothesis," *Mathematical Systems Theory,* Vol. I.

[15] Meyer, R. K. and K. Lambert, "Universally Free Logic and Standard Quantification Theory," *Journal of Symbolic Logic* (1968).

[16] Routley, R., "Exploring Meinong's Jungle," Mimeographed (1967?).

[17] Routley, R., "Some Things Do Not Exist," *Notre Dame Journal of Formal Logic* (1966).

[18] Woods, J., "Fictionality and the Logic of Relations," *Southern Journal of Philosophy* (1969).

[19] Woods, J., "On Species and Determinates," *Nous* (1967).

[20] Woods, J., "Predicate Ranges," *Philosophy and Phenomenological Research* (1969).

[21] Thomason, R. H., "Species, Determinates and Natural Kinds," *Nous* (1969).

[22] Føllesdal, D., *Referential Opacity and Modal Logic,* Ph.D. Dissertation, Harvard University (1961).

[23] Strawson, P. F., "On Referring," in *Philosophy and Ordinary Language* (ed.) Charles E. Caton, Urbana (1963).

[24] Fitch, F. B., *Symbolic Logic,* New York (1952).

[25] Aquinas, St. T., *Being and Essence* (trans.) Armand Maurer, Toronto (1949).

[26] Suarez, F., *On Formal and Universal Unity.*

[27] Leblanc, H., "On Meyer and Lambert's Quantificational Calculus," *Journal of Symbolic Logic* (1968).

[28] Marcus, R., "Modalities and Intensional Languages," in *Contemporary Readings in Logical Theory* (eds.) I. M. Copi and J. A. Gould, Toronto (1967).

[29] Bergmann, G., *Logic and Reality,* Madison (1964).

[30] Quine, W. V., *Word and Object,* Cambridge (1960).

[31] Leibniz, G., *Discourse on Metaphysics,* La Salle (1950).
[32] Thomason, R. H. and R. C. Stalnaker, "Modality and Reference," *Nous* (1968).
[33] Parsons, T., "Grades of Essentialism in Quantified Modal Logic," *Nous* (1967).
[34] Kneale, W., "Modality *De Dicto* and *De Re,*" in *Logic, Methodology and Philosophy of Science,* Stanford (1962).
[35] Woods, J., "Semantic Kinds," Mineo, University of Toronto, 1970.
[36] Hintikka, J., "Toward a Theory of Definite Descriptions," *Analysis* (1959).
[37] Van Fraassen, B. C., "Meaning Relations and Modalities," *Nous* (1969).

Identity and Reference

MICHAEL LOCKWOOD

New York University

In discussions of identity statements, it is frequently insisted that the two key substantival expressions flanking 'is' or its cognate are used in a purely referential fashion.[1] In the present paper, I intend to show that this notion of pure or genuine reference, as generally characterized in the literature, leads to paradoxical consequences when applied to the case of identity statements. Rather than take the course of denying that the substantival terms in an identity statement are purely referential, I shall propose an alternative characterization of the concept of pure reference which does not have paradoxical consequences for statements of identity.

In order to appreciate the distinction which philosophers have had in mind when they have spoken of the purely referential use of a singular term, it is simplest to consider sentences whose grammatical subjects are definite descriptions of the form 'the ϕ'. Take, for example, the sentence 'The French ambassador is ill'. We can imagine an occasion of utterance on which what the speaker intended to convey to his hearer was that some particular individual, known by the hearer to occupy the post of French ambassador, was ill; and in place of 'the French ambassador' might equally have used the man's name, 'M. Renaud' say, 'the guest of honor at the banquet', or any other expression which would successfully indicate to the hearer which individual was under discussion. Here the use of the phrase 'the French ambassador' would be

---

[1] See, for example, David Wiggins, "The Individuation of Things and Places," *Proceedings of the Aristotelian Society*, Supp. Vol. XXXVII (1963), p. 176.

said to be genuinely referential. On the other hand, exactly the same form of words might be used with the intention of conveying to someone not assumed to know who the French ambassador was, or to have any prior acquaintance with him, but who nevertheless understood the descriptive phrase—that the person, whoever he might be, who satisfied that description—was in fact ill. In this case of so-called nonreferential or attributive usage, replacement of 'the French ambassador' by another phrase nonsynonymous with the latter—although contingently characterizing the same individual—would yield a sentence which, as uttered, had an import different from that of the original.[2]

The distinction may seem pedantic at first sight. What was expressed by the sentence in a given context would, after all, have the same truth value whether or not the grammatical subject was being used referentially. Thus, a philosopher who maintains that the statement which a sentence expresses when its grammatical subject is being used referentially is different from that which it expresses when the term is being used nonreferentially is committed to the view that sameness of truth conditions is not a sufficient condition for two utterances to express the same statement. Some philosophers might therefore prefer to adopt a weaker position. Although, they might argue, we may distinguish between the referential and the nonreferential use of a singular term—on the basis of the assumptions which the speaker makes concerning the knowledge already possessed by his hearers and, consequently, on the manner in which he expects or intends them to be informed by his utterance—this distinction does not bear on the *content* of his utterance, or on what is actually being said. This view might be expressed by saying that the sentence, in its two usages, differs in force rather than in the statement it embodies.

The distinction seems to me, however, to be fairly crucial. For it can be argued that, until we know whether the grammatical subject of a sentence is being used referentially, we do not know what is the correct logical analysis of the statement being expressed. Where the substantival expression does not serve to isolate a particular individual presumed known to the hearer, it might, indeed, seem proper to deny that the statement in question is, logically, of subject-predicate form; for here a Russellian elimination of the grammatical subject in accordance with his theory of descriptions seems to do reasonable justice to the intended sense. When, in the above example, the use of the term 'the French ambassador' is nonreferential, what is being said, surely, is simply that some individual or other is both French ambassador (presuma-

---

[2] Both the terminology and this way of drawing the distinction are due to Keith S. Donnellan, "Reference and Definite Descriptions," *Philosophical Review*, LXXV (1966), pp. 281–304.

bly to the country in which the utterance is made and unique in being such) and ill. (One might without altering the essential point insert the qualification that the existence of an individual satisfying the description 'French ambassador' is presupposed by the statement rather than strictly a part of what it states.) When the descriptive phrase 'the French ambassador' is serving merely as a device for picking out an individual with whom the hearer is assumed to be familiar, it seems, in contrast, not in the least plausible to deny that the statement is logically of subject-predicate form. What, after all, is a subject-predicate statement if not one whose sole function is to identify some individual and ascribe to that individual some attribute or relation?

If the function of the subject term in a genuine subject-predicate statement may be exhaustively characterized by saying what individual it is intended to identify, it ought to be possible, so it has been argued, to substitute for the subject term any other expression with the same reference and arrive at what is merely an alternative way of expressing the selfsame statement. This property of substitutivity *salva significatione* has, in fact, seemed to philosophers to be the most natural way to characterize the genuinely referential use of a singular term.

It is undeniable that nonsynonymous but coreferential terms are often capable of standing in for one another in ordinary conversational contexts. First, in putting across a piece of information, we may sometimes try out one expression after another in subject position until we are satisfied that the hearer has 'latched on' to the intended individual. Thus we might say, for instance, 'Jane . . . [puzzled look on part of hearer] Oh! You don't know who I mean. Well, the girl I introduced you to last night . . . [smile of comprehension] told me she's going to Russia'. Secondly, in reporting a speaker's utterance it is frequently legitimate to replace the expression he used in subject position with another possessing the same reference. Thus, in reporting my assertion 'Nixon is an opportunist', someone might quite correctly say 'Michael Lockwood said that the President is an opportunist'. All this might be taken to suggest that there is a class of utterances of which it can be said that they express the same statement when and only when their subjects are identical in reference and their predicates identical in sense.[3]

If the above thesis be accepted, we have the consequence not only that sameness of truth conditions is not a sufficient condition for two utterances to express the same statement but that it is not even a necessary condition. 'Nixon is an opportunist' and 'The President is an

[3] Cf. E. J. Lemmon, "Sentences, Statements and Propositions," in Williams and Montefiore (eds.), *British Analytical Philosophy* (London, 1966), pp. 87–107.

opportunist', as uttered today, would, I have suggested, express the same statement where 'Nixon' and 'the President' are being used in a genuinely referential fashion. But it is clearly not the case that in all possible worlds these utterances would have a common truth value. They might not, say, if Humphrey had won the last election. For then the expression 'the President' would not refer to the same individual as does 'Nixon'.

It should be noted that the present point is totally distinct from that raised by Strawson in "On Referring," [4] where he makes much of the fact that the same sentence may, on different occasions of utterance, be used to make statements which differ in truth value. His argument hinges on the fact that a sentence may contain token reflexive expressions whose reference is determined by the time, place, or person at which or by whom they are uttered. What we might call 'Strawsonian ambiguity' can be eliminated by the simple device of replacing all token reflexive expressions by corresponding explicit indicators of time, place, or person. (Thus, 'I am hungry' would become 'Michael Lockwood is (timelessly) hungry at 4:30 P.M., June 3, 1970'.) Such replacement yields what Quine and others call 'eternal sentences'. It is important to appreciate that what I am claiming applies as much to eternal sentences as to those containing token reflexives. For in order to know what statement is expressed by the sentence 'The President is an opportunist', when 'the President' is being used referentially, it is not enough to know that 'the President' means 'the President of the United States in 1970'; one must also know who the President of the United States in 1970 is. Had it been Humphrey and not Nixon then, independently of token reflexivity, the sentence 'The President is an opportunist' would not, on the present account, have expressed the statement it does in fact express. The reason why utterances (even such as are free of token reflexivity) may express the same statement even though they do not possess the same truth conditions, in the sense of being true or false (or, we might add, lacking a truth value) together in all possible worlds, is that what statement a given such utterance expresses may in part be a matter of contingent, extralinguistic fact.

If, as we have been assuming, it is possible for two substantival expressions contingently to designate the same individual, it is not immediately puzzling that there can be informative identity statements. A problem arises only at the point when we attempt to apply to the substantival expressions contained in an identity statement that seemingly so plausible substitutivity criterion of pure reference. Consider the sentence 'Gaurisankar is Everest', as uttered by the explorer who (supposedly) discovered the identity of a mountain observed by the Tibetans from the north and called by them 'Gaurisankar' with one observed from Nepal and called 'Everest'. If the term 'Gaurisankar' is genuinely referential, in the sense of serving merely to pick out a certain particular, then in view of the fact that the terms do denote the same mountain we should be able, without altering the statement thereby expressed, to replace the name 'Gaurisankar' by the name 'Everest'. Patently, however, such a substitution, yielding as it does the totally uninformative 'Everest is Everest', does not preserve the force of the original statement. In fact, we are strongly tempted to say that it results in a form of words which expresses a different statement altogether and, as it happens, a trivial one.

What we might conclude, at this juncture, is that the term 'Gaurisankar', in the statement 'Gaurisankar is Everest', is not being used in a purely referential manner. It might be thought helpful, in fact, to regard both 'Gaurisankar' and 'Everest' as disguised definite descriptions and offer a Russellian analysis for the statement as a whole. Let us suppose that the descriptive packages corresponding to 'Gaurisankar' and 'Everest' respectively contain as elements 'tallest mountain visible from Tibet' and 'tallest mountain visible from Nepal'. Then such an analysis would, in effect, equate 'Gaurisankar is Everest' with a statement which says, among other things, that some mountain is both taller than any other mountain visible from Tibet and taller than any other visible from Nepal.

A preferable alternative might be to regard 'Gaurisankar is Everest' as constituting a mixed case, in which the terms 'Gaurisankar' and 'Everest' are referential, but not purely so, simultaneously playing a referential and an attributive role. On this view, the term 'Gaurisankar' would, in the above statement, have the function both of indicating a particular mountain, with which the hearer would be assumed familiar, and of attributing to the mountain indicated by 'Everest' a set of properties including, perhaps, that of being taller than any other mountain visible from Tibet. Similarly, 'Everest' would have the function both of indicating a particular mountain and of attributing to the mountain indicated by 'Gaurisankar' a set of properties including, say, that of being taller than any other mountain visible from Nepal.

There are two considerations which seem to me to render these courses unattractive. In the first place, it is notoriously difficult to offer a convincing translation of any proper name into an equivalent set of descriptions. Rather, proper names seem paradigmatically to have the function of picking out individuals without describing them. (This I take to be the element of plausibility in Mill's claim that proper names have denotation but not connotation.) At the very least, there would seem to be grounds for preferring an account of the role played by proper names in the context of identity statements which is neutral on the question of whether they possess descriptive content.

Second — though this is scarcely an argument — both the analyses I have suggested *feel* wrong. Intuitively, it should be possible, surely, to provide a uniform account of the role played by the name 'Gaurisankar', both as it occurs in a statement such as 'Gaurisankar is over twenty thousand feet high', where its referential status would hardly be questioned, and as it occurs in the making of an identity statement.

This said, we have on our hands a prima facie argument which seems to show that, whatever our intuitive feelings, the key substantival terms in an identity statement cannot be purely referential: A term is, by definition, to be characterized as purely referential if, as it occurs in the context of a declarative utterance, its sole purpose is to enable a hearer mentally to isolate, as such, the individual being talked about. If this is the sole function of a term, it should then be possible to replace it with any other expression possessing the same reference, while preserving the content of the original utterance. Within the limits set by the requirement that the hearer be able, on hearing the utterance, correctly to identify the intended individual, one expression will surely do as well as another. On the assumption, now, that the term 'Gaurisankar', as it occurs in the sentence 'Gaurisankar is Everest', is purely referential, in the sense of serving merely to indicate a certain mountain, it should be possible to replace it by the term 'Everest'. For in view of the fact that these names do in fact refer to the same mountain, the hearer will presumably continue to isolate the object intended. Yet it is clear that the content of the original utterance would not be preserved under such a substitution. Therefore, the name 'Gaurisankar', in this utterance, cannot be serving a purely referential role. This is the argument. If our intuitions are to be upheld, it will have to be exposed as invalid. The question then is where, if anywhere, the error lies.

I think the argument goes wrong at just the point where it might seem most unassailable; namely, in its assumption that, where the function of a substantival term is merely to single out some particular, its replacement by any term which singles out the same particular will yield an alternative expression of the same statement. There are, I suggest, some quite general considerations which may be brought to bear on this assumption so as to cast doubt on its validity.

In a standard conversational context, someone who, intending to make a statement, utters a sentence of the kind we are considering, makes a number of assumptions regarding the knowledge or belief state of his audience. First, he assumes that his audience is familiar with the meaning of his words both in a definitional sense and in the sense in which the meaning is, in part, a function of the particular context of utterance. But also, and more interestingly, the speaker makes two sorts of assumptions regarding the extralinguistic information which the hearer has at his disposal. These can be thought of as an assumption of knowledge and as an assumption of ignorance, respectively. The knowledge assumed is that which is required if the hearer is to identify what is being referred to by such referential terms as the sentence contains. It will be assumed that he is acquainted, in some sense, with the object or objects referred to and possesses sufficient knowledge of their attributes or relations to be able to tell from such descriptive or demonstrative content as the referential terms embody that it is these individual(s) that the speaker has in mind. What it will standardly be assumed that the hearer either does not know, or can at least be usefully reminded of, is that the individual or individuals in question possess whatever attributes or relations are being ascribed to them by the speaker as the main substance of his assertion.

Only if he satisfies all the above assumptions will a hearer be in a position to be informed, in the manner intended, by the speaker's utterance. But it is sufficient merely to satisfy the condition of ignorance and to be familiar with what is being referred to (as distinct from knowing that it is being referred to) in order to be a potential appropriate recipient, as it were, of the statement which the speaker is trying to put across. Such a person (assuming that he has command of some suitable language) is in a position, given the background knowledge he already possesses, to be informed by the statement, provided only that it is expressed in such a way as to bring this knowledge into play. Thus, even among persons who share the same linguistic knowledge, the class of people capable of being informed by a given utterance will be narrower than the class of people capable of being informed by the statement it expresses. A speaker who wishes to make a certain assertion will have, particularly in his choice of referring expression(s), to tailor his words to what he assumes his audience to possess by way of background knowledge of the subject of his assertion. One utterance may, I now suggest, be thought of as an alternative expression of the statement made by another utterance just in case the assumption of ignorance associated with each is the same and there is for each (if there is for either) a possible set of beliefs which, if possessed by a hearer, would enable him to learn from the one utterance just what an appropriately informed hearer would standardly be intended to learn from the other.

One might still be tempted to think that the replacement, within a sentence, of one purely referential term by another which in context possessed the same reference, would invariably result in what was an alternative expression, in the sense just characterized, of the statement

expressed by the original sentence. What actually follows from the foregoing discussion is, however, a somewhat stronger condition of the
interchangeability of referential expressions than mere sameness of
reference. For the substitution within a sentence of a term coreferential
with that which it replaces will fail to generate an alternative expression,
in the present sense, of the statement expressed by the original sentence if the resultant utterance differs from the latter in having associated with it an assumption of knowledge and an assumption of ignorance
which are in conflict with one another. The point is that, if the identification of the particular referred to in a sentence requires one already
to know that it possesses the attributes which are ascribed by the sentence to its subject, uttering that sentence cannot, standardly, be a way
of *informing* anyone that the individual in question possesses these attributes. As an example, consider the sentences

(1) Tom is asleep,

(2) The gardener is asleep,

and   (3) The man sleeping in the corner is asleep.

Sentences (1) and (2), provided that their respective subject terms are
being used merely as means of singling out a certain individual, appropriately referred to either as 'Tom' or as 'the gardener', could certainly
be held, in a given context of utterance, to express the same statement.
But (3), despite the fact that its subject term might be intended to pick
out the same individual as 'Tom' and 'the gardener', and indeed fitted
this individual, could not on the present view be regarded as an alternative rendering of the statement expressed by (1) and (2). For in order
to know whom 'the man sleeping in the corner' referred to, a hearer
would have, *inter alia,* already to know what someone uttering (1) or
(2) would thereby be trying to tell him, namely, that the individual in
question was asleep. And two forms of words do not, I am arguing,
constitute alternative ways of expressing a given statement unless they
also, for some imaginable audience, constitute alternative ways of im-
parting the information (if any) which the statement embodies.

Sentence (3), of course, differs from (1) and (2) in possessing just
that pleonastic character which distinguishes 'Everest is Everest'
from 'Gaurisankar is Everest'. So it will doubtless be assumed that I
wish to maintain that 'Everest is Everest' fails to express the statement embodied in 'Gaurisankar is Everest' for essentially the same reasons that (3), as I have claimed, fails to capture the statement expressed by (1) and (2). So in a sense I do; but the argument is as yet
incomplete. It is true, I think, that the reason why the replacement of
'Gaurisankar' by 'Everest', in the sentence 'Gaurisankar is Everest',
fails to produce a sentence capable of expressing the content of the
original is that the assumption of knowledge associated with the resul-

tant utterance would conflict with the corresponding assumption of ignorance. But the attempt to *state* just what the assumptions come to,
in this case, brings one up against a difficulty.

In the case of (3), the point was that the ability, on the part of a
hearer, to identify the subject of the statement expressed by (1) and (2),
under the description 'the man sleeping in the corner' would involve
his already knowing, of this individual, what it was the purpose of (1)
and (2) to say about him. If we were to maintain, analogously, that the
ability, on the part of a hearer, to identify the subject of the statement
expressed by 'Gaurisankar is Everest', under the name 'Everest',
would involve his already possessing the information which the latter
sentence has to impart, then we should have to conclude that the assumption of knowledge and the assumption of ignorance are already in
conflict here. For since *ex hypothesi* the subject of this statement just
is the object referred to by 'Everest', this ability must be possessed by
anyone who knows what 'Everest' refers to.

The obvious reply, of course, is that what is at issue is not whether
a hearer can identify, under the name 'Everest', the object in fact referred to by 'Gaurisankar' (which no doubt he can, if he is capable of
grasping the content of any utterance in which the name 'Everest' is used
referentially) but whether he can identify, under the name 'Everest',
the object referred to by 'Gaurisankar' *qua* object so referred to. But
this riposte would seem to imply that being in a position to be informed
by the *statement* expressed by 'Gaurisankar is Everest', and not merely
by this formulation of the statement, is somehow essentially bound up
with a certain combination of knowledge and ignorance concerning the
names 'Gaurisankar' and 'Everest'. This conclusion I wish to resist.

The assumption of knowledge associated with the referential use
of a definite singular term is, as I have said, that the hearer is familiar
with the individual being referred to and aware that it fulfils whatever
extralinguistic conditions are required for the term correctly to be applied to it. In the case of a definite description, these conditions amount
to the (in context unique) possession of such properties as the description connotes. In the case of a proper name, I suggest thay they
amount solely to the possession of a certain *identity*.

Rather, now, than attempt to answer 'head on' the question of what
the identity of an object consists in, let us consider what it is to answer,
satisfactorily, an identity *question*. One characteristic use of proper
names is precisely in answering questions of the form 'Who/what is
x?' where the latter does not constitute merely a request for classifica-
tion of *x*. Where a question of this kind can be satisfactorily answered
by using a proper name (as opposed to a definite description), I suggest
that one of two things must be true. Either the person asking the ques-

tion desires only to know what the individual, *x*, is *called* (in which case he is not really asking an identity question at all), or he has some prior knowledge of the individual, without knowing, however, that it is to the individual he is asking about that this knowledge relates. Consider, by way of illustration, the following exchange:

> 'Who are you?'
> 'I'm Bill Sawyer.'
> 'Oh, *you*'re Bill. I've heard a lot about you. . . .'

Here the questioner has not merely learned someone's name. He now knows whom it is he is addressing, in a sense in which he did not previously. What his newly acquired knowledge of the individual's identity comes to is just this: He is now able to bring to bear on the individual before him information he already has concerning him but which was previously filed, so to speak, not under 'man I am now speaking to' but only under 'Bill Sawyer'.

In fact, of course, one can learn an individual's name without being any the wiser with regard to the individual's identity. Only if the name *means* something to the hearer will its utterance enable him in any sense to identify the individual whose name it is. A name's 'meaning something', in this context, is not to be construed along the lines of its having a Fregean sense, or Millian connotation. (In fact, the concept I have in mind is, I think, quite neutral with respect to the question of whether names possess sense or connotation.) Rather, it is a matter of the hearer possessing a body of information, or mental 'file', relating to the individual in question, to which the name, as it were, gives access. (The name might be thought of as standing to this body of information somewhat as an address stands to a storage location in a computer.)

Something like the concept of a mental file is, I believe, crucial to the philosophical understanding, not only of identity statements, but of any statement in the expression of which one or more terms are used referentially. Previously, we have been thinking of the role of a genuinely referential expression, occurring in subject position, as being that of isolating a given particular, to which the predicate then serves to ascribe certain attributes. I propose now that we consider such an expression more from the speaker's point of view, as serving to indicate a mental file in the hearer into which the information contained in the predicate is to be placed.

Everything I said earlier about the assumptions which a speaker characteristically makes concerning the knowledge or belief state of his hearer may be restated in terms of this model. The assumption of knowledge associated with the referential use of a singular term is that the hearer possess a mental file on the individual being referred to (= familiarity or acquaintance with the latter) and that the information concerning its subject, which this file contains, corresponds sufficiently to that embodied in the referential term or inferable from its context of utterance, for its successful location to take place. The assumption of ignorance is that the file does not contain as information concerning its subject that which it is the purpose of the assertion as a whole to impart.

A given mental file is to be thought of as containing all and only such information as is known or believed by a person to hold true of a single individual. Usually, a speaker will not expect his hearer to possess more than one such file on a given particular. Thus, if the hearer is familiar at all with the individual he wishes to refer to, the file into which the information embodied in the predicate is to be directed will simply be *the* file which the hearer has on the individual in question. Here it is, for practical purposes, a matter of indifference whether we think of the referential expression as serving to indicate a particular file or merely to single out a certain individual.

In the making of an (intendedly informative) identity statement, the speaker does assume, in contrast, that the hearer has more than one file on the subject of his assertion. Consequently, the respective roles of the two substantival terms used in the making of such a statement will not be sufficiently understood when all that is known is their intended reference. Further, it must be appreciated that these terms are intended to indicate, for the hearer, *distinct* mental files. The purpose of an identity statement, which will be fulfilled if it is accepted as true, is precisely to get the hearer to merge these files or bodies of information into one.

There is no longer any problem in providing a coherent account of the assumptions of knowledge and the assumptions of ignorance associated with the assertive utterance of 'Gaurisankar is Everest'. The knowledge expected of the hearer would amount to his possession of a mental file on the mountain referred to by 'Gaurisankar', to which the name 'Gaurisankar' gives access, and similarly a mental file on that referred to by 'Everest', to which the name 'Everest' gives access. The assumption of ignorance will be satisfied insofar as the file indicated, for the hearer, by 'Gaurisankar', does not contain the information that its subject is Everest, and insofar as the file indicated by the name 'Everest' likewise does not contain the information that its subject is Gaurisankar. Since a mental file is defined as the full sum of what a person knows or believes to hold true of a single individual, to assume that these conditions are fulfilled is simply equivalent to assuming that the mental files with which the names 'Gaurisankar' and 'Everest' are respectively associated, for the hearer, are nonidentical. Since the term 'Everest' would presumably be associated, for the hearer, with the same mental file, whatever its position in the sentence, it is now obvious that its substitution for 'Gaurisankar', in the sentence 'Gaurisankar is Everest', would bring the assumption of knowledge and the assumption of ignorance into conflict.

It might be thought that it is only to accommodate identity statements that we are required to think in these terms. This is not so, however. Normally, as I said, a speaker would assume his hearer to possess but one file on an individual to which he was referring. But on such occasions as a speaker makes *any* assertion directed toward a hearer assumed to have more than one file on the individual being referred to, similar restrictions on substitutivity will apply. This is perhaps most obviously the case where the speaker himself possesses such separate files. Thus, the sentences 'Gaurisankar is over twenty thousand feet high' and 'Everest is over twenty thousand feet high' should not, in my opinion, be regarded as expressing the same statement when uttered by, or directed to, persons assumed to be unaware of the identity of Gaurisankar and Everest—for whom, that is, the terms 'Gaurisankar' and 'Everest' give access only to separate bodies of information. After all, as uttered, say, by a Himalayan explorer, these two sentences might well express what were, from his own point of view, quite distinct discoveries. This is important, since it shows that the substitutions which we must disallow are not exclusively such as would render a previously informative utterance trivial.

What, in summary, has become of our original concept of pure reference, with its associated principle of substitutivity? Well both have undergone modification. First, it was shown that, even on a standard characterization of the purely referential use of a singular term, as serving merely to pick out a certain specific individual, we should not expect the replacement of such a term, in the context of an assertion, by another possessing the same reference, invariably to yield an alternative rendering of the original statement. One term cannot, so it was argued, stand in for another when to know its reference one would have already to be in possession of the information which the utterance as a whole was intended to convey.

Second, it was shown that the standard characterization of pure reference is in any case inadequate. According to the definition with which we have replaced it, an expression is being used in a purely referential fashion if its sole purpose is to indicate, for the hearer, a particular mental file, or 'pigeon hole', which he is assumed to possess on a certain individual. Where the hearer is assumed to have more than one such file on an individual being referred to, it will not be legitimate, on the present view, to replace one expression by another which, although it refers to the same individual, cannot be expected to indicate, for the hearer, the same file.

In all, we have canvassed two rather different restrictions upon the intersubstitution of coreferential terms in purely referential contexts. Both have been shown to be violated by the substitution of 'Everest' for 'Gaurisankar' in the sentence 'Gaurisankar is Everest', where the latter is intended to express a nontrivial identity statement. If our own characterization of pure reference is accepted, the stated aims of this paper have thus been accomplished. For we have succeeded in neutralizing such arguments as are intended to show that the key substantival terms in an identity statement cannot be purely referential.

A perennial problem on which we may now be able to shed some light is that of whether identity is a genuine relation. For on the assumption, common among contemporary logicians, that a relation is expressed by any sentential context in which two or more purely referential terms are embedded, it is a straightforward corollary of what we have been maintaining that identity is indeed a relation. Whether there is some other, philosophically interesting, sense of 'relation' under which identity fails to qualify as such is a question which I shall not enter into here.

Difficulties for Mind-Body Identity Theories

JOSEPH MARGOLIS

Temple University

The contemporary literature favoring materialism is by this time so enormous that to speak of refuting the mind-body identity theory will strike the ear as either extremely naive or entirely fatuous. However, there is no single identity theory that all apparent subscribers agree upon; furthermore, although the identity theory is normally supposed to strengthen the hand of materialism, it is not necessary that it favor materialism over alternative ontologies, and it is not necessary that it be construed in narrowly ontological terms at all. Again, it is not obvious that materialists actually need subscribe to any of the usual alternative identity theories. Nevertheless, there *is* a provisional burden upon materialists to hold such a theory, failing certain alternative maneuvers, and there *are* stipulations respecting such a theory that insure maximum philosophical interest; furthermore, respecting *such* a theory, there are compelling difficulties, I am prepared to argue, blocking reasonable adoption, difficulties which, if they were allowed to stand, would be decisive. In any case, they are difficulties which I believe I have not seen any convincing way of escaping.

The chief stipulations respecting the relevant identity theories are, I think, the following: (1) that the identity posited be empirically contingent; (2) that the identity posited concern entities rather than the meanings of linguistic expressions merely; (3) that the identity posited concern psychological entities which we may have knowledge of by direct experience and introspection; (4) that, in the identity

213

posited, to speak of entities is merely to speak of the grammatical referents of the relevant reports and claims in first-, second-, and third-person discourse. I put these conditions forward more in the spirit of fixing the range within which the most fruitful and interesting disputes about the identity theory are bound to fall than with the assurance that their full import is entirely self-evident and uncontroversial. I am myself fully prepared to explore alternative ways of specifying these conditions; but to see the point of the constraints mentioned is quite sufficient for my present purpose. I cannot suppose, furthermore, that the difficulties I have in mind exhaust those that are philosophically native to the mind-body problem, but I regard them as essential difficulties, that is, difficulties each of which confronts any version of the identity theory meeting the constraints just enumerated. They are, I may say, difficulties primarily of an epistemological sort, although they have ramifications — as I hope to show — for both ontological and semantical investigations. I shall discuss them under four headings: *skepticism, Leibniz' Law, intransitivity,* and *attribution,* although, as will be seen, they are actually quite closely linked.

1. *Skepticism.* The skeptical problem arises *vis-à-vis* (at least certain) psychological states (as those of having pain, images, thoughts) because of an asymmetry between first- and second- (or third-) person discourse respecting such states. In general, we concede that claims about another's pains, images, thoughts, and the like depend on inferences from what serve as criteria, evidence, signs, symptoms, clues of such states, the occurrence of which does not necessarily follow from the occurrence of what serve as their criteria, evidence, or the like. The precise inferential connection is not important here and is, in any case, extremely controversial: it is sufficient that the admission of the occurrence of what serve as criteria, for instance, and the nonoccurrence of what they serve as the criteria for, does not entail a contradiction — regardless of what issues of doubt and certainty may or may not arise. In the first-person setting, then, we come to know that these states occur by direct awareness and without relying at all on what, in the second-person setting, serve as the criteria or evidence of the occurrence of such states.

Now, *if* the identity theory were true — if, for example, sensations were identical with brain processes *and* brain processes were not defined as unobservables — then, since brain processes (as observable in principle) would not support a comparable asymmetry, the original asymmetry admitted would have to be denied. Skepticism — "minimal skepticism," as one recent commentator puts it [1] — arises because the

---

[1] Cf. Jerry Fodor, *Psychological Explanation* (New York: Random House, 1969), Ch. 2.

inferential claims of second-person discourse do not seem to be able to recover the epistemic certainty proper to first-person discourse and because we do not seem to be able to provide suitable noninferential grounds for second-person claims themselves. *If* the identity theory were true, this skepticism could be dissolved; and if it were known to be true, it would be dissolved. We might be tempted, for example, to insist that, on Occamist grounds, materialism is ontologically more economical than dualism, hence, that the identity theory is true and that the asymmetry and attendant skepticism dissolve. There are questions, of course, whether or not the preference of a materialist ontology obliges us to accept the identity theory, and there are reasons for supposing that it may not. And there are questions about what the precise nature of ontological economy is. But, more to the point, we suppose, *ex hypothesi,* that the alleged economy of the identity theory itself lies in the fact that it describes more satisfactorily than its competitors what we know about the psychological states of others; but this is precisely the issue that generates the uncomfortable problem of skepticism. Monism — to take the tired illustration — is, trivially, more economical than dualism, but whether monism is *relevantly* more economical than dualism is a debatable matter; also, the rules governing such debates are themselves quite as debatable and as uncertain as the material in dispute.

The upshot is that the identity theory cannot legitimately be introduced in order to eliminate the skeptical problem; for, any theory that meets condition (3), that the psychological states in question be open to direct experience and inspection asymmetrically in the first- and second-person settings, must resolve the skeptical issue first in order to provide relevant evidence bearing on the adoption of the theory. *If* we cannot be sure about the mere occurrence of these states, because of the asymmetry, it is a foregone conclusion that we cannot be sure that they are identical with any specified physical state. So, if the epistemological asymmetry obtains and if "minimal skepticism" is entailed by it, we are to that extent constrained from subscribing, on rational grounds, to the identity theory. We may very well adopt an identity theory and, in doing so, discard the asymmetry posited; but I should hold that that would not count as an interesting version of the theory. That would be tantamount to reinterpreting the inferential position of second-person discourse about the relevant psychological states as an observational one. It is, in a sense, a conceivable position (and perhaps even one that would be scientifically fruitful), but it would buy its victory by denying one of the epistemologically central differences between the perception of public objects and awareness or experience of private psychological states. The shift, it is reasonable to suppose, should be supported without begging the question.

Jerry Fodor has given a recent account that indicates clearly that the matter does not arise merely as an academic possibility. Fodor concedes minimal skepticism, concedes that it is entailed by what he calls "mentalism," that is, the denial of the proposition (so-called "behaviorism") that "for each mental predicate that can be employed in a psychological explanation, there must be at least one description of behavior to which it bears a logical connection" (where, "logical connection" is very generously construed to cover entailments, definitions, necessary and/or sufficient conditions, criterial connections, and the like).[2] Fodor also holds that "the inferred-entity account of second-person mental ascriptions . . . is incoherent unless some sense can be given to the notion of direct observational verification of such ascriptions," for, although (according to his view) mental entities are introduced as "theoretical entities," that is, entities for which the evidence is inferential, statements to the effect that certain entities are theoretical entities "must invariably be contingent."[3] This is certainly the problem and, as Fodor quite rightly adds, "if some statements of psychophysical identities are true, it could be claimed that some neurological observations would count as non-inferential verifications of second-person mental ascriptions. If X has observed the neurological event N, and N is identical with the mental event E, it follows that X has observed E" (assuming, that is, a nonintentional sense of 'observe').[4]

But it is one thing to pose the problem; it is another to suggest a conditional solution; and it is quite a third to defend the solution proffered. But now, quite obviously, the problem is *to establish that* neurological observations count as observations of what is inferred in second-person mental ascriptions. Fodor supplies not the slightest argument in favor of the required assumption;[5] he merely insists that the problem can be solved and that, therefore, materialism and some form of the mind-body identity theory is (provisionally) indicated. From our present vantage, it is sufficient to seize the decisiveness of the skeptical issue *vis-à-vis* the tenability of the identity theory.

2. *Leibniz' Law.* The problem generated by Leibniz' Law arises because it is normally assumed that the identity theorist subscribes to the sense of 'identity' proper to that law: x is identical with y only if, for nonintensional contexts, what may be predicated of x may be predicated of y and what may be predicated of y may be predicated of x, *salve veritate*. Here, we shall find it useful to distinguish carefully

[2] *Ibid.*, pp. 51, 55.
[3] *Ibid.*, pp. 97–99.
[4] *Ibid.*, p. 99.
[5] Cf. *ibid.*, pp. 72–74.

between its being possible that x and y are identical and its being reasonable or proper to claim that x and y are identical. Consider the statement, "The wish happened three inches from the base of his skull."[6] (The example is Fodor's.) According to Leibniz' Law, if wishes are identical with certain neural discharges, and if the discharge may be said (observationally) to occur three inches from the base of the skull, the wish may be said to occur (to be experienced as occurring) three inches from the base of the skull. There are two considerations of the utmost importance to mention here. For one thing, Leibniz' Law presupposes the intelligibility of the relevant predications: If Fx is true and it is claimed that $x = y$, 'Fy' must be intelligible. If it is nonsense or conceded to be nonsense, the claim cannot be maintained *in accord with Leibniz' Law;* if it is said to be an "odd" expression, we are merely hedging about the truth or sense of 'Fy', and hence, to that extent, the identity is uncertain; if it is admitted that "no conventions . . . have been adopted [as yet] for 'Fy',"[7] the original claim of identity becomes downright incoherent, assuming *Leibniz' Law.*[8] For, if $x = y$, then for every predicate F, if Fx is true, then Fy is also true; and if one knows that 'Fy' has been assigned no sense though Fx is true, it is impossible to claim that $x = y$. Consequently, it *is* a substantial objection to the identity theory to challenge particular predications as "odd" or particular would-be predicates as lacking a conventional use. This is not to deny, of course, that, in some future, 'Fy' may be assigned a sense in which, if Fx is true, then Fy is also true; that is, it may be possible that $x = y$, though we must note that even this is a dubious concession *if* the expression 'Fy' must be *assigned* a sense in order to make it true. But in any case, it is simply incoherent to claim that $x = y$ knowing that the parallel ranges of would-be predications for x and y do not have comparably established conventional uses. Thus, we cannot pretend to support the claim that $x = y$ unless we are prepared to support the claim that whatever may be truly predicated of x may be truly predicated of y and that whatever may be truly predicated of y may be truly predicated of x. In particular, if a given wish is claimed to be identical with a given neural discharge, and if we claim that the discharge happened three inches from the base of a man's skull, we must be prepared to claim as well that the wish happened three inches from the base of a man's skull.

[6] *Ibid.,* p. 101.
[7] *Ibid.,* p. 104.
[8] This has, by the way, nothing to do with the Law of Transferable Epithets, which Fodor for one confuses with the conceptual truth that if a statement may be claimed to be true then that statement is intelligible; cf. *ibid.,* pp. 104–105.

Alternatively put — our second consideration — *if* we wish to maintain the identity and, at the same time, deny the intelligibility of locating wishes three inches from the base of a man's skull (because, for instance, wishes, thoughts, moods, emotions, attitudes, and the like that may be reported by way of direct experience are not, as such, assigned spatial location but are ascribed to persons — the problem takes a different form, for example, for such sensations as those of pain, aches, tickles, tingles, itches, and the like[9]) then we cannot (without further explication) be proposing the thesis compatibly with Leibniz' Law. This is not to deny that there may be alternative conceptions of identity, in accord with which the thesis may be defended; but I should hold that such a thesis would not (so far) count as an interesting version of the theory; it would be a thesis tantamount to restricting predicate expressions along dualistic lines and, given condition (2), that identity theories concern entities rather than linguistic expressions, would actually amount to dualism itself.

It also raises the baffling problem of determining the conceivable grounds for differentially restricting the extension of predicate expressions (in nonintentional contexts) where the denotata concerned are assumed to be identical. If one held, further, that perceptual contexts and contexts of direct experience and the like are inherently intentional, then *all* disputes about the identity theory based on the body of science would be disqualified. If identity theories presuppose some body of perceptual knowledge and the like which, as it will be argued, they interpret in a certain economical way, then there must be some nonintentional sense in which what is predicated of identical denotata in the context of different modes of sentience (as of perception and feeling and the like) is subject to Leibniz' Law. To return to our example, in the context of whatever sentient mode we employ in being aware of an occurrent wish, no provision is made for the discrimination of the property of the wish's "happening three inches from the base of one's skull"; but in perceptual contexts, precisely, *of* neural discharges — alleged to be identical with given wishes — we may, *ex hypothesi,* predicate their happening three inches from the base of one's skull. Now, it must be admitted that *if* the identity went through, the "odd" statement that the wish was thus located would no longer be odd; but the problem is that the identity *cannot,* in accord with

[9] Cf. Herbert Feigl, " 'The Mental' and the 'Physical'," *Minnesota Studies in the Philosophy of Science,* Vol. II, edited by Herbert Feigl, Michael Scriven, and Grover Maxwell (Minneapolis: University of Minnesota Press, 1958), p. 407. Feigl says that "my feelings or sentiments of elation, depression, delight, disgust, enthusiasm, indignation, admiration, contempt, etc. seem to me to be spread roughly through the upper half or two-thirds of my body."

Leibniz' Law, be allowed to go through if relevant predicates have no use in the context of sentience in which the relevant discriminations occur. The alleged identity presupposes that the required equivalences hold; and if they do not, it is either false or (at the very least) indeterminate.

The foregoing discussion presupposes an adoption of Leibniz' Law, with no reservations except the familiar ones governing intentional contexts and the like. I can, to be prefectly honest, see at least one possible line of theory that might justify differentially restricting ranges of (so-called mental and physical) predicates *within different contexts of sentience construed nonintentionally.* Imagine that I can only hear sounds and only smell odors, taking the verbs 'hear' and 'smell' as verbs of sentience operating in nonintentional contexts.[10] On an application of Leibniz' Law to *what* I hear and smell, namely, sounds and odors, I shall be forced to conclude, at least provisionally, that what I hear and what I smell are not one and the same. I can, however, provide a context in which the identity of *what* the sounds I hear and the odors I smell are the sounds and odors *of,* may be fixed, in virtue of which I may rightly claim that what I hear and what I smell — where the sense of the verbs has been altered to permit us to speak (as we normally do) of hearing and smelling chickens, for instance — is one and the same, in spite of the fact that the mode of sentience we call hearing and the mode we call smelling are restricted as to their range of possible discriminations. *If* a comparable maneuver could be executed respecting first-person awareness of wishes and second-person (and even first-person) perception of neural discharges, then it would be possible to hold that the spatial location of wishes is not open to the mode of sentience appropriate to certain first-person contexts, whereas it is open to modes appropriate in second-person (and certain first-person) contexts. The trouble is that the cases are not entirely comparable and that the disanalogies concern, precisely, the essential asymmetry between first- and second-person discourse. If it would be possible to disengage the resolution of the asymmetry issue — which is, in effect, the issue of skepticism — from the explication of the differentially restricted scope of the various modes of sentience that are involved, why then it would be theoretically possible, consistent with Leibniz' Law, to hold to the identity of wishes and neural discharges, in spite of the restriction that, in the context of first-person awareness of wishes, spatial location cannot be predicated of wishes. But I cannot see how the separation can be made, for the

[10] Cf. Joseph Margolis, "Fourteen Points on the Senses and Their Objects," *Theoria,* XXXVII (1962), 303–308; and " 'Nothing can be heard but sound'," *Analysis,* XX (1960), 82–87.

distinctive properties of felt wishes are precisely those assignable only within a mode of sentience that insures the asymmetry in question, and the spatial properties of neural discharges are precisely those assignable within modes of sentience that do not entail any asymmetry at all. If this difficulty cannot be overcome, the identity theory cannot be shown to be true.

It is understandable, therefore, that advocates of the identity theory should be attracted to conceptual maneuvers for eliminating mental phenomena, that is, mental states and the like *insofar as they may be reported and described by way of direct experience.* The most familiar proposal of this type may be found in J. J. C. Smart's well-known paper, "Sensations and Brain Processes," [11] which has come to be called Central-State Materialism.[12] Smart considers the objection that "it may be possible to get out of asserting the existence of irreducibly psychic processes, but not out of asserting the existence of irreducibly psychic *properties*." In pursuing his reply to this objection, Smart takes secondary qualities, colors, to instantiate "purely phenomenal or introspectible" qualities, but others are apparently prepared to extend his account to all mental states that may be directly experienced.[13] His reply is instructive:

> My suggestion is as follows. When a person says, 'I see a yellowish-orange after-image,' he is saying something like this: 'There is something going on which is like what is going on when I have my eyes open, am awake, and there is an orange illuminated in good light in front of me, that is, when I really see an orange.' (And there is no reason why a person should not say the same thing when he is having a veridical sense-datum, so long as we construe 'like' in the last sentence in such a sense that something can be like itself.) Notice that the suggested words, namely 'there is something going on which is like what is going on when,' are all quasilogical or topic-neutral words. . . . The strength of my reply depends on the possibility of our being able to report that one thing is like another without being able to state the respect in which it is like. I do not see why this should not be so.

There are, however, two decisive verbal considerations. For one, 'like' is invariably an elliptical and truncated expression, the use of

---

[11] Reprinted with revisions in *The Philosophy of Mind*, edited by V. C. Chappell (Englewood Cliffs, N.J.: Prentice-Hall, Inc., 1962).

[12] Cf. D. M. Armstrong, *A Materialist Theory of the Mind* (London: Routledge & Kegan Paul, 1968), Ch. 6.

[13] Cf. *ibid.*, pp. 79–82.

which is defective unless it is supplemented by expressions identifying such and such a respect; it is a relational term and calls for the same sort of addition as expressions like '. . . is related to . . .'. So it cannot be the case that one thing may be said to be like another without the respect in which this is so being able to be stated, though, to be sure, the one who makes the statement may not be able to supply the relevant respect articulately (think, for instance, of a machine of limited capacity) and another may do so for him or consistently with his intended meaning. Relevant to the present context, the respect in which an experienced afterimage is said to be *like* something else is, precisely, a respect governing what may be discriminated in distinct modes (or occasions) of sentient awareness. Another consideration is this: We suppose that when we make a report of an afterimage, we are reporting the details of an *experience* of a certain kind (or of an afterimage as experienced). Now, regardless of the merits of Smart's analysis of the meaning of the report itself, we cannot suppose that the afterimage experienced is nothing but the report of an afterimage experienced. Consequently, unless the very occurrence of afterimages and the like—that may well be reported—is flatly denied (and on independent grounds), Smart's suggestion is entirely irrelevant to the issue raised by Leibniz' Law. For, it may well be possible to obviate certain putative discrepancies between the extension of mental and physical predicates, as, for instance, of location,[14] without eliminating other such (and equally important) discrepancies. The qualities of experiences of pain, as distinct from the qualities of pains, may be just as difficult to assign to physical states and processes, and vice versa, as in discourse not yet improved in the way Smart suggests. Also, this last suggestion (denying afterimages and the like) would not provide us with an interesting version of the identity theory, for it would violate condition (3), that the identity posited concerns psychological entities which we may have knowledge of by direct experience and introspection.

3. *Intransitivity*. The problem raised by the intransitivity of sensations, images, thoughts, and the like depends on the fact that the modes of sentience proper to all perceptual contexts—as of observing neural discharges—provide only for transitive discriminations. If, therefore, sensations, for example, are brain processes *and* if what is discriminated in discriminating sensations is (within whatever limitations obtain for the relevant sentient modes) what is discriminated in perceptual contexts, then seemingly intransitive modes of

---

[14] Cf. Thomas Nagel, "Physicalism," *The Philosophical Review*, LXXIV (1965), 339–356. Further references to Nagel are to this article.

sentience will actually prove to be transitive. But it is, precisely, the intransitivity of the sentient modes respecting sensations and the like that generates the skeptical issue entailed by the asymmetry of first- and second-person discourse regarding such experiences.

Let me be clear about usage first. I call any sentient mode (whether termed perception or sensation) transitive if what is veridically discriminated in accord with that mode exists independently of, or may be predicated of what exists independently of, such discrimination. And I call any sentient mode intransitive if what is veridically discriminated in accord with that mode does not exist independently of such discrimination.[15] Leaving to one side speculative reforms in our theory of perception and sensation, we normally admit that pains are the objects of intransitive discrimination and that chairs and tables, or their shapes, textures, colors, are the objects of transitive discrimination. The question of transitivity, clearly, may and must be distinguished from that of the indubitability of sentient reports of any sort and has nothing to do with it. It is, however, the alleged intransitivity of certain sentient modes that specifies the epistemological (as opposed to the merely proprietary) import of the doctrine of privileged access — which, quite readily, as it happens, may misdirect us to pursue instead the question of indubitable knowledge.

The trouble with the identity theory, then, vis-à-vis intransitivity, simply parallels the difficulty already noted vis-à-vis skepticism: It puts the cart before the horse. To adopt the identity theory entails denying the intransitivity of the relevant modes of sentience asymmetrically confined to first-person discourse. But the tenability of the identity theory itself presupposes an independent argument upsetting intransitivity; it cannot legitimately be introduced merely to eliminate intransitivity, consistently with condition (3), that the identity posited concerns psychological entities which we may have knowledge of by direct experience and introspection: That would be tantamount to converting at a stroke the relevant modes of sentience into fully perceptual modes, denying the asymmetry of first- and second-person reports regarding the denotata of such reports, denying privileged access and obviating skepticism — all admirable objectives in themselves — in a word, forswearing issues to be resolved by any interesting version of the identity theory. It is, without doubt, an entirely

[15] These terms are adapted from D. M. Armstrong's account, *Bodily Sensations* (London: Routledge & Kegan Paul, 1962), though I do not subscribe to Armstrong's views about sense impressions or about the subsumability of intransitive sensations under transitive sensations. I have discussed this at more length in "Transitive and Intransitive Modes of Sentience," *Philosophy and Phenomenological Research,* forthcoming, 1971.

viable position and one which is assured of being fruitful; [16] but it is substantially irrelevant to our concern since, precisely, it provides no demonstration *that* allegedly intransitive modes of sentience are, in reality, transitive modes. And it is only on this condition that we could hold that *what* is discriminated, say, by way of sensation is one and the same with *what* is discriminated by way of perception, that is, that pain is identical with brain processes, for the denotata of the transitive and intransitive modes of sentience, if such modes be admitted, must form exclusive clusters.

Consequently, advocates of the identity theory are bound to reject intransitivity either explicitly [17] or implicitly.[18] The problem arises, characteristically, in the setting of distinguishing men and machines. Hilary Putnam, for instance, maintains that "every philosophic argument that has ever been employed in connection with the mind-body problem . . . has its exact counterpart in the case of the 'problem' of logical states and structural states in Turing machines." His claim rests on alleged parallels between two representative statements:

(1) The machine ascertained that it was in state *A*.

(2) Jones knew that he had a pain.

Questions of deviant locutions are not central to the issue. Putnam's thesis would, in effect, trivialize the mind-body problem; and, as he explains:

---

[16] Cf. Paul Feyerabend, "Mental Events and the Brain," *The Journal of Philosophy*, LX (1963), 295–296.

[17] Cf. Armstrong, *Bodily Sensations*.

[18] Cf. Hilary Putnam, "Minds and Machines," which first appeared in *Dimensions of Mind*, edited by Sidney Hook (New York: New York University Press, 1960). It has been reprinted, with extensive typographical corrections, in *Minds and Machines*, edited by Alan Ross Anderson (Englewood Cliffs, N.J.: Prentice-Hall, Inc., 1964). All references to Putnam are to this paper. It may be noted also that a more recent paper, Richard Rorty's "Mind-Body Identity, Privacy, and Categories," *The Review of Metaphysics*, XIX (1965), 24–54, suffers from precisely the same weakness as Putnam's. Rorty fails to distinguish transitive and intransitive modes of sentience, speaks only of "identification of observables with other observables" and of "identification of observables with theoretical entities." He incorrectly supposes that the distinction of discourse about sensations concerns *privacy* only. But, of course, proprioception (which is a form of perception) exhibits a distinctive kind of privacy without being an intransitive mode of sentience; and the intransitive modes are, it is true, private, but are not troublesome for their being private but for their intransitivity. In this respect, Rorty has failed to grasp the full import of Kurt Baier's argument (with which I cannot wholly agree), in "Smart on Sensations," *Australasian Journal of Philosophy*, XL (1962), 57–68. Incorrigibility, also, is *not* the issue.

A machine which is able to detect at least some of its own structural states is in a position very analogous to that of a human being, who can detect some but not all of the malfunctions of his own body, and with varying degrees of reliability.

Nevertheless, although Putnam is doubtless correct in what he says about machines, what he says has, as such, no relevant bearing on the pair of statements (1) and (2), which may, along the lines of intransitivity, be made to yield important disanalogies between men and machines. And if the counterargument may be constructed, then, contrary to Putnam's view, the mind-body problem would remain "a genuine theoretical problem."

The counterargument, of course, is quite simple. Putnam's first statement is a statement regarding a transitive mode of sentience; and the second statement is a statement regarding an intransitive mode of sentience. *That* a machine may have privileged access to its own states, in a proprietary rather than epistemological sense, does not bear at all on the privileged access proper to intransitive modes of sentience. In fact, machines apart, the so-called proprioceptive and interoceptive senses are, precisely, privileged in a proprietary respect though epistemologically dependent on modes of sentience that permit no such privilege.[19] *If* the modes of sentience proper to pain and the like behaved like the proprioceptive senses, then Putnam's thesis would be correct. But this is precisely what must be established before the identity thesis can be accepted and this is precisely what a proprioceptive model cannot provide. In a word, Putnam's thesis inherently begs the question.

There is a *caveat* to be entered, however. I hold that Putnam's two statements, *as we should now use them,* yield relevant disanalogies. I cannot deny that, in principle, the evolution of our language might, by altering in formulable respects the use of his two statements, obviate the distinction between transitive and intransitive modes of sentience. Though it is possible, it is also possible that the evolution of our language will sustain present usage. Furthermore, *if* the statements are now significantly different with respect to the identity thesis, it is reasonable to suppose that any evolutionary developments of language which eliminate the difference will have operated in *different* ways on the two statements. Consequently, we may rightly disallow the force of mere evolutionary projections that fail to account for the relevant difference, and we may disallow the force of relatively formal

[19] Cf. Joseph Margolis, "Anscombe on Knowledge without Observation," *The Personalist,* LI (1970), 46–57.

arguments that are not designed to account for the relevant difference—for instance, arguments regarding the alleged difficulty of maintaining a sharp analytic-synthetic distinction. But if this is so, then the intransitivity of certain modes of sentience poses a compelling difficulty for any identity theory.

4. *Attribution*. The problem regarding attribution concerns the avoidability of equivocating on the meaning of would-be predications regarding bodies and persons. We may assume, reasonably, that an identity (the so-called "physicalist thesis") that holds "that a person, with all his psychological attributes, is nothing over and above his body, with all its physical attributes,"[20] attributes properties to physical bodies and to persons in the same sense of 'attribute'. If 'Fb' signifies that a property F is predicated of a body b and if 'Gp' signifies that a property G is predicated of a person p, we must assume that b *has* the property F, or is in the condition of *being F*, in the same sense of 'has' and 'being' as holds when one says that p *has* the property G, or is in the condition of *being G*; that is, we must assume that the syntactical features of predication taken to capture certain aspects of what is ascribed to persons and to bodies does not obscure any possible differences in sense in saying that a person or a body has or is in a certain condition. But it is not at all clear that this thesis can be maintained, and it may well be that differences that arise here substantially affect the prospects of the identity thesis.

Consider, for instance, the following four statements: (1) "p has a pain in his tooth"; (2) "p has an unfriendly attitude"; (3) "b has a height of 5 feet 9 inches"; (4) "p has a height of 5 feet 9 inches." It is, of course, interesting, as in statements (3) and (4), that physical properties (at least some physical properties) may be predicated of persons as well as of bodies. We should not expect that psychological properties, like those ascribed in statements 1 and 2, could be predicated of bodies (as of persons) *unless* the physicalist thesis were sustained *and* unless the identity posited would justify the ascription to bodies of the particular property in question. It is entirely conceivable, given an identity weaker than strict identity (that is, weaker than an identity in accord with Leibniz' Law), that *some* psychological predicates might be applicable to bodies *and* that those that were not could be dismissed as not affecting the (weakened) identity claim. Obviously, the plausibility of such a claim would depend, precisely, on the antecedent formulability of constraints on *which* such predications would have to obtain for both persons and bodies and which could be dismissed in this regard.

---

[20] Nagel, *loc. cit.*

Now, there is no question that in attributing a height of 5 feet 9 inches to both p and b, we are not only predicating that height both of a person and of a body but are doing so in a way that preserves the univocity of 'has' that obtains in saying that p has that height and that b has that height. Whatever the difference between persons and bodies, there is no reason to suppose that persons have such attributes as height in a sense different from that in which bodies have them. The difficulty lies peculiarly with statements like the first one, that is, with statements that concern psychological states of which we are directly aware or which are open to introspection [that is, with statements in accord with our original condition (3)]. A person might well *have* an unfriendly attitude without being aware of it; but a pain is normally said to exist insofar as someone *has* a pain—where to have a pain is to *feel* pain. We can see at once that a certain equivocation on 'has' obtains here—and only here—for, the 'has' of predication is not the same as the 'has' that designates sentience. *If* we were to construe the first statement as making a predication of pain, we should have to say that "p has a having (feeling) of pain." To say, then, that p has a pain is to say that a sentient experience of some sort has occurred and that the experience may be predicated of p. On *this* reading, the use of 'has' in the original statement serves both to convey the predication *and* a distinctive feature of the property predicated, its being of the nature of a sentient experience. It is, therefore, used economically in two distinct senses, only one of which conforms to the syntactical role of predication. Consequently, it is impossible to justify any identity thesis weaker than that of strict identity unless the predications of sentient experience may be made, intelligibly and validly, of both bodies and persons (or minds) or unless their inadmissibility for bodies may be satisfactorily explained. But this is, precisely, what the physicalist thesis must establish in order to establish its claim. It is not responsive, therefore, merely to notice that the identity posited concerns terms of the same logical type, predications, or attributions.

Consider, in this connection, the views of Thomas Nagel, offered largely in explication of the truism, "For pains to exist *is* for people to have them." Nagel says:

> Instead of identifying thoughts, sensations, after-images, and so forth with brain processes, I propose to identify a person's having the sensation with his body's being in a physical state or undergoing a physical process. Notice that both terms of this identity are of the same logical type, namely (to put it in neutral terminology) a subject's possessing a certain attribute. The subjects are the person and his body (not his brain), and the attributes are

psychological conditions, happenings, and so forth, and physical ones. The psychological term of the identity must be the person's having a pain in his shin rather than the pain itself, because although it is undeniable that pains exist and people have them, it is also clear that this describes a condition of one entity, the person, rather than a relation between two entities, a person and a pain. . . . So we may regard the ascription of properties to a sensation simply as part of the specification of a psychological state's being ascribed to the person. When we assert that a person has a sensation of a certain description B, this is not to be taken as asserting that there exist an x and a y such that x is a person and y is a sensation and $B(y)$, and x *has* y. Rather we are to take it as asserting the existence of only one thing, x, such that x is a person, and moreover $C(x)$, where C is the attribute 'has a sensation of description B'.

This entirely reasonable strategy, deviating from Smart's only in substituting the body for the brain, does not in itself settle the physicalist thesis favorably. It *does* succeed in eliminating a worry about the location of sensations, but at the price of focusing attention on a worry of at least equal importance. Since, as Nagel explains, "the two sides of the identity are not a sensation and a brain process, but my *having* a certain sensation or thought and my body's *being* in a certain physical state, then they will both be going on in the same place — namely, wherever I (and my body) happen to be." But Nagel fails to see that "my *having* a certain sensation or thought" does not, relevantly for the physicalist quarrel itself, merely belong to the same logical type as "[my] body's being in a [certain] physical state or undergoing a [certain] physical process," namely, that of "a subject's possessing a certain attribute." For, the equivocation noted affects the term 'possessing' as well and thus bears directly on whether (or if not, why not) sentient states may be predicated of bodies as of minds.

It is in this connection that Nagel introduces the concept of "independent ascribability" to clarify a necessary (but not sufficient) condition of (theoretical) identities weaker than strict identities. His concept is clarified by the following:

There are certain attributes such as being hot or cold, or boiling or offensive, which cannot significantly be ascribed to a collection of molecules per se. It may be that such attributes *can* be ascribed to a collection of molecules, but such ascription is dependent for its significance on their primary ascription to something of a different kind, like a body of water or a person, with which the molecules are identical. Such attributes . . . are not independently ascribable to the molecules though they may be dependently ascribable.

On the strength of this, he formulates a necessary condition for the weaker sort of identity: "that the two terms should possess or lack in common all those attributes which can be independently ascribed to each of them individually — with the qualification that nothing is by this criterion to be identical with two things which are by the same criterion distinct."

There is an ambiguity here of decisive importance. For, (1) either the condition will be met if, when some determinate attribute is independently ascribable to persons (or bodies), it is also ascribable (independently or dependently) to bodies (or persons); or (2) for whatever determinable attributes are independently ascribable to both persons and minds, the determinate attribute ascribable to the one will be ascribable to the other. There are reasons for thinking that Nagel fails to eliminate this ambiguity.[21] But, for our purposes, it is enough to show that the condition is either too weak or is, in fact, not met by physicalism; and if this is so, then either the grounds for claiming theoretical identity have not been supplied or else the claim is false. It is obvious, for instance, that the attribute of height, as in our specimen statements (3) and (4), is independently ascribable to persons and bodies and that the causal explanation of the one will be the same as the causal explanation of the other; but this surely does not bear on the identity posited by physicalism, even if there were an enormous

---

[21] It is not a crucial matter whether Nagel does or does not provide against the ambiguity. The formulation lends itself to the ambiguity, and all the possible readings deserve to be carefully considered. If the strongest interpretation is taken, that, for (1), what is *independently* ascribed to one must be *independently* ascribed to the other, then specimen statement (1) is decisive against the thesis; if the weaker version of (1), that what is *independently* ascribed to the one may be *dependently* ascribed to the other, then either the argument is a *petitio* or an independent defense of the identity must be provided. If interpretation (2) is preferred, either it is irrelevant, for Nagel, which attributes happen to be independently ascribable to both terms or he has failed to place constraints on the range of attributes that alone could decide the identity issue. It is in the sense of interpretation (2) that Nagel construes strict identity as a species of theoretical identity; but it is in the sense of the strong version of interpretation (1) that, in his Postscript, 1968, Nagel holds that "theoretical identity is not distinct from strict identity." And if the latter were conceded, his illustration about the identity of water and the molecules that compose it is either decisive *against* the identity or he has incorrectly characterized the ascribability of attributes in the example of water (which seems false), since, on his view, boiling can only be dependently ascribed to the molecules. This is enough to suggest that the intended distinction is confused. (The Postscript, as far as I know, appears only in John O'Connor [ed.], *Modern Materialism: Readings on Mind-Body Identity* [New York: Harcourt, Brace, and Jovanovich, Inc., 1969].

number of such attributes that could be specified. The condition, therefore, on interpretation (2), is much too weak. What we lack are antecedent constraints on *which* attributes must be independently ascribable to persons (or bodies) when they are independently ascribable to bodies (or persons). But, on interpretation (1), the condition cannot be met, since statements like our first statement, or other attributions of sentience, cannot be made about bodies as they can about persons and minds; or else, as by a *petitio*, the attributes in question will be *dependently* ascribed to body (or mind). What is needed are constraints on which kinds of attributes *must* be independently ascribable to bodies and minds (or persons) and a justification for waiving the constraint for certain (seemingly relevant) attributes. For example, the attribute of location would have, on the face of it, provided a decisive test against the weaker identity, were it not for the adjustment Nagel provides. But, in precisely the same spirit, the attribute of sentient experience (of feeling pains, thinking thoughts, sensing mental images, and the like) *is* a decisive test case for the weaker identity, unless it too may be satisfactorily interpreted along similar lines. The trouble is that no comparable solution is forthcoming here, simply because the solution regarding location itself presupposes sentient states. We may speculate that if sufficiently important discrepancies regarding independent ascribability arise, it will be extremely difficult (if not impossible) to distinguish the alleged theoretical identity (if one insists on it) from a mere theory of psychophysical correlation.[22] Consequently, unless and until the physicalist explains the sense in which sentient states may be independently ascribed to bodies or provides a justification for their dependent ascription to bodies that does not beg the question, the theoretical identity of the physicalist will fail, *a fortiori*, a strict identity thesis as well.

Of course, the admission of sentient states entails at least the puzzles already collected under the headings of skepticism and intransitivity. It may be made to yield additional puzzles as well. In particular, it may be argued that, although psychological attributes (like feeling pain) may be ascribed to persons in the same syntactically relevant sense (as by predication) as physical attributes are ascribed to bodies (or persons), it nevertheless remains true that a reference to a psychological attribute (like feeling pain) is an ellipsis for a reference to *one's* having that psychological attribute (in the sense of 'have' relevant to sentience and not predication). Consequently, it is quite beside the point (a matter on which Nagel insists) to claim that "I can

---

[22] Cf. Richard Brandt and Jaegwon Kim, "The Logic of the Identity Theory," *The Journal of Philosophy*, LXIV (1967), 515–537.

. . . describe without token-reflexives the entire world and everything that is happening in it," for reference to *one's* having a sensation or thought or the like (to *my* having it or *your* having it) has to do not merely with the use of token reflexives (which we may well eliminate) but also with restrictions on the proper subjects of such psychological states: that they must be persons or minds and not bodies. Nothing follows from this alone regarding the analysis of bodies, persons, and minds, except that the physicalist thesis cannot rest solely—in dealing with the question of independent ascribability—on the purely formal features of predication and the eliminability of token-reflexive expressions. Consequently, the problem of the attribution of sentient states is a fundamental problem confronting the identity thesis.

Having offered these counterarguments, I should like to close with two further qualifications. The first is this. *If* theoretical unobservables are admitted,[23] the objections posed will not significantly bear on identity claims as between, say, sensations and microphysical unobservables. The problem of skepticism concerned second-person knowledge (as by way of inference and observation) of what is known by way of certain privileged modes of sentience proper to first-person discourse; the problem, therefore, does not arise where unobservables are admitted. The problem of intransitivity concerned the difficulty of admitting that what is discriminated by an intransitive mode of sentience and what is discriminated by a transitive mode of sentience could be one and the same; again, the problem does not arise where unobservables are admitted. Finally, to admit unobservables is to provide theoretical justification for differentially restricting the use of predicates in sentient and nonsentient contexts; hence, the problems posed by Leibniz' Law apparently can be avoided. I am, consequently, prepared to admit that the objections posed have a certain limited application—though this is precisely the point of condition (3).

The second qualification is this. It need not be the case that *all* so-called "psychological" or "mental terms" denote psychological states that are open to direct experience and introspection. Many, for instance, may be theoretical terms introduced to interpret behavior and the like in terms of purposes, functions, goals, and so forth. If it is the case that such different physical or behavioral complexes may rightly be characterized, *psychologically* characterized, in terms of *such* concepts (in terms, say, of motives, drives, purposes and the like), it is plain that physically dissimilar systems may be psychologically (or

[23] Cf. Fodor, *op. cit.*, pp. 96–99, who denies the coherence of such concepts, though entirely without argument. I am not myself, of course, here advocating an identity thesis involving theoretical unobservables or even the coherence of the concept of theoretical unobservables.

functionally) similar.[24] The identity theory, of course, *cannot* be formulated for such psychological concepts. But to say this is simply to concede that so-called "psychological" or "mental concepts" are by no means employed in uniform ways; and it is by no means potent against the construction of identity theories, since such theories, once again, are addressed to psychological states that we may have knowledge of by direct experience and introspection. It would, however, indicate that Central-State Materialism could not be defended, that is, a materialism that would posit reductions, by way of the identity thesis, for each and every distinct mental concept.

The foregoing arguments, I may say, I concede to be conditional in another respect: they depend upon a favorable—however provisional—analysis of the various modes of sentience. To the extent that the identity thesis may be assessed on the grounds of its fitting what is the case concerning sentience, the analysis of perception and sensation and the like must be supposed to be relatively independent of taking sides on the identity thesis itself. Alternatively put, the foregoing arguments may be construed, equally congenially, as a challenge to the identity thesis itself or as an invitation to partisans of the theory to supply certain needed details by which to exhibit the application of the theory (they already take to be true) to a sector of the world which they expect it to fit. On either view, these arguments are an attempt to bypass mere ideological quarrels.

[24] Cf. *ibid.*, pp. 107–120.

Physical Equations and Identity

WILLIAM RUDDICK

New York University

Logicians encourage us to read the equations of physics in familiar ways. We are to take an equation either as a universal material conditional (or biconditional), or as a contingent identity statement connecting co-referential, but nonsynonymous terms in ways Frege taught us. The latter reading is supposed to be especially suited to those equations which, like $E = mc^2$, unify diverse physical concepts or to those physical equations which, like $kT = \frac{2}{3}\bar{E}$, unify diverse physical theories. Such "bridge laws," so read, are invoked by current materialists to show the kind of identity relation they attribute to mind and body.

We know the problems which arise from reading physical laws as material conditionals. (How can a law of the form $(x)(Fx \supset Gx)$ warrant subjunctive claims about counterfactual and possible cases? Why is a law not confirmed by instances of the form, $-Fx \ \& \ -Ga$? How are we to keep lawlike statements about empty classes from being true simply in virtue of their false antecedent clauses? How are we to keep laws about ideal cases from being false for want of any confirming instances of the form, $Fa \ \& \ Ga$?) And there is a growing suspicion that this reading is more trouble than it is worth. Some nonextensional logic may be needed.

It is, however, the other reading of equations I wish to consider here. Any physical equation *may* be read as a Frege-identity statement, the nonsynonymous left and right members co-referring to the same number or to the same physical magnitude. But by so reading certain equations, we miss both the physical and metaphysical import

233

which many physicists and philosophers find in these equations. An operationalist would not object to reading '$E = mc^2$' as a statement of the co-referentiality of the energy term and the mass term. For him, left and right sides give alternative methods for arriving by measurement and calculation at the same number, and that number may serve as the common referent. Likewise, the Frege-identity reading would suit those commentators (for example, Jammer and, at times, Einstein himself) who take the equation to show that mass and energy are both really forms of something else, "massergy." This novel substance can, like numbers, stand as mutual referent for both the energy- and mass-terms.

But a Frege reading does *not* suit the most common interpretation of '$E = mc^2$'. According to that view, the equation is taken to show that mass is reducible to energy, that mass is nothing but a form of energy. This reduction may or may not eliminate mass (in the old sense) from the physicist's list of the world's properties. But, in either case, this interpretation favors energy at the expense of mass, and such an unequal treatment is not reflected in an identity reading which treats both terms alike. Identity does not capture reduction, either here or in the similar case of $kT = \frac{2}{3}\bar{E}$, an equation which is part of the reduction of temperature (in classical thermodynamics) to mean molecular energy of translation (in statistical mechanics).

To represent the reduction of mass or temperature to energy we need a different, nonsymmetrical relation. When A is reduced to B, A may be said to be "identifiable with" B. The relation of *being identifiable with* is not symmetric. To reduce A to B is not thereby to reduce B to A, nor is the fact that A is identifiable with B the fact that B is identifiable with A. Indeed, in all the cases that come to mind, the relation of identifiability is not only nonsymmetric; it is asymmetric. (Somewhat contrary to English usage, 'identifiability' shall be used here as a slightly shorter, less barbarous synonym for 'being identifiable with'.) But nonsymmetry is enough to show that identifiability is not identity. To identify A *with* B is not to identify A *and* B. To show that A is identifiable with B is not to show that A and B are identical.

The two relations I want to distinguish are, however, connected in the special case of "parallel identifiability." As we shall see in detail, to identify both A and B with the same C *is* to identify A and B — to a limited extent. To identify both A and B with C is to show that A and B are the same C, or that A and B enjoy the relation of *relative* identity (as it has come to be called in recent discussions of identity). But relative identity is not absolute identity. To show the parallel identifiability of A and B with C is *not* to show that A and B are identifiable with one another, or that A and B are (absolutely) identical.

Distinctions are beginning to abound, and I must give some hint of the work they are meant to do. If an acceptable distinction between identity and identifiability can be made out, we should benefit in at least three ways. We shall have a clearer view of certain basic physical equations and their differing interpretations in physics; we shall have an account of theory- and concept-reduction which is closer to the scientist's own sense of his accomplishments; and we shall free the (misnamed) Identity Theory of mind and body from several unnecessary objections. The logician's notion of identity is, I suggest, philosophically restrictive and distorting, at least in these matters.

I. $E.S. = M.S.$

Several examples and some subsidiary distinctions may help to clarify this promising distinction. Let us begin by taking a closer look at the Morning and Evening Star(s). In fact, we know very little about them. We do not know who identified the stars, or how he did it. We do know that the identification must have been the conclusion of an argument, for their appearances are too brief and occasional for an observation of their identity.

Let us suppose the argument went like this:

Hypotheses:

The bright lights seen briefly on successive evenings above the western horizon after sunset for short, occasional periods may be the reappearances of a single material body. Call them "the evening lights", and it, "the evening star"; for short, 'e.l.' and 'e.s.'. We can say the same, *mutatis mutandis*, for "the morning lights" (*m.l.*) and "the morning star" (*m.s.*).

Calculations:

This reappearing body, the evening star, would appear just where and when it does, if it moved through the other stars of the Zodiac in a certain closed path, *Pes*. We can say the same, *mutatis mutandis*, for the morning star and path, *Pms*.

Demonstration:

The paths *Pes* and *Pms* can be superimposed; they are congruent.

Conclusion:

The evening star and the morning star can be one and the same moving body, seen at different times and places. Call that singular body, "Venus." ('Venus' is no more a logically proper name without sense than are the names, 'the evening star' and 'the morning star'. Like them, the name 'Venus' records the striking appearance of the heavenly body in question, although not its time of appearance. The name also reflects perhaps the wanton motions of the body, for Venus from the theoretical start would have counted as a wandering star, or planet.)

In the standard notation of identity, this argument would be abbreviated as,

$e.l. = e.s.$

$m.l. = m.s.$

$e.s.$ has Pes

$m.s.$ has Pms

$Pes = Pms$

$\therefore e.s. = m.s.$

But if the identity-sign '=' is meant to connect only co-referential terms, this abbreviation is wrong in all but the line, $Pes = Pms$. In the first line, '$e.l.$' refers to a set of observed, or observable lights, while '$e.s.$' refers to a putative body which, by hypothesis, is unobservable from the earth much of the time. Moreover, the line is supposed to abbreviate the hypothesis that the evening lights are lights *from,* or *appearances* of the evening star. But neither alleged relation is symmetric; hence, '=' is not apt.

There are, however, at least two ways to allow for co-reference in this case. A phenomenalist would take the evening star to be nothing more than a set of actual and possible appearances of light, and for him the name 'the evening star' would then refer to the evening lights (or at least to the set of evening lights). Or conversely, we might argue that the terms '$e.l.$' and '$e.s.$' do not differ in reference, but only in *scope* of reference; that 'the evening lights' refers to the evening star, but only in its visible conditions or locations.

Each of these arguments restores co-reference, but not the un-biased co-reference that Frege-identity requires. Each argument allows one term to have its obvious, or patent referent, while making the other term "crossrefer" to that same referent. Thus, phenomenalism allows 'the evening lights' to refer to the evening lights patently, but makes 'the evening star' crossrefer to those same lights. The justification is, of course, that the patent, or ostensible referent of 'the evening star' is really nothing but the evening star. The appeal to scope, by contrast, reverses the crossreference by reversing the order of the reduction of one ostensible referent to the other. In diagrams, the contrast is this:

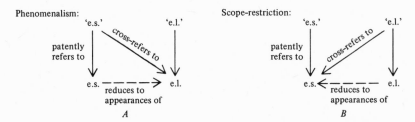

Frege once suggested that identity statements be read as metalinguistic statements about co-reference. There is a high price, as he realized, for ascent to the semantic level. Instead of being able to report directly our discovery that two supposed objects are not distinct, we would be confined to talking about their names. But, in our case, there is no need to pay this price. Ascent to the semantic level does restore co-reference, but it does not restore the symmetry needed for the standard notion of identity. If 'A' is co-referential with 'B', then 'B' is co-referential with 'A'. But if 'A' crossrefers to B, 'B' does not crossrefer to A. And it is crossreference, not co-reference, that is the semantic notion needed to state the initial hypothesis about the evening (or morning) lights and the evening (or morning) star, if we must make a semantic ascent. On the meta-level, as well as on the object level, these hypotheses express nonsymmetric relations. These are not statements of identity. The underlying reductions (represented by the horizontal arrows) show them to be identifications of stars with sets of lights (for the phenomenalist) or identifications of lights with stars (for the prototheorist whose argument we constructed).

For the sake of abbreviation, we need a new notation. Let us retain the double-bar ('=') to record co-reference of the connected terms, but add a half-arrowhead in the direction of the proposed reduction. The original hypotheses, taken at face value, can be represented

$$e.l. \geqslant e.s. \quad \text{and} \quad m.l. \geqslant m.s.$$

These formulae are to be read as "the evening lights are identifiable with the evening star" and "the morning lights are identifiable with the morning star."

By contrast, the step in our argument which identifies the two paths involves no such complications. This identification shows no preference for one of the terms and has no direction. The path of the evening star is not reduced to that of the morning star, nor vice versa. Nor is any novel theoretical object introduced. The two paths are shown to be one and the same *path*. And there is no puzzle here about two things being one. By superimposing either one on the other, we can see how two paths can be indistinguishable. It was only our original concern with apparently different objects at different times and points on that path which made us think otherwise. Here the identity sign seems appropriate, for this step in the argument states a simple, non-trivial, nonrelative (or absolute) identity. The line "*Pes = Pms*" may be left as is.

But can the conclusion, "*e.s. = m.s.*" be so abbreviated? There are obvious similarities to the case above. Again, the identification is not biased. The morning star is not identified with, or reduced to, the evening star, or vice versa. Hence, neither 'the evening star' nor 'the morning star' is made to crossrefer to the ostensible referent of the other term. Moreover, as before, the number of ostensible referents is reduced from two to one.

But here lies an important difference. In identifying *Pes* and *Pms*, we introduce no new referent, or new kind of referent. We showed that the path of the evening star and the path of the morning star are one and the same *path*. (We may want a new name for that single path, say *Ps*, but *Ps* differs from *Pes* and *Pms* in name only.) By contrast, in identifying *e.s.* and *m.s.*, we introduce a new referent, Venus. Unlike the old ostensible referents, Venus is not defined by the time of its visibility on earth. We can sensibly speculate as to whether or not Venus, if its orbit were to change in certain ways, would still be visible at dawn or at dusk, or in the middle of the night, or even at any time. But given the descriptive force of the old names, we cannot so speculate about the evening star or the morning star. If, say, the apparent object we called "the evening star" were to begin to appear at midnight, it would no longer *be* the evening star, even if we could somehow establish its continuity with what had been the evening star. Of course, we can capitalize the old names, thereby turning them into proper names which no longer exercise such restraints on counterfactual possibilities. The Evening Star (unlike the evening star) could cease to appear in the evening, just as could Venus. But then, 'The Evening Star' (unlike 'the evening star') is just another name for Venus.

The evening star was defined as a body which appeared at certain times; Venus (or The Evening Star) is defined by its peculiar path and motion, and as such is more a kinetic body fit for astronomical theory than a visible body fit for visual astronomy. By substituting Venus for the evening and morning stars, we have not only reduced the *number* of an astronomer's objects. (In this, identifying the putative

stars is like identifying their putative paths.) We have, more importantly, reduced one kind of astronomical object to another. We have
eliminated stars, defined by "secondary" visual properties in favor of a
body defined by "primary" properties, a reduction of the kind which
Galileo and Einstein would take to mark progress toward the ideal of a
geometric physical theory. In such a theory, visual properties of bodies
would be tolerated only as accidental clues to their distance, motion,
and (perhaps) composition. Venus is thus to be seen as a theoretically
preferable successor to the evening star, and not just the evening star
renamed.

In short, Venus *does* not move like other stars and, being defined
by its motion, *need* not move or appear as other stars. Thus, it is
already a borderline star, even before it and other planets were calcu-
lated to need no light of their own. We may conclude, then, that the
discovery that the path of the morning star and the path of the evening
star were one and the same *path* did not show that the morning star
and the evening star were one and the same *star*. The identity of paths
is not the ground for asserting the identity of stars, or rather, the
absolute identity of paths is not the ground for asserting the *absolute*
identity of stars. It is the ground for the *relative* identity of the morning
and evening stars, for it is the identity of paths that justifies the parallel
identifications of each supposed star with the planet Venus, and these
identifications in turn show that the morning and evening stars are one
and the same — one and the same *planet*. In suitable notation:

$$
\begin{array}{ll}
\left.\begin{array}{l} e.s. \geqslant V \\ m.s. \geqslant V \end{array}\right\} & \text{parallel identification} \\[4pt]
\dfrac{V = V}{e.s. \underset{V}{=\!\!=} m.s.} & \begin{array}{l} \text{trivial identity} \\ \text{relative identity } (= e.s. \ \& \ m.s. \text{ are the same } V) \end{array}
\end{array}
$$

Or, more briefly:

$$
\frac{e.s. \geqslant V \leqslant m.s.}{e.s. \underset{V}{=\!\!=} m.s.}
$$

This is an instance of the principle that two (putative) things identifiable with the same thing are relatively identical with one another,

$$(x)(y)(z)(x \geqslant z \,.\, y \geqslant z \,.\!\supset.\, x \underset{z}{=} y)$$

The principle proposed above resembles the familiar theorem of
identity, that two things identical with the same thing are identical

with one another:

$$(x)(y)(z)(x = z . y = z . \supset . x = y)$$

But the principles are distinct. The principle of identity follows from the transitivity and symmetry by which (with reflexivity) the identity relation is defined. But there is no corresponding derivation of the principle of identifiability above, for (as we have seen) the relation of *being identifiable with* is a biased or directed relation, and hence is not symmetric.

Besides nonsymmetry, what else distinguishes *being identifiable with* from identity? When the identity of A and B is at issue, we can expect an answer to the question, "A and B are the same *what?*" It may be (as F. Cowley has suggested to me) that only "dummy sortals" (like "the same stuff") are available for answering this question when identity of composition, or constitution, is asserted. (Water and H_2O are the same stuff, or material substance.) But not even dummy sortals are available, when *identifiability* is the relation asserted. Since identifying one putative object with another either eliminates the former from further theoretical consideration or makes some revision in the concept under which the former object was considered, we should not be surprised that we can find no answer to the question, "the same *what?*" The *identificandum* and the *identificans* may be of the same general kind (the evening star and Venus are both heavenly bodies) but differ in essential characteristics, and hence cannot be the *same* instance of that general kind. Or, *identificandum* and *identificans* may be so diverse in kind that no more general kind, not even "dummy sortals," can accommodate both. The evening lights and the evening star are not even the same phenomenon, event, or visible object.

This elimination from theory or conceptual revision suggests another difference between identifiability and identity. The former relation seems more epistemic than ontological; the latter relation, more ontological than epistemic. Presumably, it is *entities* that are identical, but it is *we* who identify them. Identifying one thing with another is a way of correcting, or simplifying the conceptual lines we have previously drawn. This seems especially so in those cases in which identification of *A* with *B* is reduction of *A* to *B*, with conceptual revision of the concept *A* and elimination of the old concept *A* from further use. (The best examples of such elimination are the identifications of temperature and mass with energy.) And this corrective elimination is reflected in our distinctive idiom for reporting identifications of *A* with *B*. We say, "*A* is *B* and nothing more," thereby dismissing whatever more *A* is wrongly thought to involve.

And yet, identifiability is not purely epistemic. Had there been no people, hence no false beliefs about, say, the evening lights, those lights would still have been identifiable with the planet Venus. Moreover, identifiability does not respect familiar grades of evidence and justified belief. The evening lights are more accessible to observation than the hypothetical evening star or the even more elusive Venus with which they are identifiable. Indeed, identifications are governed more by the metaphysician's ideals of causation, simplicity, and order than by the epistemologist's standards for "direct knowledge" and observability. And, as we know, a metaphysician is as prone as any scientist to conclusions of the form, A is B and nothing more. (Compare: "The evening lights are the appearances of an orbiting material body, and nothing more" and "Mental states are brain processes, and nothing more.")

II. $E = mc^2$

Let us turn back at last to physical equations and see how these remarks apply to more recent science.

At first glance, a physical equation gives our distinction no purchase. As noted for $E = mc^2$ at the outset, a physical equation can always be read as an identity statement about numerical values. If each side of the equation is taken, as operationalists suggest, to be a set of instructions for getting numerical values by measurement or calculation, a physical equation gives two alternative instructions for getting the same value. Or, operations apart, a physical equation can be treated as an algebraic equation, with the same result. Although variable terms and most constants are given with dimensions, these physical dimensions can always be balanced and in effect deleted by loading the constants with any otherwise unbalanced dimensions. For example, in $kT = \frac{2}{3}\bar{E}$, we can ignore the fact that T is given in degrees and E in ergs, for the Boltzmann constant k is (by complicated convention) assigned dimensions (ergs/degree) which balance the equation dimensionally. We can, accordingly, treat the equation as if it were $cx = \frac{2}{3}y$. Hence, when it is satisfied by particular values for x and y, the equation is on a logical par with, say, $3 \times 2 = \frac{2}{3} \times 9$. And surely, this is not a nonsymmetric identification. It *could* be seen as a relative identity, $3 \times 2 \underset{6}{=} \frac{2}{3} \times 9$, the conclusion of two parallel identifications, $3 \times 2 \geqslant 6$ and $\frac{2}{3} \times 9 \geqslant 6$. But this analysis is somewhat forced, unless we suppose that there are natural numbers and equally real products of natural numbers as well. There would then be point to the reductionist thesis, "3×2 is 6, and nothing more." But even so, the equation, $3 \times 2 = \frac{2}{3} \times 9$, is an identity statement, not an identifiability statement. Thus, if either this numerical equation or $cx = \frac{2}{3}y$ is to be the model for the temperature-energy "bridge law," we do not need a notion of identifiability. At best, the notion is introduced with effort.

Since mathematics is supposed to be the language of physics, we might expect physicists to reduce physical equations to algebraic or numerical equations in this way. But they do not. They do manipulate and even ignore dimensions on occasion, but they do so for the sake of physical (or metaphysical) interpretation and *not* for the sake of pure mathematical interpretation of equations. For example, Einstein and other commentators ignore the fact that m is in grams, not ergs and take '$E = mc^2$' to say or show that mass is a form of energy. That is, they read the equations as if it were '$E \leqslant m$', an identification of mass with energy.

According to dimensional analysis we can reject this interpretation out of hand. Since c^2 is a constant, m may be a measure, but not a form of energy. Only 'mc^2' has dimensions suitable for energy, namely, ML^2T^{-2}. (1 erg = 1 dyne-centimeter = 1 (gram-centimeter/second^2)-centimeter = 1 gram$-$centimeter^2/second$^2 = ML^2T^{-2}$.) Hence, only 'mc^2' might be taken to designate a form of energy. But given the traditional vagueness of the notion of form, perhaps it would be best to eschew all such identifications.

We should be content, it may seem, with taking Einstein's equation to be a statement of the co-presence and co-variation of mass and energy. This reading has much in its favor. In no way does it deprive the equation of physical or even metaphysical import. Since the time of the neoplatonists, mass had been tied to material substance. (For Newton, mass is "the quantity of matter" in a body.) There is excitement enough then in the discovery that mass and energy — even the bodiless energy of radiation — are constantly co-present and co-variable. And this reading, unlike that which identified mass with energy, honestly records the incomprehensible phenomenon of particle pair "creation" and "annihilation," one of the principal empirical supports for the equation. If "material particles" (electrons, positrons) issue from, and disappear into nonmaterial entities (photons or gamma rays), then we should not gloss this brute fact by talking of the interconversion of electronic and photonic states or forms of energy. Let us read '$E = mc^2$' in a way that admits that mass (here, the rest mass of electrons and positrons) and energy (here, the radiation energy of photons or gamma waves) co-vary in an unintelligible way. And by so doing, we will also be able to avoid the complications of identifiability. The relations of co-variation and co-presence are clearly symmetric, and we can keep to a Frege reading of the equation, without misrepresenting its physical import.

These arguments against taking mass as a form of energy are persuasive, but not decisive. The notion of form is *not* hopelessly vague, nor does it require common dimensions on both sides of an equation. Conservation principles give sense to the notion of diverse quantities, that is, quantities with different dimensions, being forms of the same *Ur*-quantity. The history of modern physics is, in large part, the joint development of the notion of energy and the energy-conservation principle. Through the nineteenth century, when it was discovered that apparent substances (like heat, electricity) vary as some recognized form of energy varies, they were themselves reclassified as novel forms of energy. The principle of energy conservation was thereby expanded in scope and, at the same time, protected from falsification by improved measurements.

There is then ample precedent for treating $E = mc^2$ as a further expansion of the domain of the principle, m designating "rest energy." Strictly speaking, 'mc^2' designates rest energy, but since c^2 is a constant whose dimensions, L^2T^{-2} have no unique physical significance (temperature has the same dimensions), we are inclined to treat it as a mere numerical conversion factor. (Indeed, Einstein's favorite analogy for the equation was Francs = K Marks. Just as francs may be exchanged at a certain rate for marks — another form of currency, or purchasing power — so mass may be exchanged for other forms of energy at a fixed rate.) There is a further reason, however, for not taking dimensional constants too seriously; their dimensions may be changed along with those of the physical variable which the constant accompanies. For example, the mass of particles is now given in millielectronvolts, Mev, the energy term most appropriate to particle accelerators.

But the history of physics does not give the only support for reading $E = mc^2$ as the identification of mass with energy. Certain derivations of the equation also favor this reading. In one standard derivation (in the 1921 Princeton lectures, published disarmingly as *The Meaning of Relativity*) Einstein derives, as the energy equation for a moving particle, $E = m/(1 - q^2)$ where the velocity q is in light seconds (and c^2 in seconds disappears). He then developed E in powers of q^2, so:

$$E = m + \frac{m}{2} q^2 + \frac{3}{8} mq^4 + \ldots$$

Since the third term is insignificant for velocities much less than the speed of light, we can ignore it. An energy term is on the left, and on the right is the sum of two terms, one of which is the expression for classical kinetic energy. What then is m? It is hard to resist the conclusion that it too is an energy term. Thus do the simplest mathematical manipulations of new equations suggest new physical interpretations of variables — a device to keep in mind for a "logic of scientific discovery."

III. $kT = \frac{2}{3}\bar{E}$

The reduction of a quasi-substance to a novel form of energy may be only a first step. Thus, heat was first reduced to a novel form of energy, thermal energy. (The reduction is familiar. Unlike a substance, it was found that heat could be produced without limit by mechanical work, and at a fixed rate first called "the mechanical *equivalent*" of heat. But as the principle of energy conservation developed, this equivalence, or co-variation came to be interpreted as interconvertibility of two forms of energy.)

The next step was reduction in a somewhat different sense. By the end of the nineteenth century, this apparently novel form of energy was shown to be, at the level of large objects, the "product" of the kinetic energy of the body's component molecules. A novel form of energy was shown to be an old form at a finer level. Just as the first reduction reduced the number of supposed physical substances, this reduction reduced the number of supposed forms of energy. We might retain the notion of thermal energy (or temperature) for the sake of experimental and theoretical convenience. (For example, the parameter β in the Boltzmann distribution law, $n_j/n_0 = e^{-\beta e_j}$ is assigned a value only by means of temperature measurement.) But, temperature is an expendable notion in any detailed physical description which is free of limits imposed by human capacities for measurement. (Most presentations of thermodynamics introduce temperature by way of the notion of thermal equilibrium, if they bother to introduce it at all.)

This very quick history ignores important distinctions (between temperature and heat, empirical temperature and absolute temperature, heat content and heat capacity, and so on). But it may be enough to cast doubt on the usual philosophers' reading of the equation, $kT = \frac{2}{3}\bar{E}$. Although this equation is an intermediate step in some derivations of the Gas Law from the kinetic model of a gas, and hence part of the "reduction" of thermodynamics to statistical mechanics, physicists do not take this equation to disparage temperature. As a bridge between the two concepts, and hence between their respective theories, it is perfectly level; the equation involves no ontological bias against temperature. Nor could it, for two reasons. As an equation, it expresses a symmetric relation. As a physical law, it expresses a contingent correlation (or possibly a causal relation), not a definitional relation between the two variables.

But the first reason begs the question. By now it should be clear that not all physical equations are best read the way logicians read them. And the second reason involves a false contrast, at least in the sciences. A law may be a definition *and* contingent, at one and the same time and in one and the same context. If our bridge law is read as an identification of temperature with energy, it is an example of such a law. It is contingent, at least in detail: Boltzmann's constant k could have had a different numerical value. But it is debatable whether the general function, $T\alpha\bar{E}$, is contingent if true. (See Saul Kripke's lecture printed in this volume.)

But let us assume that the equation is contingent, even in its more general form. To say that it is contingent is not, of course, to say that it is a correlation. I doubt that any equation which meets most of the usual standards of lawlikeness is in any sense a correlation. ("Experimental law" is, I think, a *vox nihili*, or worse.) But whatever the general case, *this* equation cannot be a correlation. There is no way of measuring, or calculating the mean translational kinetic energy other than by measuring the temperature. We are too big and slow to get at molecular kinetic energies in any other way.

Although a measure of temperature, the equation is also a definition of temperature. Of course, it is not an operational definition of temperature, for E is far more, not less removed from experience than is T. (Indeed, operationally the concepts are reversible: Temperature could be used operationally to define E.) Nor is the equation, as it is already understood, an analytic definition which gives the meaning *of* 'temperature'; nor is it a stipulative definition that gives meaning *to* a term with none. But the equation is like a stipulative definition in that it fixes the notion of temperature in a new specific context (that of the domain of assemblages of particles). And it is like an analytic definition in that this "fixing" may affect the prior meaning, or even dominate it.

An analogy may help. In the context of a plane, two lines *define* a point. That is, they fix or determine a point. (Such definition is, in German, a *Bestimmung*.) Or, to use Frege's suggestive notion, two lines "present" a point in a particular way. Such a mode of presenting is what Frege meant by the sense (*Sinn*) of a term. There are usually different modes of presenting the same thing (hence the need for, and value of identity statements), but we may come to insist on a particular mode in a certain context, to the exclusion of all others. For example, there might be reasons for adopting the definition (*Bestimmung*) or mode of presentation (*Art des Gegebenseins*) of a point by the intersection of two lines as *the* definition, for the special context of a plane. Hence, we might say, that (in a plane) a point is the intersection of two lines, and nothing more. It remains a contingent fact that a point is so presentable, but a fact that is taken to say what a point is, for the purposes of that special context. That is all we know, and all we need to know in order to work with points in a plane. Such a *Bestimmung* defines the notion of a point by stating the limits of the notion in a special context.

If this special context becomes theoretically prominent, these limits may cease to seem selective or restrictive, and the definition may be generalized to cover other contexts. Accordingly, the properties of points which the usual definitions in these contexts cited may be demoted to the rank of the inessential, even in contexts in which they were once definitive. And in such cases, we have grounds for saying that the concept of a point, or the meaning of 'point' has changed.

In a similar way, equations can constitute definitions, both limited and general, and restrict or even change meaning. And so it is, I suggest, with $kT = \frac{2}{3}\bar{E}$. Initially, it defines the notion of temperature for the special domain of statistical mechanics, namely, the domain of assemblages of point particles. But any definition for this particular special domain tends to generalize to other domains, for we (or at least our scientists) think of this domain as basic. Hence any definition within the domain of particles tends to constitute a reduction of the property so defined. A reduction here involves ontological import, or rather is what might be called "ontological export." Such a reduction shows that the macroproperty can be cast out of the list of the properties of physics in its most fully developed form.

We might then write $kT =_{df} \frac{2}{3}\bar{E}$. And so written, it is no longer symmetrical. As the notation itself shows, to define T in terms of E is not to define E by means of T. In being directed, the relation of *definability by* is like the relation of *identifiability with*. Indeed, the two relations are one and the same (relation).

IV. Mind = Body

I have not claimed that the temperature-energy equation must be read as a definition and an identification. But, as in the case of $E = mc^2$, various historical and theoretical factors favor this reading over the Frege reading common among philosophers. Those philosophers of science who wish to restrict themselves to the resources of extensional, first-order logic are free to stick with the Frege reading, and leave these nonlogical factors for the accompanying text. But philosophers of mind who wish to advance a materialist thesis should abandon the logician's reading. The proponents of "modern materialism" appeal by way of precedent and analogy to $kT = \frac{2}{3}\bar{E}$, and to the "theoretical identification" of temperature and mean translational kinetic energy of molecules. But "identification" for them is assumed or said to be an identity relation, and they read the equation as a statement of identity.

By doing so, however, they lose the force of their analogy and invite several common, and unnecessary, criticisms. I shall mention three. First, some critics of the mind-brain "Identity Theory" find the relevant notion of identity unclear and attempts to explain it misleading. For example, U. T. Place introduced the theory with a distinction between the 'is' of "composition" and definition. He gave as an example of the former, "A cloud is a mass of water droplets or other particles in suspension"; of the latter, "Red is a color." To statements of each kind we can, Place thinks, sensibly add the phrase "and nothing else." The possibility of adding this phrase distinguishes both kinds of statement from statements of predication and shows that in statements of composition and definition "both the grammatical subject and the grammatical predicate are expressions which provide an adequate characterization of the state of affairs to which they both refer." But these special kinds of 'is' statements differ from one another in that 'Red is a color' is true because of a connection in the meaning between its two "adequate characterizations" of the single state of affairs in question, while the cloud statement is true in virtue of various observations of a common state of meteorological affairs. And it is the latter contingent truth that is the model of "Consciousness is a brain process" [*The British Journal of Psychology*, XLVII (1956)].

But how, critics ask, can this be the 'is' of "composition," for conscious events are not composed of brain processes. True, but Place's example is better than his description of it. The analogy does not turn on the fact that clouds are *materially composed* of water droplets or other particles in suspension, but rather on the fact that a cloud, for scientific purposes, can be analyzed into those components. That is, a cloud's salient properties (its motion and changing shape, its translucency, and the like) can all be seen as macroproducts of the properties of its microcomponents. If the description "mass of water droplets or other particles in suspension" is an "adequate characterization" of a cloud, it is because there are no properties of a cloud which cannot be analyzed as "properties of water droplets or other particles in suspension." That is the point of saying "A cloud is a mass of water droplets . . . *and nothing else.*" And if this claim is justified, then—contrary to Place's account—the subject term may *not* be an "adequate characterization" of the same "state of affairs," for some properties of a cloud previously important to laymen, and the lay definition of 'cloud' may be ignored if they cannot be analyzed in this way. In short, the identification of clouds with suspended particles may show that 'cloud' is not an "adequate characterization" of clouds.

The phrase, "and nothing else" does not belong at the end of a claim in which both terms are unquestionably adequate descriptions. There is no point to "Red is a color and nothing else." What else did we think it might be? A sound? There *would* be point, however, to saying, "Red is visible electromagnetic radiation, and nothing else," for we suppose that red is something else, namely, an inherent property of bodies, not reflected wave motion. In short, 'and nothing else' goes not with lexical definitions, but with reductive definitions of the kind common in science. What Place misleadingly called the 'is' of composition is rather the 'is' of reduction, or of identification. His claim "Consciousness is a brain process and nothing else" is, as he supposes, like "Temperature is kinetic energy and nothing else," "Lightning is electrical discharge and nothing else." But the Frege model of identity led him to characterize "and nothing else" and the kind of 'is' statement it distinguishes incorrectly. He has recently said that the body-mind relation that he intended all along was asymmetrical, but this clarification comes late (See Place's comments on Putnam's paper in *Art, Mind and Religion*, W. H. Capitan & D. D. Merrill, editors, U. of Pittsburgh, 1967, p. 66).

Had this been said from the start, critics would have found the intended relation somewhat less puzzling. Secondly, we would have been spared much of the dispute over the Leibniz Law. By one version of the Leibniz Law, if x and y are identical, then every predicate true of x must also be true of y, and vice versa. Critics of the mind-body "identity" thesis argue that, on the one hand, brain processes have location, while conscious events do not (or at least do not have the same precisely specifiable location); on the other hand, conscious events are immediately present to only one person at most, while brain processes are public, or could be in a well-equipped surgical theater or laboratory. Therefore, if the Leibniz Law holds, conscious events cannot be identical with brain processes.

Various subtle and interesting replies have been made to try to save Identity Theory *and* the Leibniz Law. But, of course, this objection cannot arise if the Identity Theory is really the Identification Theory. Identification of A with B always involves reclassification of A, and the demotion or even denial of some of A's old properties. Any supposed properties of A which are incompatible with properties of B will, of course, henceforth be denied of A. Hence some properties of B which were previously unascribable to A without contradiction can now be sensibly ascribed to, and even true of, A. Thus, before identification with energy, the mass of a body was taken to be essentially constant, and it would have been impossible to say consistently that mass might, like kinetic energy, vary with velocity. But when mass was identified with energy, such a variation was made possible and indeed an observed fact that supports this identification. So, if conscious events are identifiable with brain processes, some revision of our notion of those events will be involved. For example, as part of the identification we may begin to make more precise locations, some no doubt arbitrary, of what are now unlocated events or even events that cannot be located at all. (Absolute) identity, the identity defined by the Leibniz Law, allows for no such adjustments.

An Identification Theory of mind with body avoids a third objection to the Identity Theory. Place himself seems to think that the materialist thesis rests solely on observed correlations of mental and neurological events. But, it is objected, correlations are no more support for materialism than they are for idealism. Indeed, they support neither form of monism nor monism *per se*. In elaborating Place's thesis, J. J. C. Smart seems to realize that correlations only suggest the *possibility* of identity, and materialism must appeal further to such metaphysical considerations as simplicity, economy, and the like. For him, the choice of materialism over other views equally compatible with correlations of mental and neurological events is ultimately a theoretical choice.

Smart is moving in the right direction, but he has not gone far enough; the choice of materialism is theoretical throughout. First, at the present time there are far fewer observed correlations than materialists seem to suppose, and those few are rather crude. For example, one of the *best* correlations of the relevant kind is that between a certain distinct brain-wave pattern and "a state of expectancy." But this state includes a variety of expectations, intentions, and other conscious states, which are indistinguishable in the electroencephalographic readings, at least in the present state of the art. There are, indeed, striking correlations between certain mental states and certain bodily movements (e.g., between dreaming and rapid eye movements), between certain mental states and certain electrical stimuli (for example, Penfield's elicitation of vivid memories by stimulation of the temporal cortex), and between certain other mental states and certain biochemical levels (e.g., between hallucinations and certain drugs). But without correlations between those movements, electrical stimuli, or drugs *and* neurological processes, these newsworthy correlations cannot be counted by materialists as encouraging evidence compatible with their thesis. We may *suppose* that these further correlations will be forthcoming, but as yet there is too little evidence to predict that research will produce mind-brain correlations without limit in number or degree of precision.

But this paucity of correlations matters less to the materialist thesis than their irrelevance. Correlations may suggest an equation, but they do not show that equation to be a law. An equation is a law only within the context of a theory that explains why that correlation holds. And one way to explain a correlation is to identify one variable with the other, in one of the ways we have discussed. Thus, mass co-varies with energy, because mass is a form of energy in that it falls under the principle of energy conservation. Temperature co-varies with mean kinetic energy, because it is the macroform of that same energy.

I doubt that restating materialism as a theory of identifiability will make it convincing. It is difficult to see how even good correlations between mental and neurological events could be given the status of law by a theory which explains them in any way, let alone by identifying mental events as forms of neurological events. The mental events in question are not quantifiable, and there seems no possibility of either bringing them under principles or finding equations which could be interpreted as statements of identification. Any correlation between mental and neurological events seems brute beyond redemption by an explanation of any sort, short of divinely preordained harmony. (Occasionalists are more clear-sighted than Descartes on the mind-body problem.)

But I mean to lessen, not increase the materialist's troubles. An identity theory is hopeless; an identifiability theory is not. As his favorite scientific analogies show, the materialist *intends* to state the identifiability of mental states with brain states, rather than their identity. But allegiance to standard logical forms leads him to misstate his thesis, and thereby invite familiar but unnecessary charges of obscurity, misanalogy, violation of Leibniz' Law, and *non sequitur*.

I do not suppose that I have made identifiability as clear as identity, and I do not propose to add a logic of identifiability to the logic of identity. I have tried to distinguish identifiability from identity and to show that our philosophy of science and philosophy of mind suffer from not making the same attempt.

On the Abstractness
of Individuals

H. HIŻ

University of Pennsylvania

Many philosophies proclaim that there are entities which are not properties or relations; these entities have properties, and there are relations that occur between them. However, these entities themselves are different in nature from properties or from relations; they are not relations which *hold* between entities, and they are not properties which entities *have,* if 'holds between' and 'has' are understood as in 'The relation of equality holds between *cos* and the derivative of *sin*' or as in 'This girl has charm'. This girl, a river, a session of the Univerity Senate, someone's toothache, are examples of such entities. Material bodies, events, facts, and sensations are often listed, not as relations, but as components of relations; not as properties, but as carriers of properties. The term 'individual' is used for them. Charm is a property which belongs to girls, and therefore it is not an individual. But the charm of this girl is not a property; it is a fact and therefore an individual.

Again, philosophies differ considerably about admitting some entities to the rank of individuals. For a radical materialist a sensation is not an individual but a property of an organism; for a phenomenalist a material body is not an individual but a set of relations of sensations. For a Cartesian dualist there are two kinds of individuals: those that are bodies in space, *res extensae,* and those that are minds, *res cogitantes.* For Arisotle Πρῶται οὐσίαι are individuals. In contemporary model theory a model is a structure composed of a class of individuals

251

and classes of those individuals, classes of pairs of the individuals, classes of pairs of the pairs of the individuals, and so on. Many philosophers considered the world to be like a model in which individuals are the fundamental building blocks.

Some philosophers think that individuals, or rather some kinds of individuals, are the only things that exist. Leaving aside the claim that existence is reserved for individuals, we may wonder what arguments are advanced in support of their existence at all. The arguments for the existence of individuals are, roughly, of four kinds: ontological, semantic, logical, and epistemological. These four are not mutually exclusive. Perhaps we should not even call them 'arguments'; they are rather declarations within a particular system of philosophy, a particular ontology, a particular semantics, a system of logic, or within an epistemology.

Hobbes provides a typical example of ontological thinking. His somatism accepts bodies as individuals. In a truly Cartesian way, he defines a body as "That which having no dependence upon our thought is coincident or coextended with some part of space."[1] More recently, Kotarbiński characterized material bodies as "localized in time and space and as having physical properties." Localization in Hobbes and in Kotarbiński is a property of material bodies. Note that material bodies are not the only things that are localized. Colors, shapes, phenomena, impressions, and events all have spatiotemporal localizations. Some localizables are material bodies. (Localization is a relation whereas the thing localized by it is thought to be not a relation but an individual.) However, the concept of localization is a troublesome one. The complications are of such magnitude that the attempt to explain individuals by means of localization is put in serious doubt. Localization is an assignment of real numbers according to a coordinate system. Three real numbers are assigned to a point; they localize that point. Of course, neither a point, nor any finite set of points has physical properties. A finite collection of points does not have a mass; it is not an electromagnetic field; it does not have a color or a shape or a smell. A body must be localized by an infinite set of points.

Which infinite set of points determines the Obelisque on the Place de la Concorde? We are tempted to answer that the set of points on the surface of the Obelisque determines the Obelisque. But then we face two essential difficulties. First, no matter how carefully we study the Obelisque, it will be impossible to say whether certain points are inside, outside, or just on its surface. In order to overcome

[1] *De corpore*, VIII, 1.

this difficulty, science accepts the principle of continuity which, in this case, amounts to a supposition of the existence of a unique surface of the Obelisque. But, then we meet the second difficulty. That part of the Place de la Concorde which surrounds the Obelisque, that is, that part which is not the Obelisque itself, is also a body. It is bounded by the river, by a garden, by buildings, and by the streets around it. It is slipped over the Obelisque like a ring over a finger. Now, the internal contour of the rest of the Place de la Concorde is identical with the external contour of the Obelisque. Do, therefore, the points of that contour belong to the Obelisque, or do they belong to the surrounding square? You may be inclined to say that the points do not belong to either. But the points do belong to the total Place de la Concorde, now inderstood to be a total body including the Obelisque. It seems that an essential source of both difficulties is the concept of a point. This concept seems to be too delicate an instrument for the study of the rough reality surrounding us. Thus, a reexamination of the concept of localization is required. Perhaps a reasonable substitute would be the geometry of solids suggested by Whitehead, Nicod, and Tarski. It has the advantage of considering spheres to be individuals and then defining abstract concepts, such as points, as classes of spheres.[2] A geometry of solids is based on mereology (or on its elementary part, corresponding to what today is called 'the calculus of individuals'). But, of course, it adds powerful postulates of a geometric kind. Concluding only that the concept of localization needs to be modernized, note that there are some importnat reasons for considering certain entities as individuals, which are not localizable. For example, facts are such possible individuals. The nondivisibility of 9 by 2 is a fact; it has several properties and it has relations to other facts. But it itself is not a class, a property, or a relation. Nondivisibility by 2 is a property. Nondivisibility is a relation, but the nondivisibility of 9 by 2 is neither of them. Rather it is a fact. Events differ from facts in being localizable in time or in space. Events happen; facts just are.

Let us now turn to some semantic and logical considerations about individuals. These are the central problems about individuals. I stated at the beginning that individuals are not properties or relations; rather that they enter into relations and have properties. This statement is ontological. The semantic counterpart of it is that some phrases occur as arguments and never as functors in logical formulae. Thus in '$\Lambda p[p \supset p]$' the implication sign is a functor and 'p' is an argument. The relation of implication therefore is not an individual

---

[2] See Tarski, *Logic, Semantics, Metamathematics*, pp. 24–29.

because its sign is used as a functor. The distinction between functor and argument reminds us of the distinction between subject and predicate. Throughout most of the history of philosophy the problems concerning individuals were formulated in terms of subject and predicate. According to Aristotle, individuals are those things of which predications can be made but which themselves are never predicates. Aristotle's writings are often interpreted in two ways:

(1) The first treats them as defending a syntactic theory according to which there are nouns that cannot stand in the predicate position of a correct sentence whereas these same nouns can stand in the subject position;

(2) The second treats them as defending a semantico-logical theory according to which there are things of which predications can be made; that is, there are x's such that 'x is y' is true for some y but the utterance 'y is x' is either meaningless or changes the meaning of *is*.

For instance *This man is Callias* is not a predicative statement but an identity statement. I am inclined to interpret Aristotle in the semantic rather than the purely syntactic way. The Oxford translation of Aristotle was made at a time when the nominal interpretation of definitions was popular, and Ross and his colleagues tried to impose a similar view on Aristotle. Now, if Aristotle is speaking about things and not only about their names. then he gives some arguments for the existence of individuals. Aristotle argues in *The Posterior Analytics* that if x is predicated of y and y of z and z of something, and so on, then the descending series of predicates cannot continue *ad infinitum;* there must be a final term, a term that is not attributable to a subject but is itself a subject of attributes. And similarly the ascending series $x(y)$, $z(x)$, $w(z)$, and so on will terminate. Among arguments that we cannot ascend infinitely with predication or descend infinitely, we find the idea that essential attributes of nature must be finite in number; otherwise definitions would be impossible.[3] There is also the idea that an infinite series cannot be traversed.[4] Today these arguments seem vague or wrong. Although we try to avoid the appeal to all-inclusive classes since they lead to contradictions, there is no reason whatsoever to think that every descending series of predications terminates. To use today's terminology,[5] it is questionable whether the relation of predication is founded or not.

The axiom of *Fundirung* (or of regularity) excludes all infinite

[3] *Post. Analyt.* (84a25).
[4] *Post. Analyt.* (82b38).
[5] Quine, *Set Theory and Its Logic,* p. 141.

descending series of predication, circular or not, "It forbids any endless descent, repetitive or not with respect to membership."[6] Aristotle did not think about circular membership, but today it is regarded as a possible source of antinomies. The logical discussion about individuals requires examining the correctness of the axiom of regularity. I will argue that it should be abandoned.

Before seeing why, recall that Frege argued that the old distinction between subject and predicate is useless. It is interesting to see exactly how Frege argues his case. He says

> ... the contents of two judgments may differ in two ways: either the consequences derivable from the first, when it is combined with certain other judgments, always follow from the second, when it is combined with the same judgments (and conversely), or this is not the case. The two propositions "The Greeks defeated the Persians at Platea" and "The Persians were defeated by the Greeks at Platea" differ in the first way. ... Now, I call that part of the content that is the same in both the conceptual content. Since it alone is of significance for our ideography, we need not introduce any distinction between propositions having the same conceptual content. ... One would do violence to the formula language of mathematics if he were to distinguish between subject and predicate in it.

Instead of a subject-predicate structure, Frege prefers the use of a function-argument structure for a sentence, or as it is better to say, a functor-argument structure. "Let us assume that the circumstance that hydrogen is lighter than carbon dioxide is expressed in (the) formula language. ... 'Hydrogen' is here taken as the argument and 'is lighter than carbon dioxide' as the functor; 'being lighter than carbon dioxide (hydrogen)' is the way we may write it. "But," Frege remarks, "we can also conceive of the same conceptual content in such a way that 'carbon dioxide' becomes the argument and 'being heavier than hydrogen' the function." Then we write 'being heavier than hydrogen (carbon dioxide)'. Frege maintains that there are different ways of analyzing a sentence and that the same content may be expressed by a functor with an argument or by the inverse functor and a different argument. To follow the Fregean example:

being heavier than ⟨hydrogen⟩ (carbon dioxide)
being heavier^{-1} than ⟨carbon dioxide⟩ (hydrogen)

are equivalent sentences; they express the same content.[7]

---

[6] Quine, *Set Theory and Its Logic*, p. 285.
[7] Jean van Heijenoort, *From Frege to Gödel*, 1967, pp. 12, 21, and 22.

To study this further, take a modified logic of Leśniewski as the standard logic. In it one has $\Lambda x[\text{ob } (x) \equiv x \neq \phi \ \& \ \Lambda y[y \neq \phi \ \& \ y \subset x \supset y = x]]$. The concept of an object is not identical with the concept of an individual. Note, for example, that in this sense negation is an object for it is true that $\sim \neq \phi$ (that is, there are p such that $\sim(p)$) and $\Lambda y[y \neq \phi \ \& \ \Lambda z[y(z) \supset \sim (z)] \supset y = \sim]$ but not ob $(\supset)$ because, for example, $\equiv \ \subset \ \supset$ but not $\equiv \ = \ \supset$. (That is to say, equivalence is included in but not identical with implication.) Thus some objects are not individuals. Only those objects which are spoken about in the lowest grammatical category are individuals. Besides sentences, the only other lowest grammatical category is that of names.

Let us indicate carefully the grammatical categories involved and the grammatical structure of the sentence which is the axiom of Leśniewski's "Ontology":

$$\Lambda x\Lambda y[x \ \epsilon \qquad y \equiv V \ z[x \ \epsilon \qquad z \ \& \ z \ \epsilon \qquad y]]$$
$$\quad i \ (s; \ ii) \ i \qquad \quad i \ (s; \ ii) \ i \qquad i \ (s; \ ii) \ i$$

where i indicates the grammatical category of an individual phrase and (s, ii) the category of a functor which together with two phrases of the category i forms a sentence. Generally, a phrase is of the grammatical category $(a; \ b_1, \ b_2, \ \ldots, \ b_k)$ if together with phrases of the grammatical categories $b_1, \ b_2, \ \ldots, \ b_k$ respectively, it forms a phrase of the grammatical category a. Among phrases of the grammatical category i there are two constant phrases ϕ and U. They are defined, for example, by

$$\Lambda x[x \ \epsilon \ \phi \equiv \ \sim x \ \epsilon \ x]$$

$$\Lambda x[x \ \epsilon \ U \equiv x \ \epsilon \ x]$$

It is easy to prove that

$$\Lambda x[x \ \epsilon \ U \equiv \text{ob } x]$$

In the grammatical category i there are phrases which are not meant to name single individuals. Examples of such phrases in English are *man* and *centaur,* and in the language of logic ϕ and U. It is a remarkable fact that logic does not have the means of defining individuals.

An essential feature of Leśniewski's logic, as well as of many other systems of logic, is that there is a lowest grammatical category of which phrases cannot appear as functors. This grammatical category is represented in the axiomatization. Phrases of other grammatical categories are then defined by means of this elementary, lowest grammatical category. However, such a limitation can be overcome. Some preliminary comments will help explain how it is possible to enlarge a system of logic of this kind.

$$\Lambda x \Lambda y [x \quad\quad \supset \quad\quad\quad\quad y \quad\quad \equiv$$
$$(s;\,s)\,(s;\,(s;\,s)(s;\,s))\,(s;\,s)$$

$$\Lambda z [x \quad (z) \supset \quad y \quad (z)]]$$
$$(s;\,s)\,s \quad (s;\,ss)\,(s;\,s)\,s$$

Here the symbol '$\supset$' occurs in two different grammatical categories. Theoretically a different symbol could be used in '$\supset$
$$\iota s;\,(s;\,s)(s;\,s))'.$$
But there are intuitive reasons for preserving the same sign. In a natural language, such as English, the same phrase which occurs in two different grammatical categories may have closely and systematically related meanings.

In the sentence 'Friendship permits differences' the word 'permits' belongs to a different grammatical category from that in the sentence 'One permits a friend to be different'. In the latter case it is a verb which takes a name of an individual as its subject. Similarly while the word 'result' occurs in two different grammatical categories in the following two sentences, its use in the two is closely related.

Peace and prosperity result in happiness.
The result of peace and prosperity is happiness.

That is, although one occurrence of 'result' is a verb, and the other a noun, they are really the same word. Logic has not as yet accounted for such facts. On the contrary, it often obscures the issue by introducing two signs instead of one. A typical example is the notation for the unit class: ιx.

$$\iota xy \equiv x = y$$

More exactly,

$$\iota \quad\quad\quad x\,y \equiv x = \quad\quad y$$
$$((s;\,a);\,a)\,a\,a \quad a\,(s;\,aa)\,a$$
$$2 \quad 1\ 1\ 2 \quad 3 \quad 34\ 4$$

(Here the numerals indicate the grouping; the argument for 'ι' is 'x', the argument for 'ιx' is 'y'; the arguments for '$=$' are 'x' and 'y'.) It would be much more natural to use the sign '$=$' than to use the iota.

$$= \qquad x\, y \equiv x = \qquad y$$
$$((s;\, a);\, a)\, a\, a \qquad a\, (s;\, aa)\, a$$
$$2 \quad 1\ \ 1\ 2 \qquad 3 \qquad 34\ \ 4$$

Logic does allow the use of the same sign in two grammatical categories. But, there is no systematic treatment of such use. In order to provide a systematic treatment, variables as well as constants should be used in more than one grammatical category. In general we should be able to write

$$\Lambda f[f \qquad x\, y \equiv x\, f \qquad y]$$
$$((s;\, a);\, a)\, a\, a \qquad a\, (s;\, aa)\, a$$
$$2 \quad 1\ \ 1\ 2 \qquad 3 \qquad 34\ \ 4$$

Once a variable can occur in more than one grammatical category in the same formula, or more precisely, if in a single formula two different occurrences of a variable which are bound by the same quantifier can be of two different grammatical categories, the old prejudices about individuals can be overcome. If '*x(y)*' is used, we should be able to use '*y(x)*' as an equivalent of it, provided we assign suitable grammatical categories.

$$x \qquad (y) \equiv y \qquad (x)$$
$$(s;\, a) \quad a \qquad (s;\, (s;\, a))\ (s;\, a)$$
$$1 \quad 1 \qquad 2 \qquad 2$$

Here, we change the position of '*y*' adjusting its grammatical category. (Note, however, that we keep the grammatical category of '*x*' unchanged. An old principle stipulates that we make one change at a time. Incidentally, this has an application for constructing definitions; one new concept is defined at a time.) If we apply a similar change to individuals we obtain

$$\Lambda x \Lambda y[x \qquad (y) \equiv y \qquad (x)$$
$$(s;\, i) \quad i \qquad (s;\, (s;\, i))\ (s;\, i)$$
$$1 \quad 1 \qquad 2 \qquad 2$$

Thus an individual may be construed as a set of properties of an individual. This corresponds exactly to a fundamental intuition of what an individual is. It is a set of properties. As an example, a girl is, perhaps, just the set of properties which apply to her: they may be charm, being over 5 feet tall, being in New York, listening to a lecture, sitting next to a man in the audience, wondering what individuals really are, and so on. She has infinitely many properties, and all of them are her constituent elements. But if individuals are the same as sets of their properties, then any other entity can be identified with the set of its properties. In consequence, an individual can also be identified with the set of properties of the set of the properties of an individual. And similarly with even more complicated and remote sets. However, this is a peculiar use, maybe abuse, of the word 'identity'. We use the same variable, or the same constant for two entities and this is the only sense of their identity. Their categories and their ontological statuses are different.

The relaxation of logic which is being proposed is not minor. As a matter of fact it may immediately raise suspicions that an antinomy similar to Russell's antinomy is reconstructable in a relaxed logic of this sort. But a moment's reflection suffices to see that under proper precautions the antinomy is not obtainable here.

Ordinarily Russell's antinomy is presented as follows:

1.1 $\Lambda x[R(x) \equiv \sim(x(x))]$

1.2 $R(R) \equiv \sim(R(R))$

by substitution of 'R' for 'x' in 1.1.

If we take a formula as a structured string we can have two different structures assigned to 1.1:

2.1 $\Lambda x[R \quad (x) \equiv \sim (x \quad (x))]$
$\quad\quad (s; a) \; a \quad\quad (s; a) \; a$

and

2.2 $\Lambda x[R \quad\quad (x) \quad \equiv \sim (x \quad (x))]$
$\quad\quad (s; (s; a)) \; (s; a) \quad\quad (s; a) \; a$

For it is possible either to take the second occurrence of 'x' in 1.1 as of the same grammatical category as that of the last occurrence of 'x' or to take the second occurrence of 'x' in 1.1 as of the same grammatical category as that of the third occurrence of 'x'. In the first case, 2.1, we obtain an antinomy if we allow a uniform substitution for a variable appearing in more than one grammatical category, that is, with a spectrum greater than 1. With the same kind of substitution, the second way of looking at 1.1, namely that shown in 2.2, does not lead to a contradiction. If in 2.2 we substitute 'R' for all occurrences of 'x', we obtain

On the Abstractness of Individuals

$$2.3 \quad R_{(s;\,(s;\,a))}\,(R)_{(s;\,a)} \equiv \sim(R_{(s;\,a)}\,(R)_{a})]$$

R occurs in 2.3 in three different grammatical categories. Each of the structures 2.1 and 2.2 is equally justified, for each meets the requirement that every variable of the definiendum appear freely in the same grammatical category in the definiens. And neither of them meets another requirement calling for each free variable of the definiens to appear in the same grammatical category in the definiendum. But once variables are allowed to appear with spectra greater than 1, the second requirement should be abandoned.

Expression 2.3 is not a contradiction. It asserts only that the Russellian property of properties has the Russellian property of property of properties if and only if the Russellian property does not have the Russellian property of properties; or the Russellian class of classes belongs to the Russellian class of classes of classes exactly when the Russellian class does not belong to the Russellian class of classes.

The intended distinction can be phrased by saying that in the case of 2.1 a class is Russellian if it is not a member of itself, and that in the case of 2.2, a class is Russellian if it does not contain itself as a member. Expression 2.2 is in the spirit of thinking that a class is determined by its members; 2.1 looks at a class as determined by its membership in some classes.

The amendment to the rule of definition which will favor 2.2 over 2.1 is that, when in doubt, the grammatical category of a variable in the definiendum should be taken as the highest in which this variable occurs as free in the definiens. This harmonizes well with the fact that a definition may introduce a new grammatical category, as 2.2 does and 2.1 does not. And the new constant must express a concept which is of a higher order than any of the arguments. It is only the lower Russell class (as in 2.1) that cannot be allowed, and which, in fact, is excluded by the condition on definition just stated; this requires that the newly defined constant be of a higher order than any of its arguments. The higher Russell class is introduced by a definition 2.2 that satisfies this condition.

A few comments about the alleged epistemic status of individuals are in order. Many ontological somatists claim that the material bodies are immediately given. Kotarbiński argues this way. Others take sensations as immediately given and consider sensations to be individuals. This is the way Carnap and Goodman proceed. We may question the entire dispute about what is immediately given. Perhaps nothing is immediately given: Maybe everything is known together with other known objects, facts, and entities of all kinds of ontological levels. We must be careful to distinguish several senses of the phrase "immediately given." According to one sense, discussed in the *Logische Aufbau der Welt* of Carnap, "given" means "known," and "immediately given" means "known without further reflection." Some sentences are descriptions of the immediately given, namely *Protokolsätze*. But this is very different from the given as indicated by pointing gestures and demonstrative phrases such as 'this' and 'it'.

There are many reasons to think that what is given is not bodies, not objects of any kind, not sensory qualities but certain sentences. I advocate epistemic aletheism. In addition, it is very doubtful whether sentences of the sort 'This river is the Nile' constitute a solid base for our knowledge. Sentences with demonstratives are often vague.

An individual is not given by a demonstrative. We only abstract the individual from a mass of facts.